D0298453

A REFERENCE GUIDE TO
AUDIOVISUAL INFORMATION

A REFERENCE GUIDE TO
AUDIOVISUAL
INFORMATION

By James L. Limbacher

R. R. BOWKER COMPANY

NEW YORK & LONDON, 1972

A XEROX EDUCATION COMPANY

XEROX

Published by R. R. Bowker Co. (A Xerox Education Company)
1180 Avenue of the Americas, New York, N.Y. 10036

Printed and bound in the United States of America.

Library of Congress Cataloging in Publication Data

Limbacher, James L
  A reference guide to audiovisual information.

  1. Audio-visual education—Bibliography. I. Title.
Z5814.V8L55   016.00155'3   72-1737
ISBN 0-8352-0546-0

Contents

Preface

It seems difficult to believe that only five years ago there was a serious dearth of good reference works in the audiovisual field. But five years ago there wasn't as much need for them as there is today. The tremendous "information explosion" in all fields of knowledge has perhaps spurred the sudden plethora of books on films, recordings, radio, and television.

At one time the humanities librarian took care of all questions in a large public or university library, and the general reference librarian did his best in the smaller libraries. Today, however, because of the unprecedented growth of the nonprint sections of the library, many reference questions are now directed to the audiovisual librarian, who must provide the answers quickly and efficiently. The questions have become so varied and so specific that a few general reference books can no longer provide the answers.

We have also entered the era of the "film buff," the "trivia" groups, the specialized record collector, the TV addict and the "nostalgia radio buff," all of whom want and need information of far greater depth than in the past. Today we must know who sang the highest note ever sung, the names of all the actors who played Tarzan, the release date and original titles of Czechoslovakian films, the titles of all the Bowery Boys films, the availability of all the albums and tapes by Jo Stafford, Istvan Kertesz, and hundreds of other recording artists, the names of the actors who played "Vic and Sade" on radio and when *Gunsmoke* transferred from radio to TV and—well, you name it. The audiovisual librarian must somehow find such information.

Books like the *American Film Institute Catalogs*, the *New York*

Times and *Variety* film reviews, *Feature Films on 8mm and 16mm*, the *Filmgoer's Companion*, and a rapidly growing list of other audiovisual reference books, have been added to the list of such indispensable works as the *Schwann Record and Tape Guide*, the now defunct *Film Daily Yearbook*, and the *Library of Congress* record and film volumes, as basic research aids for the audiovisual librarian.

This reference guide was developed to aid the librarian in finding the material which both he and the public he serves need. The term "audiovisual" has been construed to include basically motion pictures, filmstrips, disc recordings, tapes, theater, music, dance, radio, and television. The majority of library users get their musical knowledge and enjoyment from *recordings* of music on discs and tapes. The theater buffs have discovered that some of the great works of the living theater are now preserved on film, videotapes, and recordings. The same applies to the dance. Today's audiovisual librarian must therefore become more knowledgeable and versatile in these fields.

This book in no way intends to suggest that the performing arts reference libraries and humanities librarians can be done away with. Rather, the rapid development of the public's acceptance of the audiovisual media has presented the librarian with a new breed of library patron, reared in an era when audiovisual media are commonplace in schools, universities, and television. He differs from the patron who had only theatrical films and radio in his background. Today's library patron listens and watches more and perhaps reads a bit less, yet he uses the library more than ever before. As more people use libraries for their information, librarians need more and quicker sources for that information.

The reference works cited in this guide are divided into two sections: books and periodicals. The works appear in alphabetical order by title, followed by publication information, and a brief description of the contents. Prices (based on 1972 prices) are given with each entry when available, together with the number of pages and other important information, making this list also useful as a purchasing guide. The addresses of publishers are listed in a separate section. Film and recording reviews listed in the *Multi-Media Reviews Index* (MMRI) are so indicated in the annotation.

Titles preceded by an asterisk (*) are the author's personal selections for a basic reference book collection. Because some of the cited reference works, such as encyclopedias and library book catalogs, are usually available in the general reference section of most libraries, they are not designated as basic audiovisual reference works, although they are of much value for searching and answering reference questions. Certain types of material, such as scripts, general histories and criticisms, technical crafts, "fan" magazines, and biographies without indexes, which can be found in the regular humanities section of the library, have not been included in this volume.

The reference works cited in the Books and Periodicals sections are indexed by subject in a separate section. To find information on a particular topic, the reader can check the appropriate subject category and refer to the entries in the Books and Periodicals sections.

Another section, "A Selected Bibliography of Other Audiovisual Books," is included as a guide to sources for further supplementary reading or more in-depth study of audiovisually related topics. This bibliography is also arranged alphabetically by title under specific subject headings. Full publishing information and prices are included when available, to aid the reader in purchasing these materials.

This first edition of *A Reference Guide to Audiovisual Information* is to be updated regularly, and this updating process will keep pace with the development of the audiovisual field. Comments, suggestions, additions, and even corrections by those who read and use this guide are welcomed by the editor.

The editor would personally like to hear from anyone who has ways of making the audiovisual reference librarian's job easier. That's what this book is for.

James L. Limbacher

The Ready Reference File

Most libraries find that developing a "ready reference" card file pays off in several ways: (1) it saves repeating the search process on often-asked questions; (2) it gathers in one place all sorts of information needed for both telephone and in-person reference service; and (3) it gives each reference desk a personal and localized information center.

When a question is asked the first time, a reference form should be filled out (see examples) and then transferred to a 3 by 5 file card, listing the answer and, if possible, the source. If proper headings and cross-headings are given, the ready reference file can be the most valuable adjunct to the reference book collection that any library can have.

The ready reference card file for audiovisual information differs from the one for a general reference desk in its focus on specific areas, rather than general information. A local source directory for a variety of services can be included, such as names, addresses, and telephone numbers of those offering out-of-print records, used films, and audiovisual equipment. Addresses of music, film, record and tape buffs and their interests can also be included. The ready reference file can also include the policies and procedures which the staff may need while on duty.

Headings for Card File

Some possible headings are listed here to help the librarian develop a personal reference file which will be valuable to the staff in serving the public.

1

```
                                    DATE _____
PATRON'S NAME _____
ADDRESS _____ PHONE _____
QUESTION: _____
_____
_____

ANSWER NEEDED BY: _____ WILL CALL _____
ANSWER: _____
_____
_____
_____

SOURCES USED TO FIND ANSWER: (1) _____
(2) _____ (3) _____
NO ANSWER FOUND _____ DATE _____
                            _____
                                    name of researcher
```

REFERENCE FORM

PATRON Address Phone	
	Elementary High School College Adult
Needed for	Question
	Job, Assignment, General Reading, etc.
To be ready	Called for
SOURCES	
	Per _____

REFERENCE FORM

Appraisals—Records. The policy on what price is given to records donated to the library for use on the donor's income tax report. Also the policy as to what kinds of records (78 rpm, 45 rpm, $33\frac{1}{3}$, etc.) the library accepts as donations.

Ballet. See DANCE.

Blind. The address and telephone number of the nearest service center for recordings and braille books for the blind or partially sighted.

Camera Clubs. A list of addresses and telephone numbers of camera clubs in the area.

Camera Shops. A list of local camera shops where films and photographic equipment may be purchased.

Cartridges. See TAPES.

Cassettes. See TAPES.

Classification—Film. A list of classification of films used by the Motion Picture Association of America.

Collectors. A list of addresses and telephone numbers of persons who collect, sell, and trade films, records, tapes, and other audiovisual materials.

Concerts. A list of organizations in the area who give musical concerts on a regular basis, such as college and high school music departments, symphonies, commercial theaters and concert halls, and ballet and opera companies.

   Printed materials on these concerts and showcards should be posted on library bulletin boards.

Damage—Records and Films. The library's policy on damaged records and films with chart of costs and how billing, if any, is to be handled.

Dance. A list of ballet and modern dance troupes, dance studios, dance films, and area dance presentations.

Donations (see also APPRAISALS). A policy on what items are accepted by the library as donations.

Equipment—Branches. A list of the audiovisual equipment available at each library branch and when and by whom it can be used.

Equipment—Phonographs. A listing of phonographs (inventory) and their locations in the library system.

Equipment—Projectors. The policy on whether the library lends film and filmstrip projectors to its borrowers and, if not, where these items can be rented, with address and telephone number.

Equipment—Purchase. A list of stores which feature projectors, phonographs, slide, and filmstrip projectors, and other equipment.

Film Festivals. A list of local film festivals and the entrance rules, plus addresses, names, and telephone numbers of those to contact.

Film Libraries—Area. A list of addresses and telephone numbers of area commercial film libraries.

A file of the catalogs or holdings of these film libraries.

Film-makers. A list of local and area film-makers, both amateur and professional.

Film Production—Local. A list of addresses and telephone numbers of schools, colleges, and private production units in the area.

Film Programs—Area. A list of area organizations, film societies, colleges, service groups, etc., who offer film programs to the public, together with addresses and telephone numbers.

Printed material on any of these film series.

Film Programs—Library. A list of types of film programs shown at the library on a regular basis. Times and place of showings should be included.

Brochures describing these programs.

Films—Borrowing Rules. A list of the policies governing the borrowing of library films by the public, together with costs, availability, and the obligations of the borrower in regard to damage, theft, etc.

Films—Free-loan. A list of commercial films for rental free-of-charge to organizations in the area.

A file of these catalogs and listings.

See also *Educator's Guide To Free Films.*

Films—Sale. A list of companies who offer "used films" for sale to collectors and the general public.

A list of film catalogs which are on file for public use.

A list of commercial places which sell 8mm and 16mm films, filmstrips, and other film materials to the general public.

Gifts. See DONATIONS.

Holidays. A list of holidays on which the library will be closed.

Hours—Library. The days and hours that the library is open and the same information for the audiovisual section, if it differs.

Hours—Nearby Libraries. A list of open hours for other libraries for the convenience of library patrons.

Laboratories—Film. A list of laboratories which process films.

Listening Facilities. A location and policy of record listening facilities in your library, and its branches.

Lost and Found. The location of where lost and found items may be picked up.

Music Appreciation. A list of courses being given in your area in music appreciation, both credit and noncredit.

Music Lessons. A list of teachers, especially piano teachers, who are available for teaching in your area, together with addresses and telephone numbers.

Musical Instruments. A list of music stores which sell, rent, and appraise musical instruments.

Nitrate Film—Law. Your local law on the possession of 35mm nitrate film.

Opera. A list of opera companies, opera interest groups, and courses on opera appreciation in your area.

Periodicals. A list of library periodicals available (together with what runs are on hand) which the public may check out on audiovisual subjects.

Policies—Film Selection. The written policies governing the selection of films purchased for the library collection.

Policies—Record and Tape Selection. The written policies governing the selection of records and tapes for circulation at the library.

Posters. A list of places which sell old movie and concert posters to collectors and for special occasions.

Projection Lamps. A list of sources where projector bulbs can be purchased and their approximate costs.

Radio Shows—Recordings and Tapes. A list of collectors and agencies which sell and/or make recordings of old radio shows.

Ratings—Films. A list of rating services available in your library.

Reading Improvement. A list of schools which offer reading improvement courses, plus a checklist of recordings available on the subject at your library.

Record Companies—Addresses. Addresses of lesser-known labels which do not appear in the usual record company address lists.

Recording Studios. A list of commercial establishments which specialize in disc and tape recordings.

Records—Imported. A list of importers of foreign recordings in your area.

Records—Out-of-print. A list of addresses of those dealing in out-of-print recordings and collectors items.

Records—Rare. See COLLECTORS.

Records—Sale (classical). A list of record stores in your area which specialize in classical recordings.

Records—Sale (popular). A list of record stores in your area which specialize in "pop" music.

Records—Specialty. A list of stores which specialize in dance rhythm records, foreign language discs, instructional tapes, religious albums, etc.

Records and Tapes—Dialog. The following albums contain dialog from motion pictures.

The Alamo (Columbia CS-8358)
Beneath The Planet of the Apes (Amos AAS-8001)
Bonnie and Clyde (Warner Brothers WS-1742)
Cromwell (Capitol St-640)
Inn of the Sixth Happiness (20th-Fox 3001)
Joe (Mercury SRM-1-607)

> The Longest Day (20th-Fox 5007)
> Love Story (Paramount 7000)
> M*A*S*H (Columbia OS-3520)
> A Man for All Seasons (RCA Victor VDM-116)
> My Side of the Mountain (Capitol SF-245)
> Owl and the Pussycat (Columbia S-30401)
> The Producers (RCA Victor LSP-4008)
> Romeo and Juliet (Capitol SWDR-289)
> Who's Afraid of Virginia Woolf? (Warner Brothers 2B 1657)
> The Wonderful World of the Brothers Grimm (MGM 1E3)
> (Check *Schwann* for availability and for new additions
> to this list)

Reels—Sale. A list of shops which handle 8mm and 16mm take-up reels.

Religious Films. A list of commercial rental libraries in your area which specialize in films for churches and synagogues.

Repairs—Equipment. The policy on the repairing of audiovisual equipment owned by the library and the addresses and telephone numbers of companies who do such work.

These addresses and telephone numbers may also be passed on to library patrons who may need their own equipment repaired.

Screens. A list of stores who rent movie screens for film and slide programs.

A paragraph on the library's policy on renting screens.

Sheet Music. The policies governing the distribution of sheet music to the public, together with the procedures for checking it out.

Sleep Teaching. A list of those who specialize in the sleep teaching method. (A very popular question!)

Stills. A list of collectors and commercial establishments which sell or trade "stills" from old movies and portraits of actors and recording personalities.

Tape Recorders and Players. A list of stores who sell and/or rent tape recorders and players.

Tapes—Auto. A list of stores which sell audio tapes to be played in cars.

Tapes—Sale. A list of commercial stores which sell prerecorded tapes (cassettes and cartridges) in your area.

Television—Cable. The status of cable television in your area, and who to contact about it.

Television Sets for Viewing. A list of locations of TV sets available to the public in your library.

Theaters. A list of movie theaters and legitimate theaters in your city with opening and closing times (and perhaps the types of presentations and phone numbers).

Transparencies. A list of companies who sell and rent transparencies for overhead projectors.

Travel Films. A list of travel film programs and clubs in your area. (See also FILMS—FREE LOAN.)

Information for Card File

In a check of some of the more active audiovisual centers in the United States, the following information was requested most often. The majority of such information would be considered under the term "trivia," but most people in the field find that this is the type of information which is needed most often. Even with the spate of detailed reference books on the media which have appeared in the last few years, much of this information must be researched until an answer is found.

Some audiovisual staffs comb the Sunday magazine "question and answer" sections of newspapers for items relating to films, recordings, and other media, and paste them on 3 by 5 cards for the ready reference file, together with a heading and the source. Over the years, these items can become a useful file of information without the need for each library to research each item.

For convenience, some of the "most-asked-for" information is listed on the next few pages. The data may be typed on cards as the basis for the ready reference file, along with questions the staff has previously researched. There are, of course, hundreds of others, but this is a good sampling of information to have at your fingertips.

Actor—Name Changes
Some of the actors who had their names changed *after* appearing in films are:
>Julie Bishop (originally Jacqueline Wells)
>Peter Lupus (originally Rock Stevens)
>Hedy Lamarr (originally Hedwig Keisler)
>Gig Young (originally Byron Barr)
>Shepperd Strudwick (to John Shepperd, then back)
>(See *Filmgoer's Companion* for some other name changes.)

Cagney, James
James Cagney uttered the line "You dirty rat" in *Taxi*, a Warner Brothers film of 1932.

Chan, Charlie
Among the actors who have played detective Charlie Chan on the

screen are George Kuwa, Sojin, Warner Oland, Sidney Toler, Roland Winters, J. Carroll Naish (TV), and Ross Martin (in a TV pilot film).

On radio, the role was played by Santos Ortega, Walter Connolly, and Ed Begley.

Films—16mm
The 16mm films came on the market in the early 1920s and the gauge is usually designated as "nontheatrical" film.

Films—Oldest
The first copyrighted movie was *Fred Ott's Sneeze*, which ran for just a few seconds.

The Great Train Robbery (1903) gets credit for having the first story line, but actually there were many others before it.

Any photographic record made before 1896 could be considered one of the "oldest" movies of all time.

Fu Manchu
The following actors have played Fu Manchu on the screen: Boris Karloff, Christopher Lee, Warner Oland, and Henry Brandon.

There have been ten features, a serial, a radio series, a TV series, and eleven short subjects made on Fu Manchu.

Horses—Cowboy's
The following movie cowboys had horses with these names:
Rex Allen: Koko
Gene Autry: Champion
Bob Baker: Apache
Johnny Mack Brown: Rebel
Rod Cameron: Knight
Hopalong Cassidy: Topper
Bill Cody: Starlight
Buster Crabbe: Falcon
Eddie Dean: Copper
Hoot Gibson: Goldie
Monte Hale: Pardner
Tim Holt: Lightning
Jack Hoxie: Scout
Buck Jones: Silver
Lash Larue: Rush
Allen Lane: Black Jack
The Lone Ranger: Silver (originally "Dusty" but changed when Silver Cup Bread became the radio sponsor)
Tim McCoy: Baron (later Ace)

Ken Maynard: Tarzan
Tom Mix: Tony
George O'Brien: Mike
Jack Perrin: Starlight (later Midnight)
Duncan Renaldo: Diablo
Tex Ritter: White Flash
Roy Rogers: Trigger
Reb Russell: Rebel
Charles Starrett: Raider
Bob Steele: Brownie
"Tonto": Scout
Tom Tyler: Ace (later Baron)
John Wayne: Duke

Marlowe, Phillip

The character of detective Philip Marlowe has been played on the screen by:
Dick Powell (*Murder My Sweet*)
Robert Montgomery (*Lady in the Lake*)
George Montgomery (*The Brasher Doubloon*)
Humphrey Bogart (*The Big Sleep*)
James Garner (*Marlowe*)

Motion Pictures—Most Expensive

The most expensive picture ever made is said to be Russia's *War and Peace* (1967) at a cost of nearly $100,000,000.

Second place goes to Twentieth Century Fox's *Cleopatra* (1963) at a cost of an estimated $42,000,000.

Never on Sunday

Based on an original screen play by Jules Dassin, who also produced, directed, and acted in the 1960 film. The same screen play was later adapted by the author into a Broadway musical called *Illya Darling*.

Opera

The world's most popular and most performed operas are said to be: *Aida*, *La Boheme*, and *Carmen*.

Opera—Singers

The highest note ever sung was C above high C by Lucrezia Agujari (recorded by composer W. A. Mozart).

Singers who have sung the longest at the "Met" include:
George Cehanovsky (40 yrs)   Giovanni Martinelli (32)
Antonio Scotti (34)   Angelo Bada (30)

Leon Rothier (29)
Lily Pons (28)
Lawrence Tibbett (27)

Alessio de Paolis (26)
Adamo Didur (25)
Nicola Moscona (25)

Riley, Chester
Jackie Gleason was the first Chester Riley on the DuMont TV network's *The Life of Riley*. William Bendix took over the role on TV and later in a Universal Picture. Rosemary DeCamp was Gleason's "wife" in the series and Marjorie Reynolds was Bendix's "wife."

Ryan's Daughter
Based on an original screenplay by Robert Bolt.

Tarzan
The following actors have played Tarzan in the movies and on TV:

Elmo Lincoln
Gene Polar
P. Dempsey Tabler
James H. Pierce
Frank Merrill
Johnny Weismuller
Mike Henry

Buster Crabbe
Herman Brix (later named Bruce Bennett)
Glenn Morris
Lex Barker
Gordon Scott
Jock Mahoney
Ron Ely

Theater—Drive-ins
The first drive-in theater (as opposed to the conventional indoor or "hard-top" theater) was opened in a parking lot behind a Camden, N.J. machine shop in 1934.

Theaters—Film
The Soviet Union has 140,900 movie theaters, compared to 19,000 for the United States and Canada combined.

The largest movie theater in the United States is the Radio City Music Hall in New York City with 5,959 seats, followed by the Fox Theater in Detroit with 5,049 seats.

Theaters—Opera Houses
The original Metropolitan Opera House in New York City opened on October 22, 1883. The New Metropolitan Opera House opened on September 16, 1966.

The Paris Opera House is the largest in the world.

Welles, Orson
Orson Welles made two films before *Citizen Kane: The Hearts of Age* in 1934 and *Too Much Johnson* in 1938 with Joseph

Cotten. All prints of the latter have reportedly been lost or destroyed.

Citizen Kane was released in 1941 and has been called by critics "the greatest film of all time." (Brussels)

Books

ALA Rules for Filing Catalog Cards (2nd ed., abridged). Pauline A. Seely, ed. American Library Association, 1968. 94 pp. $2.00. A basic reference work covering the alphabetical arrangement and filing of entries in a card catalog.

A–Z of Movie Making. Wolf Rilla. Viking, 1970. 128 pp. illus. $6.95. The technique of shooting film on a professional basis. Bibliography, but no index.

The Academy Awards: A Pictorial History (rev. ed.). Paul Michael. Crown, 1968. 341 pp. illus. $7.95. Covers Academy Award winners from 1927 to 1968 with name and film title indexes.

*Academy Awards Illustrated. Robert Osborne. Marvin Miller Enterprises, 1965. illus. $9.95 ($5.00 paperbound). A history of the Academy Awards, complete with biographies of winners and list of nominees who lost. Only major honors are covered: best picture, actor, actress, supporting players, and special Oscars.

Academy Players Directory. Margaret Herrick, ed. Academy of Motion Picture Arts and Sciences, 1970. 2 vols. 1,000+ pp. illus. $60.00 (paperbound). A pictorial directory of actors currently in films, with photographs. Volume 1 is devoted to women (characters, ingenues, and leading), children, racial ("colored" and Oriental), and names and addresses of studio casting, artist's, and writer's representatives. Volume 2 covers men in the same categories.

*An Actor's Guide to the Talkies. Richard B. Dimmitt, ed. Scarecrow, 1967. 2 vols. 1,000+ pp. $35.00. A companion

series to *A Title Guide to the Talkies* with alphabetical listing of actors and their pictures. Volume 1 is an index to Vol. 2, which lists the casts.

Agee on Film. James Agee. Beacon, 1958. 432 pp. $2.45 (paperbound). Reviews of theatrical films and comments by critic James Agee on films from 1944 to 1960. Index.

Allan Dwan: The Last Pioneer. Peter Bogdanovich. Praeger, 1971. 200 pp. illus. $2.95 (paperbound). Traces the 45-year career of director Allan Dwan with a complete list of his films and credits.

All-Talking, All-Singing, All-Dancing. John Springer. Citadel, 1966. 256 pp. illus. $10.00. A picture history of the Hollywood musical film from the beginning of the sound era through the middle 1960s. Complete index of titles and actors.

*An Alphabetical Guide to Motion Picture, Television and Video Tape Production. E. L. Levitan. McGraw-Hill, 1970. 797 pp. illus. $24.50. Complete, heavily illustrated encyclopedia of film, TV, and tape techniques. Leans toward the technical side.

*The American Cinema: Directors and Directions 1929–1968. Andrew Sarris. Dutton, 1968. 383 pp. $2.95 (paperbound). The assessments of 200 directors with a directorial chronology and index.

*American Film Institute Catalog of Motion Pictures Produced in the United States: Feature Films, 1921–1930. 2 vols. Kenneth Munden, ed. R. R. Bowker, 1971. 1,653 pp. $55.00. A detailed reference source for credits, synopsis, and related information on American feature films of the twenties. Volume 1 covers the films themselves in alphabetical order. Volume 2 has the performers' and technicians' filmographies, films by production companies, and a list of the films by subject and content. This is the first of a series of books which will cover the 75-year output of American features and short subjects.

The American Movies Reference Book: The Sound Era. Paul Michael. Prentice-Hall, 1969. 629 pp. illus. $29.95. An alphabetical film encyclopedia divided into six parts: history, actors, titles, directors, producers, and awards. Bibliography and index included.

The American Musical. Tom Vallance. Barnes, 1971. 192 pp. illus. $3.50. The titles of 1,750 Hollywood film musicals are indexed together with filmographies on over 500 actors, directors, composers, choreographers, and conductors who made the musical film an art form.

Animation in the Cinema. Ralph Stevenson. Barnes, 1971. 176 pp. illus. $2.95 (paperbound). A history of the animated film with an index of titles.

Antonioni. Ian Cameron and Robin Wood. Praeger, 1969. 140 pp. illus. $4.95 (paperbound). The films of Italian director Michelangelo Antonioni are discussed. Complete filmography is included.

Archaeology of the Cinema. C. W. Ceram (Kurt W. Marek). Harcourt, Brace and World, 1965. 264 pp. illus. $6.50. A complete and accurate history of the motion picture up to 1896 when films were first projected. Bibliography and index.

The Art of Animation. Bob Thomas. Golden, 1958. 188 pp. illus. $5.95. Information on the Walt Disney Studios and its animation work. Index.

The Art of W. C. Fields. William K. Everson. Bobbs-Merrill, 1967. 232 pp. illus. $7.50. A survey of the career of comedian W. C. Fields.

Arthur Penn. Robin Wood. Praeger, 1969. 144 pp. illus. $2.50 (paperbound). A survey of the films of director Arthur Penn with filmography and credits.

*The Audiovisual Equipment Directory. Kathleen A. Ryan, ed. National Audiovisual Association, 1954– . Annually. illus. $7.00. Illustrated catalog of audiovisual equipment with complete details on each item. Includes projectors, phonographs, radios, TV receivers, and tape players. Indexes and appendixes are heavily cross-referenced to aid searching.

*Audiovisual Market Place. Editor unlisted. R. R. Bowker, 1969– . Annually. $15.00. A source directory of addresses and information on films, educational radio, libraries, associations, audiovisual facilities, bibliographies, reference materials, producers, and manufacturers. A classified directory of services.

Audiovisual Resource Guide. Alva I. Cox, ed. National Council of Churches of Christ, 1966. $3.95. An alphabetical, annotated list of nontheatrical short films with special emphasis on use in religious situations. Source addresses by geographical area.

Audiovisual Source Directory. Elaine George, ed. Motion Picture Enterprises. Semiannually. Free. A national directory with addresses and telephone numbers of selected film services, including animation, tapes, film inspection machines, laboratories, filmstrips, sound effects, optical effects, projectors and equipment, phonographs, tape recorders and players, theatrical equipment, and video recordings.

The Bad Guys. William K. Everson. Citadel, 1964. 241 pp. illus. $6.95. A survey of movie villains with index.

*Baker's Biographical Dictionary of Musicians (5th ed. with supp). Nicholas Slonimsky, ed. G. Schirmer, 1971. 1,885 pp. $35.00. Published in 1958, this fifth edition is now bound with a 1971 supplement and covers dates of first performances on all major musical works, bibliography of music books and magazine articles, debut dates for performers, and their biographies. The supplement gives much space to popular and modern music, jazz, rock, country, western, and their performers.

A Basic Record Library. W. W. Schwann, ed. W. W. Schwann. 16 pp. Free. A list of recommended basic recordings, divided by musical period (medieval and renaissance, baroque, etc.). No specific versions or labels are recommended.

The Basic Repertoire. Martin Bookspan. 1966. Stereo Review. Free. Ratings of various versions of classical music recordings with recommendations for "best versions." Updated on a more or less regular basis in monthly *Stereo Review* columns.

Behind the Screen. Kenneth Macgowan. Delacorte, 1965. 528 pp. illus. $12.50 ($2.95 paperbound). A general history of the American cinema with index of names and film titles.

The Best Remaining Seats. Ben M. Hall. Bramhall, 1961. 266 pp. illus. $12.50. A survey of the lavish movie theaters which appeared in the 1920s and which are now disappearing. Full name and theater index.

Billy Wilder. Axel Madsen. Indiana University, 1969. 168 pp. illus. $2.95. A study of the works of director Billy Wilder with a complete filmography and credits.

The Birth of a Nation Story. Roy E. Aitken (as told to Al P. Nelson). Al Nelson, 1965. 96 pp. illus. $4.50. A history of *The Birth of a Nation*, a 1915 film which became one of the most famous films ever made. No index.

Blacks in American Films: Today and Yesterday. Edward Mapp. 1972. Scarecrow. $7.50. A history of the Negro in motion pictures from the early days of the movies through 1961. From 1962 to 1970, specific appearances are cited and evaluated. Old and new stereotypes are compared, followed by a bibliography and index.

*Blue Book of Hollywood Musicals. Jack Burton. Century, 1953. 296 pp. (OP). The songs sung in Hollywood musicals from 1927–1952 are chronicled and indexed. Now out of print (dealers are

charging approx. $20 a copy), this valuable reference book should eventually reappear, since its sister volume, *Blue Book of Broadway Musicals*, reappeared in a revised edition in 1969.

Bogey: The Films of Humphrey Bogart. Clifford McCarty. Citadel, 1965. 191 pp. illus. $3.95 (paperbound). A survey of the career of actor Humphrey Bogart with full credits.

Books in Print and *Subject Guide to Books in Print.* No editor listed. R. R. Bowker. 2,000+ pp. annually. $42.50 for both. A guide to books currently available, listed by authors, title, and series. Acts as an index to *Publisher's Trade List Annual.*

Bound and Gagged: The Story of the Silent Serials. Kalton C. Lahue. Barnes, 1968. 352 pp. illus. $7.50. A history of the silent film serial with name and title index.

*British Cinema. Denis Gifford, ed. Barnes, 1968. 176 pp. illus. $2.95 (paperbound). A small but exceedingly complete encyclopedia of actors, directors, and technicians in British films. Does not include American actors and directors. An excellent cross-index.

The British National Film Catalog. Michael Moulds, ed. British Film Institute, 1963– . Annually. $20.00 per year. All film production in Great Britain is chronicled by nonfiction films and fiction films which are arranged and divided by the universal decimal classification system. A complete name and producer index.

*Broadcasting Yearbook. Editor unlisted. Broadcasting, n.d. Annually. $12.35. Basic information on TV and radio, facilities, equipment, FCC rules, NAB codes, program service agencies, networks (national and regional), and station representatives.

Bunuel: The Man and His Work. Ado Kyrou. Simon and Schuster, 1963. 208 pp. illus. $1.95 (paperbound). A study of the films of Spanish director Luis Bunuel with complete credits and large bibliography.

Burt Lancaster: A Pictorial Treasury of His Films. Jerry Vermilye. Falcon, 1971. 159 pp. illus. $3.95. A filmography of the films of actor Burt Lancaster.

Buster Keaton. Jean P. Lebel. Barnes, 1967. 179 pp. illus. $2.95 (paperbound). A survey of the career of comedian Buster Keaton.

Canadian Feature Films. 1913-1969. Peter Morris, ed. Canadian Film Institute, 1972. 2 vols. 40 pp. $6.00. A two-volume set covering and documenting feature films made in Canada. Volume 1 covers the years 1913 to 1940 and Vol. 2 ranges from 1941 to 1969. Production data and credits are given, plus plot synopses and review excerpts.

Catalog of Copyright Entries. Editor unlisted. Library of Congress, 1896–   . Every 10 years. Price varies. Copyright information (and some credits) for all theatrical and nontheatrical films copyrighted since 1896. Comes in the following volumes: 1896-1912, 1912-1939, 1940-1949, 1950-1959, 1960-1969. Supplements are issued on a more-or-less regular basis. The films are indexed by releasing companies and copyright claimants.

Censorship of the Movies. Richard S. Randall. University of Wisconsin, 1968. 280 pp. $7.95. An analysis of the social and political control of the film medium with a detailed name and subject index.

Charles Laughton. William Brown. Falcon, 1970. 159 pp. illus. $3.95. A study of the films of actor Charles Laughton with cast credits and short synopsis of each film.

The Cinema as Art. Ralph Stephenson and J. R. Debrix. Penguin, 1965. 272 pp. illus. $1.45 (paperbound). The aesthetics of the cinema with a director's index.

The Cinema of Alain Resnais. Roy Armes. Barnes, 1968. 175 pp. illus. $2.95 (paperbound). An analysis of the films of French director Alain Resnais.

The Cinema of Alfred Hitchcock. Peter Bogdanovich. Museum of Modern Art, 1963. 48 pp. illus. (OP). A review of the career of director Alfred Hitchcock.

The Cinema of Francois Truffaut. Graham Petrie. Barnes, 1970. 240 pp. illus. $2.95 (paperbound). A filmography of the work of French director Francois Truffaut.

The Cinema of Fritz Lang. Paul M. Jensen. Barnes, 1969. 223 pp. illus. $2.95 (paperbound). A filmography of the works of director Fritz Lang.

The Cinema of Howard Hawks. Peter Bogdanovich. Museum of Modern Art, 1962. 38 pp. illus. (OP). A filmography of the work of director Howard Hawks.

The Cinema of John Frankenheimer. Gerald Pratley. Barnes, 1969. 240 pp. illus. $2.95 (paperbound). A review of the career and work of director John Frankenheimer. Complete credits and synopses of all films.

The Cinema of Joseph Losey. James Leahy. Barnes, 1967. 175 pp. illus. $2.95 (paperbound). The film career of director Joseph Losey.

The Cinema of Orson Welles. Peter Bogdanovich. Museum of Modern Art, 1961. 16 pp. illus. (OP). A review of the career of director Orson Welles.

The Cinema of Roman Polanski. Ivan Butler. Barnes, 1970. 192 pp. illus. $2.95 (paperbound). A filmography of the work of Polish director Roman Polanski.

Cinema: The Arts of Man. Thomas Wiseman. Barnes, 1964. 181 pp. illus. $10.00. A history of films, concentrating on the sound era. Index.

Classic Motion Pictures. David Zinman. Crown, 1971. 310 pp. illus. $9.95. Complete credits, production details, running times, release dates, and comments on 50 movie milestones.

Classics of the Foreign Film. Parker Tyler. Citadel, 1962. 243 pp. illus. $8.50. Comments on silent and sound foreign films. No index.

Classics of the Silent Screen. Joe Franklin. Citadel, 1959. 255 pp. illus. $6.95. A detailed selection of famous silent films and biographies of top Hollywood stars of the period. The appendix contains the casts of films cited, plus answers to many questions frequently asked about the movies.

Clown Princes and Court Jesters. Kalton C. Lahue and Sam Gill. Barnes, 1970. 406 pp. illus. $8.50. Short biographies of comedy actors of the silent film era who did not become major stars.

Code for Cataloging Music and Phonorecords. Joint Committee on Cataloging, eds. Music Library Association of the American Library Association, 1958. 88 pp. (price unavailable.) A basic reference work for music and record (as well as tape) cataloging for libraries covering various forms and entries with filing rules, glossary, and index. Basic reference work.

Collecting Classic Films. Kalton C. Lahue. Hastings, 1970. 159 pp. illus. $6.95. An information book listing distributors of classic silent films and how to collect them.

The College Film Library Collection—A Selected List of Films. Emily S. Jones, ed. Bro-Dart, 1971. 2 vols. 16mm: $7.95; 8mm and filmstrips: $9.95. An annotated list of films and filmstrips arranged by subjects followed by a directory of distributors and a title index. Special section on feature films which were milestones in film history.

Collier's Encyclopedia. Louis Shores, ed. Crowell-Collier, 1964. 23 vols. illus. $234.50. Entries under "Motion Pictures" include origins, early films, feature films, World War I, the 1920s, the 1930s, World War II, postwar years, types of films, technical aspects, wide-screen processes, production, distribution, exhibition, censorship, classification, and a few short biographies on selected actors and directors. There are entries under radio history, radio and television broadcasting, and color television.

*The Complete Book of the American Musical Theater (rev. ed.). David Ewen. Holt, 1971. 455 pp. $15.00. A thorough history of the American musical theater divided by major composers and lyricists, an analysis and content outline of each show, a name and title index and a song index. Basic reference work.

Compton's Encyclopedia and Fact Index (originally *Compton's Pictured Enclycopedia*). F. E. Compton, ed. William Benton, 1922–   . 24 vols. illus. $124.50. Entries under "Motion Pictures" include prehistory, audiences, persistence of vision, studios, producing, directing, acting, trick effects, sound, dubbing, projection, animation, foreign markets, film-making, and bibliography. There are short entries on phonographs and television and a detailed section on radio.

A Concise Biographical Dictionary of Singers. Harry Earl Jones, ed. Chilton, 1969. 487 pp. $14.95. Classical singers from almost every part of the world have their biographies in this book, translated from the original German into English in 1969. The biography includes the record labels for which they recorded, their voice register, and the major roles they have sung.

Confessions of a Cultist. Andrew Sarris. Simon and Schuster, 1971. 490 pp. $3.95 (paperbound). Reviews of theatrical films from 1955 to 1969 with title and name index.

Continued Next Week. Kalton C. Lahue. University of Oklahoma, 1964. 294 pp. illus. $6.95. Serials from 1912–1930 with casts and chapter titles are listed, along with an index of serial titles, serial actors, and general names and subjects. Sound serials are not covered.

Creative Film-Making. Kirk Smallman. Macmillan, 1969. 245 pp. illus. $7.95. A handy book of fundamental film-making techniques for use by the amateur or the classroom teacher.

Cukor and Co: The Films of George Cukor and His Collaborators. Gary Carey. Museum of Modern Art, 1970. 168 pp. illus. $2.95 (paperbound). A study of the films of director George Cukor.

Current Biography. Charles Moritz, ed. H. W. Wilson, 1940– .
monthly ex. August. $6.00 per year. Biographies of major film
people since 1940. Includes all Oscar winners, famous singers, and
musicians.

Current Film Periodicals in English. Adam Reilly, ed. Educational Film Library Association, 1972. 25 pp. $2.00. An
annotated bibliography of current film periodicals with appendixes
indexing them by place of origin.

D. W. Griffith: American Film Master. Iris Barry. Museum of
Modern Art, 1965. 88 pp. illus. $6.95. An analysis of the
films of director D. W. Griffith with character names of the actors.

Dames. Ian and Elizabeth Cameron. Praeger, 1969. 144 pp.
illus. $4.95 ($2.95 paperbound). Biographies and complete filmographies of the best-known "dames" (good-bad girls, wisecrack-
ing sidekicks, villainesses, tarts, singers, gun molls, and
"phenomena") in sound motion pictures.

Days of Thrills and Adventures. Alan G. Barbour. Macmillan,
1970. 168 pp. illus. $6.95. A historical study of movie serials
during the sound era.

Dialogue with the World. Editor unlisted. Films Incorporated,
1969. 206 pp. illus. $3.00. Plot synopses and discussion guides
on many films released in 16mm by Films Incorporated. No
index.

Dictionary of 1000 Best Films. R. A. E. Pickard. Association
Press, 1971. $12.00. An alphabetical listing of 1,000 famous
films made between 1903 and 1970 with story synopses and
production credits.

A Dictionary of the Cinema. (rev. ed.). Peter Graham, ed.
Barnes, 1964. 158 pp. $4.95 ($2.95 paperbound). A dictionary
on films and film people.

A Directory of Film Libraries in the USA. Joan Clark, ed. Film
Library Information Council, 1971. $3.00. Information on
libraries which have 16mm film collections, complete with
addresses and extent of collections.

Early American Cinema. Anthony Slide. Praeger, 1970. 192 pp.
illus. $2.95 (paperbound). A study of early film studios—Kalem,
Lubin, Biograph, IMP, Essanay, and the independents, plus
chapters on comedies and serials. Bibliography and index.

Eastern Europe. Nina Hibbin, ed. Barnes, 1970. 239 pp. illus.
$3.50 (paperbound). A guide to postwar Eastern European actors,

directors, and technicians, complete with full credits. The countries covered are Albania, Bulgaria, Czechoslovakia, East Germany, Hungary, Poland, Romania, the Soviet Union, and Yugoslavia.

Educator's Guide to Free Films. Mary Foley Horkheimer and John W. Diffor, eds. Educator's Progress Service, 1949– . Annually. $10.00 (paperbound). A directory of nontheatrical films (mostly shorts) which are available without charge from sponsors. Annual edition lists films by general subject matter with annotations, then by alphabet and specific subject. A complete source list is also included.

Educator's Guide to Free Filmstrips. Mary Foley Horkheimer and John W. Diffor, eds. Educator's Progress Service, 1949– . Annually. $8.50 (paperbound). A companion volume to *Educator's Guide to Free Films*, arranged in the same way, except listing filmstrips.

Educator's Guide to Free Tapes, Scripts and Transcriptions. Walter A. Wittich and Raymond H. Suttles, eds. Educator's Progress Service, 1955– . Annually. $7.75. An annotated list by subject of nearly 400 free-loan scripts, tapes, and recordings with speed and running time listed, plus distributor source. A title index, subject index, and distributor index also are included.

EFLA Evaluation Cards. Esme Dick, ed. Educational Film Library Association, 1946– . Bimonthly. EFLA membership only. Evaluations of new nontheatrical films rated by committees in various parts of the United States. Released in ready-to-file catalog card form. All EFLA cards are entered in MMRI.

800 Films for Film Study. D. John Turner, ed. Canadian Film Institute, 1969. 112 pp. $6.00. Information on and descriptions of 800 16mm films for use in film study courses.

8mm Film Directory. Grace Kone, ed. Comprehensive Service, 1969. 532 pp. $10.50 (paperbound). The first comprehensive 8mm film catalog, listing all types of 8mm films in all formats.

The Emmy Awards: A Pictorial History. Paul Michael and James Robert Parish. Crown, 1970. 378 pp. illus. $9.95. A listing of the winners in television's annual Emmy awards, including all nominees. Index.

Encyclopaedia Britannica. John V. Dodge, ed. Encyclopaedia Britannica, 1964. 24 vols. illus. $459.00. Entries under "Motion Pictures" cover history, sound, color, wide-screen systems, film art, production, direction, theater management, exhibition, distribution, animation, educational films, documentaries, film festivals, and awards. There are detailed sections on the phonograph, magnetic recording, radio, and television.

Encyclopedia Americana. Editors unlisted. Americana, 1963. 36 vols. illus. $35.00. Entered under "Moving Pictures" are articles on history, nickelodeon era, color, censorship, techniques, financing, film art, Griffith, the German school, Chaplin, montage, von Stroheim, Flaherty, documentaries, World War II, and educational films. A short entry on the phonograph and detailed sections on radio and television are included.

L'Encyclopedie du Cinema. Roger Boussinot, ed. Bordas (Paris), 1967. 1,550 pp. illus. $30.00. An in-depth encyclopedia of performers, titles, directors, and film people. Text in French.

L'Encyclopedie du Cinema par L'Image. Roger Boussinot, ed. Bordas (Paris), 1970. 772 pp. illus. $30.00. A fully illustrated (some in color) history of the great sound films and stars from all countries. Text in French.

Encyclopedia of Music for Pictures. Erno Rapee. Arno, 1970 (originally published in 1925). 510 pp. illus. $15.50. A handy work for pianists and organists who accompany silent films, written by the top expert in the field in 1925.

Errol Flynn. James Robert Parish, Alan C. Barbour, and Alvin H. Marill. Cinefax, 1969. 64 pp. illus. $2.95 (paperbound). Contains a short introduction and a filmography of actor Errol Flynn with most of the pages devoted entirely to pictures from his films. Unpaginated.

Experiment in the Film. Roger Manvell, ed. Arno, 1970 (originally published in 1949). 285 pp. illus. $10.00. A definitive treatise on experimental films and film-makers originally written by many different authors in 1949.

Exploring the Film. William Kuhns and Robert Stanley. Pflaum, 1968. 2 vols. 190 pp. illus. $3.20 each. An enrichment set aimed at high schools who offer film history appreciation and study courses. Bibliography after each chapter. No index. Second volume is a teaching guide to the first.

The Face on the Cutting Room Floor. Murray Schumach. Morrow, 1964. 305 pp. illus. $6.95. The story of movie and television censorship with a detailed subject and name index.

*Feature Films on 8mm and 16mm. James L. Limbacher, ed. R. R. Bowker, 1971– . Biennial. $13.50. An alphabetical listing of all 16mm feature films generally available in the United

States with information on running time, color, major stars, and director. Complete director's index. Supplements appear five times a year in *Sightlines* magazine.

Federico Fellini. Gilbert Salachas. Crown, 1969. 224 pp. illus. $2.95 (paperbound). The films of Italian director Federico Fellini are discussed.

Fellini. Angelo Solmi. Humanities, 1968. 183 pp. illus. $7.50. An analysis of the films of Italian director Federico Fellini.

Film. Editors vary. Simon and Schuster, 1967–68– . Annually. $6.95. An anthology of film criticism written and edited by members of the National Society of Film Critics. Among the editors of the various editions have been Richard Schickel, Hollis Alpert, Andrew Sarris, and Joseph Morgenstern.

Film and TV Festival Directory. Shirley Zwerdling, ed. Back-stage, 1971. 174 pp. $10.00. Contains a list with detailed information on the many film and television festivals held around the world each year. Each listing contains the sponsor, director, location, year established, month held, categories, types of entries, and eligibility, among other items. There is a cross-index by subject of festival, plus a special index of amateur festivals, and film TV awards.

Film Collector's Registry. Ted Riggs, ed. Ted Riggs, 1969– . 16 pp. Annually. $3.00. Information on movies and movie people of special interest to film collectors.

Film Collector's Yearbook. Ted Riggs, ed. Ted Riggs, 1971– . Annually. $1.00. A directory of film collectors divided by their collecting interests.

A Film Course Manual. Charles Sweeting, ed. McCutchan, 1971. 60 pp. $2.25 (paperbound). Articles on various phases of teaching a course in the motion picture: history, reviewing, exhibition, acting, writing, directing, the documentary, aesthetics, and research.

Film Daily Yearbook. Hugh Fordin, ed. Arno, 1918–1970. Annually. $25.00 each. The information book of the international motion picture industry contains a complete alphabetical listing of theatrical films released since 1916 with company and date, statistics, comprehensive booklist, credits, and award lists. Series ends with 1970 edition.

Film Evaluation Guide. Emily S. Jones and Esme Dick, eds. Educational Film Library Association, 1965 with 1968 and 1971 supplements. 528 pp. $30.00. A book version of the EFLA evaluation cards in alphabetical order, revised, and updated.

The Film Index. Harold Leonard, ed. Arno, 1966 (originally published in 1941). 723 pp. $22.50. A valuable retrospective bibliography of writings on the film compiled by the WPA New York City Writer's Project. Covers articles and material up to the beginning of World War II only. Excellent subject and name index.

Film Music. Kurt London. Arno, 1970 (originally published in 1936). 280 pp. $9.50. A summary of the history, aesthetics, and techniques of film music.

*Film Music: From Violins to Video. James L. Limbacher, ed. 1973. Scarecrow. 400 pp. price not set. Articles about film music by noted film composers and critics, taken from the now defunct *Film and TV Music* magazine, plus a discography of recorded film music, a list of composers and their scores are the main portions of this reference work.

Film Notes. Eileen Bowser, ed. Museum of Modern Art, 1969. 128 pp. $5.00. Study notes on 16mm films in the Museum of Modern Art circulating film collection with bibliography, titles, and director indexes.

Film Review Index. Wesley A. Doak and William Speed, eds. Audiovisual Associates, 1970–   . Annually. $30.00 per year. An index to critical reviews on educational films. Quarterly supplements.

*Film Sneaks Annual. James L. Limbacher, ed. 1972–   . Pierian. 121 pp. $6.95 (paperbound). Annually. A title guide to evaluations of over 4,500 nontheatrical 16mm sound films contributed by 40 major film librarians in public libraries. Films are rated for community use and not for school use.

The Film Till Now. (3rd. ed.). Paul Rotha and Richard Griffith. Twayne, 1967. An in-depth history of motion pictures in America, England, France, Germany, and other countries. Detailed index.

Filmed Books and Plays. 1928-1967. A. G. S. Enser. London House and Maxwell, 1968. 448 pp. $16.95. An alphabetical list of film titles derived from books and plays, followed by author and "change of title" indexes.

*Filmgoer's Companion. (3rd ed.). Leslie Halliwell, ed. Hill and Wang, 1970. 1,072 pp. $15.00. $3.95 (paperbound). An encyclopedia of film information in alphabetical form including titles, performers, themes, and techniques from both the silent and sound eras.

Filmographic Dictionary of World Literature. Johan Daisne, ed.
Humanities Press, 1971. 2 vols. $53.50. A compilation of
authors and the films based on their works, supplemented by a
large section of photographs.

Films. Editor unlisted. National Catholic Office for Motion
Pictures, 1969–   . Annually. Reprints of the top film reviews
from the *Catholic Film Newsletter* with sections on film education, a bibliography on best books and periodicals of the year,
statistics, and an alphabetical list of NCOMP ratings.

Films for Children. Editor unlisted. Educational Film Library
Association, 1965. 59 pp. $2.00 with supplement (paperbound).
An annotated list of nontheatrical films recommended for viewing
by youngsters. Due for revision this year.

Films for Young Adults (rev. ed.). Esther Hefland, ed. Educational Film Library Association, 1970. 54 pp. $2.00 (paper-
bound). An alphabetical list of annotated reviews of films
especially recommended for viewing by young people. Cross index
of subjects is a help to program planners. Bibliography.

Films in America. 1929–1969. Martin Quigley, Jr., and Richard
Gertner. Golden, 1971. 379 pp. illus. $12.95. Selected feature
films over a 40-year period are commented upon and major credits
given. Films are divided by year of release. Index.

The Films of Akira Kurosawa. Donald Richie. University of
California, 1965. 218 pp. illus. $5.95. A historical study of the
films of Japanese director Akira Kurosawa.

The Films of Alfred Hitchcock. George Perry. Dutton, 1965. (no.
of pp. unavailable.) illus. $1.95 (paperbound). The career and
films of director Alfred Hitchcock are covered.

The Films of Alice Faye. W. Franklyn Moshier. W. Franklyn
Moshier, 1971. 182 pp. illus. $7.50. The career of Alice Faye
is chronicled, together with complete credits, storyline, and
review excerpts from all her films.

The Films of Bette Davis. Gene Ringgold. Citadel, 1966. 191 pp.
illus. $6.95 ($3.95 paperbound). The film career of actress Bette
Davis is reviewed.

The Films of Cecil B. DeMille. Gene Ringgold and DeWitt Bodeen.
Citadel, 1969. 377 pp. illus. $10.00. The film career of
producer-director Cecil B. DeMille is presented with a complete
index of his films.

The Films of Charlie Chaplin. Gerald McDonald, Michael Conway, and Mark Ricci. Citadel, 1965. 224 pp. illus. $7.95. A survey of the film career of Charlie Chaplin.

The Films of Clark Gable. Gabe Essoe. Citadel, 1970. 253 pp. illus. $10.00. A filmography of the films of actor Clark Gable.

The Films of Errol Flynn. Tony Thomas, Rudy Behlmer and Clifford McCarthy. Citadel, 1969. 221 pp. illus. $8.95. An illustrated filmography of actor Errol Flynn.

The Films of Gary Cooper. Homer Dickens. Citadel, 1970. 281 pp. illus. $10.00. A filmography of actor Gary Cooper with complete credits.

The Films of Greta Garbo. Michael Conway, Dion McGregor, and Mark Ricci. Citadel, 1963. 155 pp. illus. $7.95. A review of the film career of actress Greta Garbo.

The Films of Hal Roach. William K. Everson. Museum of Modern Art, 1970. 96 pp. illus. $2.50 (paperbound). A study of the films of producer-director Hal Roach and the comedians who appeared in them.

The Films of Ingrid Bergman. Lawrence J. Quirk. Cadillac, 1970. 224 pp. illus. $9.95. An illustrated filmography of actress Ingrid Bergman.

The Films of James Stewart. Arthur F. McClure, Ken D. Jones, and Alfred E. Twomey. Barnes, 1970. 256 pp. illus. $8.50. A complete history of the films of actor James Stewart with plot synopses, credits, and critical comments.

The Films of Jean Harlow. Michael Conway and Mark Ricci. Citadel, 1965. 159 pp. illus. $5.95. A review of the career of actress Jean Harlow.

The Films of Jean-Luc Godard. Various authors. Praeger, 1969. 192 pp. illus. $2.95 (paperbound). An analysis and filmography of the work of French director Jean-Luc Godard.

The Films of Joan Crawford. Lawrence J. Quirk. Citadel, 1968. 222 pp. illus. $7.95. Covers the film career of actress Joan Crawford.

The Films of John Wayne. Mark Ricci, Boris and Steve Zmijewsky. Citadel, 1970. 285 pp. illus. $9.95. An illustrated history of John Wayne with complete filmography and credits.

The Films of Josef Von Sternberg. Andrew Sarris. Museum of Modern Art, 1966. 56 pp. illus. $4.95. An analysis of the films of director Josef von Sternberg with credits and character names of actors.

The Films of Katharine Hepburn. Homer Dickens. Citadel, 1971. 244 pp. illus. $9.95. A review of the film career of actress Katharine Hepburn with complete casts and credits.

The Films of Laurel and Hardy. William K. Everson. Citadel, 1967. 223 pp. illus. $7.95. A survey of the career of comedians Stan Laurel and Oliver Hardy.

The Films of Marilyn Monroe. Michael Conway and Mark Ricci. Citadel, 1964. 160 pp. illus. $5.95. A history of the films of actress Marilyn Monroe with plot synopses and full credits.

The Films of Marlene Dietrich. Homer Dickens. Citadel, 1968. 223 pp. illus. $7.95 ($3.95 paperbound). A review of the career of actress Marlene Dietrich.

The Films of Mary Pickford. Raymond Lee. Barnes, 1970. 175 pp. illus. $8.95. A filmography of the films of actress Mary Pickford with rudimentary credits.

The Films of Nancy Carroll. Paul Nemcek. Lyle Stuart, 1969. 224 pp. illus. $7.95. Casts, credits, synopses, and reviews of all actress Nancy Carroll's films, plus her life story and 280 photographs.

The Films of Orson Welles. Charles Higham. University of California, 1970. 210 pp. illus. $10.95. Revealing and detailed synopsis and analysis of the work of American film director Orson Welles, complete with title and name index.

The Films of Robert Bresson. Various authors. Praeger, 1969. 143 pp. illus. $2.50 (paperbound). An analysis and filmography of the work of French director Robert Bresson.

The Films of Robert Rossen. Alan Casty. Graphic Society, 1969. 96 pp. illus. $2.50 (paperbound). The films of director Robert Rossen are discussed.

The Films of Spencer Tracy. Donald Deschner. Citadel, 1969. 253 pp. illus. $8.95. The film career of actor Spencer Tracy is presented with complete film credits.

The Films of W. C. Fields. Donald Deschner. Citadel, 1966. 192 pp. illus. $2.95 (paperbound). A review of the career of comedian W. C. Fields.

Films on the Campus. Thomas Fensch. Barnes, 1970. 534 pp. illus. $15.00. A report on film-making on today's college campus, complete with sample scripts and an analysis of the production facilities on American campuses. Index.

The Filmviewer's Handbook. Rev. Emile McAnany. Deus, 1965. 208 pp. illus. $.95 (paperbound). Covers history, language, and sample series of films plus a survey of film societies in the United States.

The First Twenty Years. Kemp R. Niver. Locare Group, 1968. 176 pp. illus. $7.50. One hundred pre-1912 films are selected from the 3,000 films restored by the Library of Congress and described in detail. A title index and stills are included.

The Focal Encyclopedia of Film and Television Technique. Raymond Spottiswoode, ed. Hastings, 1969. 1,100 pp. illus. $37.50. A complete and technically detailed encyclopedia on all technique forms for both TV and films.

The Fondas: The Films of Henry, Jane, and Peter Fonda. John Springer. Cadillac, 1970. 279 pp. illus. $10.00. A filmography for the acting Fonda family.

Foreign Films on American Screens. Michael F. Mayer. Arco, 1965. 119 pp. illus. $2.00 (paperbound). Articles on censorship, classification, theaters, and award-winning foreign films.

Foreign Language Audiovisual Guide. Bertha Landers, ed. Landers Associates, 1961. 172 pp. $7.50 (paperbound). A descriptive listing of over 2,000 recordings, films, tapes, etc., appearing in 12 foreign languages.

*Forty Years of Screen Credits. John T. Weaver, ed. Scarecrow, 1970. 2 vols. 1,458 pp. $35.00. An alphabetical listing of film actors and the films in which they appeared.

Four Aspects of the Film. James L. Limbacher. Brussel and Brussel, 1969. 386 pp. illus. $7.95. Historical studies of 3-D, widescreen, color, and sound films with complete filmography and index.

4 Great Comedians. Donald W. McCaffrey. Barnes, 1968. 175 pp. illus. $2.95 (paperbound). A survey of Charlie Chaplin, Harold Lloyd, Buster Keaton, and Harry Langdon.

France. Marcel Martin, ed. Barnes, 1971. 191 pp. $3.50 (paperbound). An alphabetical biographical listing of hundreds of performers, directors, and technicians involved in the French film industry. Titles of films mentioned are indexed at the end.

Fred Astaire: A Pictorial Treasury of His Films. Howard Thompson. Falcon, 1970. 158 pp. illus. $3.95. An illustrated history of the films of Fred Astaire.

French Cinema (enlarged ed.). Roy Armes, ed. Barnes, 1970. 2 vols. 438 pp. illus. $5.90. A survey of French films since World War II, concentrating on directors and actors. Complete index, but no credits.

Fritz Lang in America. Peter Bogdanovich. Praeger, 1969. 144 pp. illus. $4.95 ($2.50 paperbound). A review of the career of director Fritz Lang with complete filmography.

The Gangster Film. John Baxter. Barnes, 1970. 160 pp. illus. $3.50 (paperbound). An index of gangster film titles plus biographies and filmographies of actors and directors who specialized in this film genre.

The Gary Cooper Story. George Carpozi, Jr. Arlington, 1970. 263 pp. illus. $6.95. A biography of actor Gary Cooper with a complete filmography.

George Stevens: An American Romantic. Donald Richie. Museum of Modern Art, 1970. 104 pp. illus. $2.50. A study of the films of director George Stevens with complete credits.

Germany. Felix Bucher. Barnes, 1970. 298 pp. illus. $3.50 (paperbound). An index to over 6,000 German film titles, plus biographies of over 400 German actors, directors, and technicians.

Gloria Swanson. Richard Hudson and Raymond Lee. Barnes, 1970. 269 pp. illus. $8.50. A complete film career book on actress Gloria Swanson with casts and short plot synopses. No index.

A Glossary of Motion Picture Terminology. Thurston C. Jordan. Pacific Coast, 1968. 64 pp. illus. $1.95 (paperbound). An alphabetical glossary of film terms used in commercial film-making.

Godard. Richard Roud. Doubleday, 1968. 176 pp. illus. $2.95 (paperbound). A study of the films of French director Jean-Luc Godard with complete filmography and credits.

The Golden Web. Eric Barnouw. Oxford University, 1968. 391 pp. illus. $9.00. A history of broadcasting from 1933 to 1953. Index.

The Great Films. Bosley Crowther. Putnam's, 1967. 258 pp. illus. $10.00. Fifty selected films covering 50 years of the movies with plot synopsis, analysis, and complete credits for each title. Index.

The Great Movie Series. James Robert Parish, ed. Barnes, 1971. 333 pp. $15.00. illus. Twenty-five of the most popular film series from *Andy Hardy* to *James Bond* are covered, including an essay on each series; complete casts and credits are also given. Index.

The Great Movie Stars. David Shipman. Crown, 1970. 576 pp. illus. $10.00. Biographies of major stars with photographs and credits.

The Great Radio Comedians. Jim Harmon. Doubleday, 1970. 195 pp. illus. $6.95. An analysis of some of the great radio comedians with name and subject index.

The Greatest Stunts Ever. John G. Hagner. El-Jon, 1967. 32 pp. illus. (price unavailable.) Pictures of stunts and stuntmen in Hollywood. No index.

*Grove's Dictionary of Music and Musicians (5th ed.). Eric Blom, ed. St. Martin's, 1961. (10 vols. including supplement). Last published in 1954, this is a detailed encyclopedic dictionary of the world of music, covering folk, classical, ethnic, popular, and other forms of music, biographies of composers and musicians, and other important information on the subject. The tenth volume is an updated supplement to 1961. Addenda and corrections are also included in the supplement. *Grove's Dictionary* is of great help in cataloging musical recordings.

Guide to Educational Recordings: Volume I. American And British Poetry. Editor unlisted. Serinas, 1971. 52 pp. (price unavailable.) Readings of poems by nearly 400 American and British poets on records, cassettes, and audiotapes are listed and described, together with a source list and an alphabetical listing of the poets.

A Guide to Film Courses in Canada. Linda Beath, ed. Canadian Film Institute, 1971. 100 pp. $1.50 (paperbound). Annually. A directory of film courses offered in Canadian colleges and universities. Revised almost every year.

Guide to Films (16mm) about Ecology, Adaptation and Pollution. Editor unlisted. Serinas, 1971. 54 pp. $2.95. Synopses of 350 films on ecology, environmental adaptation, and pollution are listed, together with rental sources.

A Guide to Films about Famous People. Daniel Sprecher. Serinas, 1970. 206 pp. $5.45 (paperbound). A cross-index of famous personalities appearing in short, nonfiction films.

Guide to Films (16mm) about Negroes. Editor unlisted. Serinas, 1971. 86 pp. $3.95. Synopses of over 740 films about the history, culture, problems, and lives of blacks in Africa and the United States. Subjects include racial discrimination, ghetto life, African cultures, the civil rights movement, Black Power, and prominent black leaders from the past and present.

Guide to Films (16mm) about the Use of Dangerous Drugs, Narcotics, Alcohol and Tobacco. Editor unlisted. Serinas, 1971. 58 pp. $2.95. Synopses of 225 films and 60 filmstrips concerning drugs, alcohol, and tobacco, together with sources and rental information. Filmstrips are listed separately from films.

A Guide to Films (for) Discussion and Study. Rev. Ronald L. Holloway. National Center for Film Study, 1968. 62 pp. illus. (price unavailable.) (paperbound). Alphabetically arranged by title, this film study guide is divided into two sections—shorts and features in 16mm.

Guide to Foreign Government-Loan Film (16mm). Editor unlisted. Serinas, 1971. 133 pp. $4.95. A list of over 3,000 films available for free loan in the United States from foreign sources, covering the arts, culture, international relations, history, science, sports, and travel. Many are in the native languages and the countries covered range from Argentina to Zambia.

Guide to Free-Loan Films (16mm) for Entertainment. Editor unlisted. Serinas, 1971. 77 pp. (price unavailable.) An alphabetical list of over 900 films of value for showing on entertainment programs, each with its own synopsis and rental source. Films on sports, the arts, animation, animals, and from many foreign countries are listed.

Guide to Free-Loan Training Films (16mm). Editor unlisted. Serinas, 1971. 205 pp. $5.95. Synopses of nearly 2,000 films available for public showings on a free basis from 310 different sources. Listed alphabetically, the subjects run from training in agriculture through writing.

A Guide to Government-Loan Film (16mm). Editor unlisted. Serinas, 1970. (no. of pp. unavailable.) $4.95 (paperbound). Synopses of over 900 general interest government films, and an alphabetical listing of over 2,000 general and specialized government films, with borrowing sources and index.

Guide to Government-Loan Filmstrips, Slides and Audio Tapes. Editor unlisted. Serinas, 1971. 46 pp. $2.45. Over 150 free-loan filmstrips, slide programs and audiotapes available from U. S. Government agencies are listed with sources for rental.

A Guide to Military-Loan Film (16mm). Editor unlisted. Serinas, 1970. 149 pp. $4.95. Synopses of over 1,430 free military government films with source list and index.

Guide to State-Loan Film (16mm). Editor unlisted. Serinas, 1971. 56 pp. $2.95. Synopses of over 540 films from 60 state agencies are listed together with the borrowing sources. The titles include films about the various states, conservation, sports, historic sites and personalities, travel, and economic development.

Guide to the Ford Film Collection in the National Archives. Mayfield Bray, ed. National Archives, 1970. 118 pp. illus. $5.00. An illustrated and annotated list of films from the Ford Film Collection on file at the National Archives. All entries are divided by subject.

Guidebook to Film. Ronald Gottesman and Harry M. Geduld, eds. Holt, Rinehart and Winston, 1972. 230 pp. (price unavailable.) A reference book of film information, including an annotated book list, theses and dissertations about film, museums and archives, film schools, equipment and supplies, distributors, bookstores, publishers, still pictures and posters, film organizations and services, film festivals and contests, film awards, and film terminology.

Guidelines for Audiovisual Materials and Services, for Public Libraries. Audio-Visual Committee, Public Library Association, eds. American Library Association, 1970. 33 pp. $1.00. Policies for standards in library audiovisual areas are defined and divided into services, materials, personnel, space, equipment, responsibilities, and statistics. Indexed.

Guides to Newer Educational Media. (3rd ed.). Margaret I. Rufsvold and Carolyn Guss, eds. American Library Association, 1971. 62 pp. $2.50. An annotated bibliography of reference books and bibliographies on films, filmstrips, recordings, tapes, programmed instruction materials, slides, transparencies, and video recordings.

A Half Century of American Film. Editor unlisted. Films Incorporated, 1968. 160 pp. illus. $1.00 (paperbound). Descriptions and subject area classification of 500 feature films available from Films Incorporated.

The Hall of Fame of Western Film Stars. Ernest N. Corneau. Christopher, 1969. 307 pp. illus. $9.75. A very complete biographical book on western heroes, villains, and supporting players (but no heroines) with a filmography on each.

A Handbook of Film, Theater and Television Music on Record. 1948-1969. Steve Smolian, ed. Record Undertaker, 1970. 128

pp. $7.00. A compilation of phonorecords including most film and TV scores listed in alphabetical order with an index.

Harvard Dictionary of Music (2nd ed.). Willi Apel, ed. Belknap Press, 1969. 935 pp. $20.00. A dictionary of music literature, including such items as musical terms, genres, operas, ballet, musical instruments, and movements; biographies of musicians and composers are not included. Excellent for finding musical definitions.

The Heavies. Ian and Elisabeth Cameron. Praeger, 1967. 144 pp. illus. $4.95 ($2.95 paperbound). A list of actors who specialize in villain roles in films with complete credits.

The History of the British Film. Rachel Low. Allen and Unwin, 1950. 4 vols. Treats the development of the British film from 1896 to 1929 with complete title and name indexes.

The History of Motion Pictures. Maurice Bardeche and Robert Brassilach. Arno, 1970 (originally published in 1938). 412 pp. illus. $14.00. A history of the motion picture industry with a name and title index.

A History of the Kinetograph, Kinetoscope and Kinetophone. W. E. A. Dickenson. Arno, 1970 (originally published in 1895). 55 pp. illus. $4.00. A history of the earliest film inventions, written soon after they were invented. Valuable historical data.

A History of the Movies. Benjamin B. Hampton. Arno, 1970 (originally published in 1931). 456 pp. illus. $20.00. A history of the silent film and of the transition to sound, including some biographical material of people who developed the movies. Complete index.

Hitchcock's Films. Robin Wood. Barnes, 1965. 204 pp. illus. $2.95 (paperbound). A discussion of the films of director Alfred Hitchcock.

Hollywood. Leo E. Rosten. Arno, 1970 (originially published in 1941). 436 pp. illus. $13.50. One of the definitive histories of the film about actors and film-makers, originally written just before World War II. Index.

Hollywood and the Academy Awards. Nathalie Fredrick. Award, 1968. 191 pp. illus. $1.50 (paperbound). A survey of Academy Awards year by year.

Hollywood and the Great Fan Magazines. Martin Levin. Arbor, 1970. 222 pp. illus. $10.00. A reprinting of some of the fan magazine articles on some of the top Hollywood stars.

Hollywood in the Forties. Charles Higham and Joel Greenberg. Barnes, 1968. 192 pp. illus. $2.95 (paperbound). A general survey of films of the 1940s. Index.

Hollywood in the Thirties. John Baxter. Barnes, 1968. 160 pp. illus. $2.95 (paperbound). A survey of the films of the 1930s. Index.

Hollywood in the Twenties. David Robinson. Barnes, 1968. 176 pp. illus. $2.95 (paperbound). An anlysis of the golden age of the silent film. Index.

The Hollywood Musical. John Russell Taylor and Arthur Jackson. Secker and Warburn, 1971. 278 pp. illus. $12.95. An encyclopedic reference work of 1,443 film musicals, filmographies of 275 of the best known musical films, an index of 2,750 song titles from these films and a biographical index of 1,100 people involved in performing and preparing the musical films. Over 130 photographs.

Hollywood: The Golden Era. Jack Spears. Barnes, 1971. 440 pp. $12.00. Articles which originally appeared in *Films in Review* have been grouped to cover the history of the film from World War I to the advent of sound. Articles include those on World War I movies, comic strips, doctors, Indians, baseball on the screen, and career articles on Norma Talmadge, Max Linder, Mary Pickford's directors, Colleen Moore, Marshall Neilan, Robert Florey, and Charlie Chaplin's collaborators. A name and film title index are included, along with filmographies of the articles.

Hollywood Today. Pat Billings and Allen Eyles. Barnes, 1971. 192 pp. $2.95 (paperbound). Biographies of 370 actors, directors, producers, writers, and cinematographers in contemporary films. All credits since 1960 are listed.

Hope Reports. Thomas W. Hope, ed. Hope Reports, 1969. $115.00. Annually. A full subscription service to trends in audiovisual education, motion pictures, and video cassettes, consisting of three separate reports. Covers markets, production, award winners, analysis, religion, film libraries, and surveys on various aspects of the audiovisual field.

Horizons West. Jim Kitses. Indiana University, 1970. 176 pp. illus. $2.95 (paperbound). A study of the western film as exemplified by three directors—Anthony Mann, Budd Boetticher, and Sam Peckinpah, with a filmography·on each.

Horror. Douglas Drake. Macmillan, 1966. 277 pp. illus. $6.95 ($1.50 paperbound). A general survey of the horror film with title and general indexes.

Horror in the Cinema. Ivan Butler. Barnes, 1970. 208 pp. illus. $2.95 (paperbound). A history of the horror film with an index of titles.

How Sweet It Was. Arthur Shulman and Roger Youman. Shorecrest, 1966. 448 pp. illus. $12.50. A pictorial history of commercial television with a complete index.

How to Make Animated Movies. Anthony Kinsey. Viking, 1970. 95 pp. illus. $6.95. A guide to film animation. Index.

Howard Hawks. Robin Wood. Doubleday, 1968. 200 pp. illus. $4.95 ($2.95 paperbound). A study of the works of director Howard Hawks with filmography and credits.

The Human Adventure Through Film. Editor unlisted. Films Incorporated, 1970. 36 pp. illus. Free. A guide for screen education teachers with annotations of many feature films, plus a bibliography and a glossary of film terms.

Humphrey Bogart: The Man and His Films. Paul Michael. Bobbs-Merrill, 1965. 190 pp. illus. $7.95. A survey of the career of actor Humphrey Bogart.

IFIDA Film Directory—A Listing of Available Film Product. Myron Saland and Paul Sawyer, eds. International film Importers and Distributors of America, 1965. Annually. Free. A paperbound directory of American companies and their foreign film product. The list is published by the distributor's name, then by an alphabetical list of the films.

I Lost It at the Movies. Pauline Kael. Bantam, 1965. 323 pp. $.95 (paperbound). Hundreds of film reviews by Pauline Kael with a complete title and name index.

An Illustrated History of the Horror Film. Carlos Clarens. Putnam's, 1967. 256 pp. illus. $6.95. A history of the horror film with casts, credits, and index.

Immortals of the Screen. Ray Stuart. Sherbourne, 1965. 224 pp. illus. $7.50. Biographies of famous screen actors, many with heights and other personal material given. No index.

In the Beginning. Kemp R. Niver. University of California, 1967. 402 pp. $2.00. Annotations of early films in the Library of Congress paper print collection.

An Index to Films in Review 1950-1964. Marion Fawcett, ed. National Board of Review of Motion Pictures, 1965. 2 vols. 301 pp. $10.00. A complete index to the periodical *Films in Review* through 1964 by name, subject, author, and illustrations.

Information Please Almanac, Atlas and Yearbook. Dan Golenpaul Associates, eds. Simon and Schuster, 1946–   . Annually.
$2.95 (paperbound). Contains Academy Award winners, and
information on sound, inventions, actors, theaters, and top-
grossing films.

Ingmar Bergman. Birgitte Steene. Twayne, 1968. 158 pp. illus.
$4.95. An analysis of the films of Swedish director Ingmar Berg-
man.

Ingmar Bergman. Robin Wood. Praeger, 1969. 191 pp. illus.
$5.95 ($2.95 paperbound). A discussion of the films of Swedish
director Ingmar Bergman.

International Directory of 16mm Film Collectors. Evan Forman,
ed. Filmland, 1971. (no. of pp. unavailable.) $15.00. A direc-
tory of over 3,000 16mm film collectors in the United States and
Europe.

*International Film Guide. Peter Cowie, ed. Barnes, 1966–   .
Annually. 480 pp. $5.95 ($3.95 paperbound). An almanac of
facts, figures, surveys, and opinions about film-making during each
year. Lists of new film books, bookshops, record albums, rental
libraries, etc., are included.

*International Motion Picture Almanac. Charles S. Aaronson, ed.
Quigley, 1928–   . Annually. Covers all films released since
1944 with major cast names. Also includes biographies of film
people with birthdates, addresses of industry personnel, and complete index of contents.

International Television Almanac. Charles S. Aaronson, ed.
Quigley, 1956–   . Annually. $12.50. Television industry
statistics, a Who's Who, addresses, names of TV press members,
and a survey of the world television market are some of the features of this annual volume.

An Introduction to the Egyptian Cinema. M. Khan, ed. Informatics (London), 1969. 93 pp. (price unavailable.) illus. Filmographies of the people involved in making films in Egypt, with
a complete list of Omar Sharif's films, and statistics on the industry.

Japan. Arne Svensson. Barnes, 1970. 192 pp. illus. $3.50
(paperbound). Filmographies on all major Japanese film actors,
directors, and technicians are listed together with credits and
plot synopsis on every film mentioned in the book.

Jean-Luc Godard. Richard Roud. Doubleday, 1967. 176 pp.
illus. $2.95. An analysis of the films of French director Jean-
Luc Godard.

John Ford. Peter Bogdanovich. Harcourt, 1968. 144 pp. illus. $4.95 ($2.25 paperbound). The film career of director John Ford, with complete credits and index.

John Huston: A Pictorial Treasury of His Films. Romano Tozzi. Falcon, 1971. 160 pp. illus. (price unavailable.) A filmography of the work of director John Huston.

Judy: The Films and Career of Judy Garland. Joe Morella and Edward Z. Epstein. Citadel, 1969. 216 pp. illus. $8.95 ($3.95 paperbound). Covers the film career of singer-actress Judy Garland.

Karloff. Alan G. Barbour, Alvin H. Marill, and James Robert Parish. Cinefax, 1969. 64 pp. illus. $2.95 (paperbound). Contains a short introduction and a filmography of actor Boris Karloff with most of the pages devoted to pictures from his films. Unpaginated.

Laurel and Hardy. Charles Barr. University of California, 1968. 144 pp. illus. $1.95 (paperbound). An illustrated history of the films of comedians Stan Laurel and Oliver Hardy with complete filmography.

Library of Congress Catalog—Motion Pictures and Filmstrips. Library of Congress, 1951–   . Quarterly. $20.00 per year. A dictionary catalog of subject and title entries of all LC cards for films and filmstrips. Annual paperbound issue. Also available are bound volumes covering 1948–1952, 1953–1957, and 1958–1962.

Library of Congress Catalog—Music and Phonorecords. Editor unlisted. Library of Congress, 1947–   . Quarterly. $20.00 per year. An alphabetical master list of recordings and music reproduced from Library of Congress catalog cards which comes in three quarterly editions and a cumulative annual. A subject index is included with each issue.

Lindsay Anderson. Elisabeth Sussex. Praeger, 1969. 96 pp. illus. $1.95 (paperbound). An analysis and filmography of the work of English director Lindsay Anderson.

Listening Bibliography. Sam Duker, ed. Scarecrow, 1964. 211 pp. $7.00. An annotated listing of readings on listening skills. Cross-referenced by authors and by subjects.

List-O-Tapes. Editor unlisted. Trade Service Publications, 1968–   . $36.00. Biweekly. A cumulative list of popular and classical tapes currently available by type of tape (cartridge, reel-to-reel, or cassette), speed, and content. A companion volume to the *Phonolog.* In loose-leaf notebook form. Constantly updated.

The Liveliest Art. Arthur Knight. Mentor, 1957. 352 pp. illus.
$1.25 (paperbound). A general history of the motion picture with
index.

Losey on Losey. Tom Milne. Doubleday, 1968. 192 pp. illus.
$2.95 (paperbound). A study of the films of director Joseph
Losey with filmography.

Lost Films. Gary Carey. Museum of Modern Art, 1970. 91 pp.
illus. $4.00. Plot synopses and still photographs from a series
of silent films of the 1920s which are presumed to be "lost" by
the Hollywood studios.

Low Budget Features. William O. Brown, ed. 1971. 240 pp.
$20.00. A "How-to-do it" handbook for independent producers
and film-makers which gives information on financing, organization, script breakdown, production boards, shooting schedules,
cost estimating, union and talent contracts, equipment and crew
requirements, among others, plus a source and a craft dictionary.
A 27-page sample film budget is also included. It does not take
into consideration anything about the "art" of the film, but
concentrates on the cold hard facts of good planning and getting
the most for the production dollar.

The Lubitsch Touch. Herman G. Weinberg. Dutton, 1968. 334
pp. illus. $2.45 (paperbound). A critical study of the films of
director Ernst Lubitsch.

Luis Bunuel: An Introduction. Ado Kyrou. Simon and Schuster,
1963. 208 pp. illus. $4.50. The 45-year career of Spanish di-
rector Luis Bunuel is covered, along with a chronology of his films
and a detailed bibliography.

Magic Shadows. Martin Quigley, Jr. Quigley, 1960. 191 pp.
illus. $4.50. A study of the origin of motion pictures up to 1896,
with a complete chronology and large bibliography.

Mamoulian. Tom Milne. Indiana University, 1970. 176 pp. illus.
$2.95 (paperbound). A study of the works of director Rouben
Mamoulian with complete filmography and credits.

The Marx Brothers: Their World of Comedy. (2nd ed.). Allen
Eyles. Barnes, 1969. 176 pp. illus. $2.95 (paperbound). A
survey of the career of the Marx brothers.

Media One and Two for Christian Formation. Rev. William A.
Daglish, ed. Pflaum, 1970. 2 vols. 895 pp. illus. $7.50 each.
An alphabetical annotated and evaluated list of nontheatrical
films, filmstrips, tapes, and recordings with a subject index for
possible church utilization.

Michelangelo Antonioni. Pierre Leprohon. Simon and Schuster, 1963. 207 pp. illus. $1.95 (paperbound). A study of the films of Italian director Michelangelo Antonioni with complete filmography and extensive bibliography.

A Million and One Nights. Terry Ramsaye. Simon and Schuster, 1964 (originally published in 1926). 868 pp. $10.00. A thorough history of silent films with index.

Mr. Laurel and Mr. Hardy. John McCabe. Grosset and Dunlap, 1966. 262 pp. illus. $3.95. A survey of the careers of Stan Laurel and Oliver Hardy.

Moonlight Serenade. John Flower. Arlington, 1972. $10.00. A chronological discography and diary of the Glenn Miller Orchestra concerts and broadcasts during the 1930s and up to 1942.

Motion Picture Almanac. See *International Motion Picture Almanac.*

The Motion Picture and the Teaching of English. National Council of Teachers of English, eds. Appleton, 1965. 168 pp. illus. $1.95 (paperbound). A guide to teaching films in the classroom.

Motion Picture Moods for Pianists and Organists. Erno Rapee. Arno, 1970 (originally published in 1924). 678 pp. illus. $30.00. A rapid-reference of pieces used to accompany silent films.

*Motion Picture Performers. Mel Schuster, ed. Scarecrow, 1971. 702 pp. illus. $15.00. A bibliography of magazine articles about film actors covering the period from 1900 to 1969 in major film and general periodicals. Indexed.

*Motion Pictures from the Library of Congress Paper Print Collection. 1894-1912. Kemp R. Niver, ed. University of California, 1967. 402 pp. $27.50. A completely annotated and indexed list of films restored in the Library of Congress film archives during the early days of the movies.

Motion Pictures: The Development of an Art from Silent Films to the Age of Television. A. R. Fulton. University of Oklahoma, 1960. 320 pp. illus. $5.95. A general survey of film history with index.

Movie Comedy Teams. Leonard Maltin. Signet, 1970. 352 pp. illus. $1.50 (paperbound). Biographies and filmographies of the best-known film comedy teams, including Laurel and Hardy, Wheeler and Woolsey, the Marx Brothers, and others.

The Movie Industry Book. Johnny Minus and William Storm Hale (pseuds.). Seven Arts, 1970. 603 pp. illus. $25.00. A book about the business and distribution facets of the film industry, chock-full of information on contracts, censorship, copyrights, budgets, and the legal elements of the industry.

The Movies (rev. ed.). Richard Griffith and Arthur Mayer. Simon and Schuster, 1970. 442 pp. illus. $19.95. An informal history of the movies.

Movies and Censorship. Bosley Crowther. Public Affairs Committee, 1962. 28 pp. $.25 (pamphlet). A concise overview of film censorship.

Movies for TV: 6180 Ratings. Fannie Donchin, ed. Consumer's Union, 1970. 52 pp. $1.00 (paperbound). Ratings for theatrical films now being shown on television have been compiled from the ratings in *Consumer's Union* and *Consumer's Reports*, which sometimes show conflicting ratings for the quality of any film in the alphabetical list.

Movies on TV (4th ed.). Steven H. Scheuer. Bantam, 1968. 393 pp. $1.25 (paperbound). An alphabetical listing of nearly 7,000 feature films being shown on television with a list of major stars, short plot synopses, and a rating. Formerly published as *TV Key Movie Guide* in earlier editions.

Multi-Media Reviews Index. C. Edward Wall and B. Penny Northern, eds. Pierian, 1971. Annually. $19.50. An alphabetical index to reviews of over 10,000 films, filmstrips, spoken records, tapes, slides, transparencies, illustrations, globes, charts, media kits, and other audiovisual media. Each review citation indicates the positive or negative feeling of the review. Over 70 periodicals and services were used in compiling the index.

Music Reference and Research Materials (2nd ed.). Vincent Duckles, ed. Free Press (Macmillan), 1967. 385 pp. $8.50. An annotated bibliography on music, containing corrections and reviews from previous edition.

Music Since 1900 (4th ed.). Nicholas Slonimsky, ed. Scribner's, 1971. 1,600 pp. $49.50. This chronology covers music and events up to 1969, in addition to having a dictionary of terms and a "letters and documents" section. Dates of world premieres of opera, symphonies and other musical works, developments in popular music and other data are listed.

Musical Accompaniment of Moving Pictures. Edith Lang and George West. Arno, 1970 (originally published in 1920). 64 pp. $4.00. A manual for pianists and organists accompanying silent films.

The Musical Film. Douglas McVay. Barnes, 1967. 175 pp. illus. $2.95 (paperbound). A history of the musical sound film arranged by year, followed by an alphabetical title index.

Musician's Diary. Editor unlisted. Boosey and Hawkes. $3.50 ($2.00 paperbound). Annually. A handy reference book which lists major musical events, a festival calendar, holidays, a musician index, world currencies and exchange rates and addresses, composers' birthdates, and first performances of noted musical works.

NICEM Index to 8mm Motion Cartridges. Editor unlisted. University of Southern California, 1970. 400+ pp. Every three years. $8.50. A companion piece to *Nicem Index to 16mm Educational Films* and arranged in the same manner.

*NICEM Index to Producers and Distributors. Editor unlisted. University of Southern California, 1971–   . Annually. $12.50 per year. A cumulative list of addresses of film producers and distributors. Listed alphabetically.

*NICEM Index to 16mm Educational Films. Editor unlisted. University of Southern California, 1971–   . Every three years. $18.50 (paperbound). An alphabetical listing of the majority of nontheatrical films currently available (as well as those out of print) plus a short annotation with rental and purchase information. A subject guide and distributor's directory are also included.

NICEM Index to 35mm Educational Filmstrips. Editor unlisted. University of Southern California, 1971–   . Every three years. $12.00 (paperbound). A companion volume to the above with like arrangement except for silent and sound filmstrips.

*National Union Catalog: Motion Pictures and Filmstrips. 2 vols. Library of Congress, 1953–   . Every five years. $20.00. A photo-offset listing of film catalog cards copyrighted during a given period. All entries are annotated and a companion volume consists of a subject list to the entries.

The New American Cinema. Gregory Battcock, ed. Dutton, 1967. 256 pp. illus. $1.75 (paperbound). A critical anthology of contemporary film-making with index.

The New Catalogue of Historical Records—1898–1908/09 (2nd ed.). Robert Bauer. Greenwood, 1970 (originally published in 1947). $17.00. A reprint of the original 1947 edition of the earliest recordings released at the turn of the century up to 1909. Of value for collectors and for evaluating collections presented to libraries.

New Cinema in the USA. Roger Manvell. Dutton, 1968. 160 pp. illus. $1.95 (paperbound). A study of American feature films since World War II with index.

A New Pictorial History of the Talkies. Daniel Blum (rev. by John Kobal). Grosset and Dunlap, 1970. 352 pp. illus. $10.00. A history of sound films and actors with a complete index.

The New Wave. Peter Graham, ed. Doubleday, 1968. 184 pp. illus. $2.95 (paperbound). Writings on the "New Wave" group of filmmakers, including Truffaut, Godard, Chabrol, and others. Bibliography but no index.

The New York Times Directory of the Film. Editor unlisted. Arno, Random House, 1971. 1,000+ pp. illus. $25.00. A spin-off from the six-volume *New York Times Film Reviews*, this book contains over 2,000 photos of film actors, over 500 film reviews, an index of performers, directors, writers, producers, and companies with the titles of the pictures they made.

*New York Times Film Reviews—1913-1968. Editor unlisted. Arno, 1970. 7 vols. 3,816 pp. illus. $395.00. A complete re-printing of all reviews of theatrical films appearing in the *New York Times* by the day the review appeared. The index, a separate volume, features complete credits by name of person and of film, plus 2,000 photographs of film stars.

*The New York Times Film Reviews—1969-1970. Editor un-listed. 1971. Arno Press. 300 pp. $27.00. Over 800 film reviews plus name and title index appear in this first companion volume to the *New York Times Film Reviews—1913-1968.*

The New York Times Guide to Movies on TV. Howard Thompson, ed. Quadrangle, 1971. 223 pp. $1.95 (paperbound). An anno-tated critical list of theatrical films now on television with source, director, and actors listed.

Next Time, Drive Off the Cliff! Gene Fernett. Cinememories, 1968. 205 pp. illus. $10.00. An illustrated history, with com-plete credits, of Mascot Pictures, and the films produced there in the 1930s. No index.

99+ Films on Drugs. Editor unlisted. Educational Film Library Association, 1970. 68 pp. $3.00. An alphabetical annotated listing of drug films together with ratings and category, classifica-tion, rating, and series listing indexes. A list of films on drugs not reviewed is also cited.

Outline of Czechoslovakian Cinema. Langdon Dewy, ed. Informa-tics (London), 1971. 122 pp. A study of the Czech cinema and the actors and technicians who developed the film movement in that country. The films are divided into major periods and fully indexed.

The Parade's Gone By. Kevin Brownlow. Knopf, 1968. 580 pp. illus. $15.00. Ballantine (3.95 paperbound). A series of interviews with motion picture pioneers. Index.

Phonograph Record Libraries—Their Organization and Practice. Henry F. J. Curral, ed. Archon, 1963. 183 pp. illus. $9.50. A survey of record libraries in England with data and statistics, plus a list of sources and a bibliography. Chapters cover policies, development, materials, storage, and other record data.

A Pictorial History of Burlesque. Bernard Sobel. Putnam's, 1956. 194 pp. illus. $5.95. A history of the burlesque stage through its heyday and its all but complete demise. Fully indexed with the names of personalities who started and starred in burlesque.

A Pictorial History of the Great Comedians. William Cahn. Grosset and Dunlap, 1971. 223 pp. illus. $7.95. Biographies and information on famous film and TV comics with complete index.

A Pictorial History of Radio. Irving Settel. Citadel, 1967. 176 pp. illus. $6.95. A history of radio with complete index.

*A Pictorial History of Television. Daniel Blum. Chilton, 1959. 288 pp. illus. $10.00. A history of television from its inception through 1959. Title and actor index.

A Pictorial History of Television. Irving Settel and William Laas. Grosset and Dunlap, 1969. 210 pp. illus. $7.95. A history of television from its beginnings to 1969. Index.

A Pictorial History of the Silent Screen. Daniel Blum. Putnam's, 1953. 334 pp. illus. $6.95. Lavish illustrations of actors and stills from silent movie era from 1893 to 1929. Index.

A Pictorial History of Vaudeville. Bernard Sobel. Citadel, 1961. 224 pp. illus. $6.95. A history of vaudeville and the great personalities who appeared in it, with a complete name index located in the front of the book.

A Pictorial History of the Western Film. William K. Everson. Citadel, 1970. 246 pp. illus. $10.00. An illustrated history of westerns.

The Private Eye, the Cowboy and the Very Naked Girl. Judith Crist. Holt, 1968. 301 pp. $.95 (paperbound). Reviews of theatrical films from 1963 to 1969 with complete name and title index.

Published Screenplays: A Checklist. Clifford McCarty, ed. Kent State University, 1971. 124 pp. $6.95. An alphabetical list of published screenplays and excerpts from screenplays with writing credits and sources.

*Radio's Golden Age. Frank Buxton and Bill Owen. Easton Valley, 1966. 417 pp. $9.95. An alphabetical list of radio programs with credits and stars. Bibliography and index.

The Real Tinsel. Bernard Rosenberg and Harry Silverstein. Macmillan, 1970. 436 pp. illus. $9.95. Interviews with film pioneers, directors, actors, distributors, etc. Photos and index.

Recordings in the Public Library. Mary D. Pearson. American Library Association, 1963. 153 pp. $4.00. A complete analysis of selecting, purchasing, processing, and circulation recordings in public libraries with a list of sources for equipment, supplies, suggested subject classification, and subject headings, glossary, bibliography, and index.

Rediscovering the American Cinema. Editor unlisted. Films Incorporated, 1970. 112 pp. illus. $3.00 (paperbound). A catalog of silent and sound 16mm films divided by directors and themes. Films are limited to those distributed by Films Incorporated.

Reference Guide to Fantastic Films. Walt Lee, ed. Walt Lee, 1972. 3 vols. $28.00. An alphabetical listing of 20,000 long and short films on the subjects of science fiction, fantasy, and horror. Each entry lists production data, cast and credits, fantastic content, story source, references, and cross-references to alternate titles, sequels, other versions, and related titles. The guide covers 75 years of film-making in 50 countries. Titles are in the original language with English equivalents in parentheses.

Remember Radio? Ron Lackmann. Putnam's, 1970. 128 pp. illus. $6.95. A pictorial history of radio and those personalities who were most popular. Name and title index.

Revue. Robert Baral. Fleet, 1962. 288 pp. illus. $15.00. A nostalgic look at the revue with a complete history of each revue and a content analysis. Full credits and index.

Ring Bells! Sing Songs! Broadway Musicals of the 1930's. Stanley Green. Arlington, 1971. 384 pp. illus. $14.95. A history of the 1930s musicals—68 musical comedies, 32 operettas, 56 revues, and 2 operas—plus listings of film versions, readings, and 138 photographes. Indexed.

Rock Encyclopedia. Lillian Roxon. Grosset and Dunlap, 1971 (originally published in 1969). 613 pp. illus. $9.95. $3.95 (paperbound). The biographies of 1,202 rock-and-roll stars in alphabetical order and a discography on 22,000 rock song titles are two of the major features of this encyclopedia. Also 122 photographs.

Scandinavian Film. Forsyth Hardy. Arno, 1972 (originally published in 1952). 62 pp. illus. $13.00. A brief history of Scandinavian films with title index (most titles are in the original language) and name index.

The School and the Art of the Motion Picture. David Mallery. National Association of Independent Schools, 1964. 101 pp. $1.00 (paperbound). A teacher's guide to leading discussions on theatrical films and teaching film courses in schools. Annotations on several hundred films. Index.

Science Fiction in the Cinema. John Baxter. Barnes, 1970. 240 pp. illus. $2.95 (paperbound). A survey of the science fiction film on a worldwide basis with credits and index.

*Screen World. John Willis, ed. Crown, 1949–   . Annually. illus. $8.95. A survey of the American and foreign film with pictures and complete credits, plus index.

Second Wave. Various authors. Praeger, 1970. 144 pp. illus. $2.50 (paperbound). An analysis of the latest European directors and a filmography of their works to date.

See No Evil. Jack Vizzard. Simon and Schuster, 1970. 381 pp. $6.95. The story of the censoring of films by the industry, with a complete reprinting of the Motion Picture Production Code.

Selznick. Bob Thomas. Doubleday, 1970. 302 pp. illus. $7.95. A biography of producer David O. Selznick and a complete survey of his films with casts and credits.

The Serial. Alan G. Barbour. Screen Facts, 1967. 2 vols., 300 pp. each. illus. $5.00 (paperbound). The plots (chapter by chapter) of sound serials are chronicled in these two volumes. Each volume is indexed and has illustrations from serial ads.

The Serials: Suspense and Drama by Installment. Raymond William Stedman. University of Oklahoma, 1971. 514 pp. illus. $9.95. A historical study of movie serials, radio serials, and television serials with complete appendixes on radio and TV serials, plus a title index and bibliography.

Shakespeare on Film. An Index to William Shakespeare's Plays on Film (rev. ed.). Peter Morris, ed. Canadian Film Institute, 1972. 30 pp. $3.00. A survey of film adaptations of Shakespeare's plays from the earliest silent films to *King Lear* in 1971.

Simon Says—The Sights and Sounds of the Swing Era, 1935-1955.
George T. Simon. Arlington, 1971. 492 pp. illus. $19.95. Illus-
trated biographies and historical facts about bandleaders and musicians of the thirties, forties, and fifties with reviews, popular music
charts, orchestra personnel, and a complete index.

*Sound Recordings Collections in the United States of America and
Canada.* Committee of the Association for Recorded Sound Collections, eds. New York Public Library, 1967. 157 pp. A geo-
graphic listing of recorded sound collections in the United States
and Canada with addresses and basic types of holdings. No cross-
references.

Sounds for Silents. Charles Hofmann. Drama Book Specialists,
1970. 100 pp. illus. $10.00. Covers the subject of creating musi-
cal backgrounds for silent films, including score examples.

Spellbound in Darkness. George C. Pratt. University of Rochester,
1966. 2 vols. 452 pp. $12.95 (in plastic spiral binding). A series
of readings in the history and criticism of the silent film. No index.

Spencer Tracy. Larry Swindell. World, 1969. 319 pp. illus.
$7.95. The film career of actor Spencer Tracy is illustrated with
complete credits and index.

Spoken Records. Helen Roach. 3 vols. Scarecrow Press, 1963,
1966, 1970. Annotated reviews of recordings dealing with readings, lectures, interviews, documentaries, and drama.

Standards for Cataloging Nonprint Materials (rev. ed.). Editor unlisted. Association for Educational Communications and Technology, 1971. $3.50. Catalog standards for nonprint materials
are listed to aid librarians in developing consistency in cataloging.

Stanley Kubrick Directs. Alexander Walker. Harcourt Brace
Jovanovich, 1971. $8.95. This biography of director Stanley
Kubrick is followed by a complete filmography and includes over
350 illustrations.

Starring John Wayne. Gene Fernett. Cinememories, 1970. 189
pp. illus. $7.95. A filmography of actor John Wayne with full
credits.

The Stars. Richard Schickel. Dial, 1962. 287 pp. illus. $12.50.
Biographies of the most famous star "personalities" from the silent
and sound eras. Index.

Sweden. Peter Cowie, ed. Barnes, 1970. 2 vols. 480 pp. illus.
$2.95 each (paperbound). Volume 1 is devoted to over 1,000 titles
and biographies of leading directors, players, and technicians in

Swedish films. Volume 2 covers the works of noted Swedish directors.

TV. Dave Kaufman. Signet, 1968–   . Annually. $1.00 (paperbound). An annual volume listing the television season to come. Complete name and title index.

*TV Feature Film Source Book. Avra Fliegelman, ed. Broadcast Information Bureau, 1964–   . Annually. $75.00 (paperbound). A title listing of feature films available for television showing. Includes many titles which never saw U.S. theatrical release. The book is divided into four sections: title index, packages, features, and sources. Midyear supplement.

*TV Movies. Leonard Maltin, ed. Signet, 1969. 535 pp. illus. $1.25 (paperbound). An alphabetical listing of films generally available for showing on television. Gives quality rating, short synopses, major stars, and director when possible. Also lists original running time. Does not cover standard westerns or "B" films which have been through the TV grind many years ago.

Tarzan of the Movies. Gabe Essoe. Citadel, 1968. 108 pp. illus. $8.95. A review of the Tarzan films and the actors who played the leading role.

The Technique of Film Animation. John Halas and Roger Manvell. Hastings, 1968. 360 pp. illus. $10.95. Techniques of animation in motion pictures are discussed along with a film list, bibliography, and index.

The Technique of Film Editing. Karel Reisz, ed. Hastings, 1958. 286 pp. illus. $7.50. The styles and techniques of editing film for the movies and television.

The Technique of Film Music. Roger Manvell and John Huntley. Hastings, 1957. 299 pp. illus. $9.00. The history and techniques of composing for the screen.

The Technique of Special Effects Cinematography. Raymond Fielding. Hastings, 1968. 396 pp. illus. $15.00. The techniques of "trick" shots and process work.

A Technological History of Motion Pictures and Television. Raymond Fielding, ed. University of California, 1967. 256 pp. illus. $14.00. A compilation of articles from the *Journal of the Society of Motion Picture and Television Engineers.*

*Theatre World. John Willis, ed. Crown, 1944–   . Annually. illus. $8.95. A thorough review of each theatrical season with complete credits on each production, number of performances, opening

and closing dates, plays which closed out of town, and productions of regional groups as well as Broadway and off-Broadway shows. Complete list of Pulitzer Prize plays, New York Drama Circle Awards, and the Tony Awards. Biographies of actors, directors, and designers active in each season are listed along with a complete name and title index. At least one picture is included of each production. Indexed.

Theatrical Events on Records and Tape. James L. Limbacher, ed. Pierian Press, 1972. A discography of plays, musical comedies, revues, burlesque, etc., with an index of composers, playwrights, and performers.

Themes—Short Films for Discussion. William Kuhns. Pflaum, 1968. 207 pp. $12.45. A revised version of *Short Films in Religious Education* aimed at the more general film user.

*30 Years of Motion Picture Music. Editor unlisted. American Society of Composers, Authors and Publishers (ASCAP), 1960. 150 pp. Subscription only. The songs from Hollywood musical films from 1928 to 1959 are indexed with recorded versions of each song listed. Originally sent free to ASCAP members, copies may still be purchased from them as long as the supply lasts.

*A Title Guide to the Talkies. Richard B. Dimmitt, ed. Scarecrow, 1963. 2 vols. 2,133 pp. $47.50. An alphabetical list of sound films together with basic credits and literary sources.

A Tower in Babel. Eric Barnouw. Oxford University, 1966. 344 pp. illus. $8.50. A history of radio from its beginnings to 1933. Index.

Tune in Tomorrow. Mary Jane Higby. Cowles, 1968. 226 pp. illus. $5.95. The story of radio serials by one of the stars who played in them. Bibliography but no index.

The Turned-on Hollywood 7. Jackie Lynn Taylor. Pacifica, 1970. 76 pp. illus. (no price listed.) (paperbound.) A history of those involved in Hal Roach's "Our Gang" movie comedies.

Twenty Years of Silents, 1908–1928. John T. Weaver (comp.). Scarecrow, 1971. 514 pp. The credits for silent screen actors are given in this compilation. Arranged alphabetically by name of actor, titles of their films are given chronologically. Also listed are the Wampas Baby Stars and the original members of *Our Gang.*

Ulrich's International Periodicals Directory (13th ed.). Editor unlisted. R. R. Bowker, 1969. 2 vols. Addresses and current subscription prices for periodicals divided by subject and country, cross-indexed by title. Indexed.

Using Films. James L. Limbacher, ed. Educational Film Library Association, 1967. 130 pp. $3.50 (paperbound). Utilization of films in public libraries, small towns, museums, schools, film societies, churches, and homes is discussed in article form. The reference section contains names and addresses of film distributors, publications, and periodicals.

The Versatiles. Alfred E. Twomey and Arthur F. McClure. Barnes, 1970. 304 pp. illus. $10.00. Biographies of some of the great character actors in films.

Visconti. Geoffrey Nowell-Smith. Doubleday, 1968. 192 pp. illus. $2.95 (paperbound). A study of the films of Italian director Luchino Visconti, with bibliography.

Warner Brothers Presents. Arlington, 1971. 428 pp. illus. $11.95. A history of the 1930s and 1940s at the Warner Brothers Studio in Hollywood with a complete index of all Warner's, releases from 1930 to 1950 with cast names, brief synopses, and review quotes. Indexed.

The Western: An Illustrated Guide. Allen Eyles. Barnes, 1967. 183 pp. illus. $2.95 (paperbound). A survey of the American western film.

The Western: From Silents to Cinerama. George M. Fenin and William K. Everson. Crown, 1962. 361 pp. illus. (price unavailable.) A survey of the Hollywood western film with complete index.

*What Did They Sing at the Met? Robert J. Wayner. Wayner Publications, 1971. 84 pp. $3.95 (paperbound). An alphabetical index of noted singers who performed at the old Metropolitan opera house, together with their roles and number of performances per season.

*Whatever Became of . . . ? Richard Lamparski. Crown, 1967–1970. 3 vols. illus. $4.95 each. A handy guide to film actors and sports figures who have retired.

*Who Wrote the Movie—and What Else Did He Write? Academy of Motion Picture Arts and Sciences and Writers Guild of America (West Coast), eds. AMPAS, 1970. 491 pp. $35.00. A complete directory of the writers of motion picture features and material from other media with a title index and awards list (both nominees and winners).

Who's Who in TV. Richard H. Heller. Dell, 1967. 192 pp. illus. $.60 (paperbound). Biographies of TV personalities, including the names of characters played on television programs.

Wide-Screen Cinema and Stereophonic Sound. Michael Z. Wysot-sky. Hastings, 1971. 284 pp. $15.00. An English translation of a Russian book dealing with the technical side of wide-screen motion pictures and stereophonic sound. A reprint of the 1965 book.

Wid's Year Book. Joseph Dannenberg, ed. Arno, 1971. 4 vols. $45.00. *Wid's Year Book* evolved into the *Film Daily Yearbook* and these first four editions chronicle the film industry between the years 1918 and 1922. Volumes are listed as 1918, 1919-1920, 1920-1921, and 1921-1922. The last volume features a cumulative list of 4,000 feature films released during the period, together with release date and distributor. Each volume lists actors, directors, and cameramen and their films of that year. An analysis of the foreign market, a list of first-run theaters, and other valuable information is made available in these previously hard-to-get books. (See also *Film Daily Yearbook.*)

Winners of the West: The Sagebrush Heroes of the Silent Screen. Kalton C. Lahue. Barnes, 1971. $10.00. illus. Biographies of major and minor western heroes and their sidekicks in silent films.

The Work of the Film Director. A. J. Reynertson. Communication Arts, 1970. 259 pp. illus. $13.50. An analysis of the work of the motion picture director with bibliography and title list.

The World Almanac and Book of Facts. Lyman H. Long. Newspaper Enterprise Association, 1868-   . Annually. $1.95 (paperbound). Academy Awards, development of sound, major film releases of the year, actors' and directors' birthdates, and deceased film personalities are all included.

World Book Encyclopedia. Editor unlisted. Field Enterprises, 1969. 20 vols. illus. $184.30. Entries under "Motion Pictures" include audiences, film-makers, sound, color, the industry, film terms, history, red-letter dates, sound, the 1940s, Academy Award winners, and a list of related articles. There are sections on amateur and professional radio broadcasting, television production, and color television, together with "famous firsts" for all these topics.

The World of Laughter: The Motion Picture Comedy Short, 1910-1930. Kalton C. Lahue. University of California, 1966. 240 pp. illus. $4.95. A survey of silent film comedy short subjects with index.

The World of Musical Comedy. Stanley Green. Ziff-Davis, 1960. 391 pp. $10.00. A selected history of the major composers and lyricists of each era. A musical discography and an index of names and songs are included.

The World of Robert Flaherty. Richard Griffith. Duell, Little, 1953. 165 pp. illus. $1.25 (paperbound). A study of the films of documentary film pioneer Robert Flaherty.

World Radio-TV Handbook. Editor unlisted. World Radio–TV Handbook Co. Hellerup, Denmark. Annually. This detailed handbook lists shortwave, medium wave, and television stations with frequencies, programs, world maps, and other data about radio and television. Indexed.

The World's Encyclopedia of Recorded Music. Francis F. Clough and G. J. Cuming, comp. Greenwood, 1970. 890 pp. $70.00. Published in England and known as WERM, this is an exhaustive and detailed listing of recordings by composer, complete with label number, personnel, and other relevant information such as reissues and arrangements. There is no attempt to evaluate the individual recordings or cite critical reviews. This is a valuable retrospective discography and phonograph reference work. Reprint of the 1952 book.

*World-Wide Record Collectors' Directory. Roy Will Hearne, ed. Hollywood Premium Record Guide, 1970. 48 pp. $3.00. A directory of record collectors, their special interests, and their addresses arranged by country and state. Covers the entire world in alphabetical order by country.

Periodicals

Action! Editor unlisted. Director's Guild of America, 1966– .
illus. six times a year. $4.00. Articles on directors and film-
makers of the past and present, and special features. No reviews.

The American Cinematographer. Herb A. Lightman, ed. ASC
Holding Corp., 1919– . illus. monthly. $6.00. Articles on
cinematography, photographic effects, and film techniques, written for the technical reader.

American Record Guide. James Lyons, ed. American Record
Guide 1935– . monthly. $6.00. In-depth record reviews, dis-
cographies, biographies, and articles of interest to serious record
listeners are the highlights of each issue of this long-published
periodical. Reviews indexed in *Multi-Media Reviews Index.*

The Audio-Visual Equipment Directory. Kathleen A. Ryan, ed.
National Audio-Visual Association, 1954– . illus. annually.
$7.00. An illustrated catalog of audiovisual equipment with com-
plete details on each item, including projectors, phonographs,
radios, TV receivers, and tape players. Indexes and appendixes are
heavily cross-referenced to aid searching.

Audiovisual Instruction. Howard B. Hitchens, Jr., ed. Association
for Educational Communications and Technology, 1956– .
illus. ten times a year. $12.00. A periodical aimed at the school
audiovisual field featuring articles and bibliographies as well as the
supplements to the *Multi-Media Reviews Index.* Not of great value
to public libraries except for the above-mentioned supplements,
which are valuable.

Backstage. Allen Zwerdling, ed. Backstage, 1960–   . weekly. $15.00 per year. Reviews of theatrical and nontheatrical films as well as stage information. Film reviews indexed in *MMRI*.

Billboard. Lee Zhito and Paul Ackerman, ed. Billboard Publications, 1930–   . weekly. $35.00. A weekly magazine covering the national and international news of the music, record, and tape industry with emphasis on popular music, the "charts," jukeboxes, and reviews. Special annual issues on country and western music, a buyer's guide, and others.

The Booklist. Edna Vanek, ed. American Library Association, 1905–   . semimonthly. $10.00 per year. Reviews of nontheatrical 16mm sound films, 8mm loops, and 35mm filmstrips. Reviews indexed in MMRI.

Boxoffice. Ben Sklyen, ed. Associated Publications, 1920– weekly. $7.00 per year. Reviews of new theatrical films and theater news.

Business Screen. Lon B. Gregory, ed. Harbrace, 1938– monthly. $5.00 per year. Articles on instructional and sponsored films and equipment. Reviews indexed in MMRI.

(Cinema-TV Digest) CTVD. Ben Hamilton, ed. Hamilton-Hampton Books, 1961–   . quarterly. $4.00 per year. Information from foreign film magazines, some reviews. Reviews are indexed in MMRI.

Canyon Cinema News. Emory Menefee, ed. Canyon Cinema. 1960–   . illus. monthly. $3.00 a year. News and articles on experimental films and contemporary cinema.

Catholic Film Newsletter. Editor unlisted. National Catholic Office of Motion Pictures, 1964–   . illus. monthly. $6.00 per year. Reviews of contemporary theatrical films and editorials, plus NCOMP ratings as to moral values. Reviews indexed in MMRI.

Christian Century. Editor unlisted. Christian Century Foundation 1884–   . weekly. $8.50 per year. Contains some film reviews and is indexed in *Reader's Guide.*

Cineaste. Gary Crowdus, ed. Crowdus, 1967–   . quarterly. $2.00 per year. Reviews and interviews on films with a political slant.

Cinema. Rod Dyer and Michael Lindsay, eds. Cinema, 1963– . triannually. $4.00 per year. Articles, interviews, book, and film reviews slanted toward the film buff. Reviews indexed in MMRI.

Cinema Canada. Art C. Benson, ed. Canadian Society of Cinematologists, 1961–   . illus. bimonthly. $3.00 per year. Interviews with film-makers, film festival schedules, and film reviews.

Cinema Journal. Richard Dyer MacCann, ed. Society for Cinema Studies, 1966–   . semiannually. $4.00 per year. In-depth articles on the cinema and book reviews.

Cinema Trails. Bill McDowell, ed. Remuda, 1971–   . quarterly. illus. Articles on western stars.

Classic Film Collector. Samuel K. Rubin, ed. Samuel K. Rubin, 1964–   . quarterly. illus. $5.00 per year. A newspaper chock-full of information for film buffs and collectors. Articles on stars, a necrology, reviews, new 8mm and 16mm releases, features, and news of the Society of Cinephiles (film collectors). Reviews indexed in MMRI.

The Commonweal. Editor unlisted. Commonweal, 1924–   . weekly. $12.00 per year. Film reviews are a feature of each issue and they are indexed in *Reader's Guide.*

Concert Artists Directory. see *High Fidelity/Musical America.*

Cue. Stanley Newman, ed. Cue, 1935–   . weekly. $8.50 per year. Theatrical reviews of new feature films, an annotated alphabetical list of features currently playing in New York City. Reviews indexed in MMRI.

Daily Variety. Thomas M. Pryor, ed. Daily Variety, 1933–   . five days a week. $20.00 per year. Film reviews and news of the commercial film industry. Reviews indexed in MMRI.

Deadwood. Larry M. Byrd, ed. Hamlin, 1970–   . bimonthly. $6.00 per year. Articles on western films and actors.

Ebony. John H. Johnson, ed. Johnson, 1945–   . monthly. $6.00 per year. Film reviews are part of this periodical, accenting black actors and directors.

Educational Screen and AV Guide. Henry Ruark, ed. Educational Screen, 1922–   . monthly. $5.00 per year. Nontheatrical film reviews and news and articles on the educational film. Reviews indexed in MMRI.

Educational Television. Charles S. Tepfer, ed. C. S. Tepfer Publishing Co., 1969–   . illus. eight times a year. $8.00. The subjects of public television, schools and colleges, medicine, business, industry, and military uses of television are covered in this periodical. A new products section, a list of sponsored films cleared for TV use, and an editorial are also included in each issue.

Esquire. Arnold Gingrich, ed. Esquire, 1933–   . monthly. $7.50 per year. Detailed reviews of new theatrical films.

Facts on File. Lester A. Sobel, ed. Facts on File, 1940–   . weekly. $200 per year. Contains information on film personalities and review sources for the major theatrical films of the year. Annual bound volume.

Falling for Stars Newsletter. John G. Hagner, ed. John G. Hagner, 1968–   . six times a year. $4.00 per year. News and information on Hollywood stuntmen of the past and present.

Film Canadiana. editor unlisted. Canadian Film Institute, 1970–   . quarterly. $25.00 per year. Covers film-making in Canada with complete information and credits on films made there. Index.

Film Comment. Richard Corliss, ed. Film Comment, 1962–   . quarterly. $6.00 per year. Articles on films and film history. Reviews indexed in MMRI.

Film Culture. Jonas Mekas, ed. Jonas Mekas, 1954–   . quarterly. $4.00 per year. Articles on contemporary cinema and book reviews. Reviews indexed in MMRI.

Film Fan Monthly. Leonard Maltin, ed. Film Fan Monthly, 1965–   . monthly. $5.00 per year. Career articles on famous and not-so-famous film people with complete filmographies and credits.

Film Heritage. F. Anthony Macklin, ed. University of Dayton, 1965–   . quarterly. $2.00 per year. Articles on films and actors, plus book reviews.

Film Index. John Howard Reid, ed. John Howard Reid (Australia), 1970–   . monthly. $8.00 per year. Interviews and alphabetical credits on sound films (12 pages in each issue).

Film Information. James Wall, ed. National Council of Churches, 1970–   . monthly. illus. $4.00 per year. Film reviews with audience ratings for Protestants and general public. Reviews indexed in MMRI.

Film Library Quarterly. William J. Sloan, ed. Film Library Information Council, 1968–   . quarterly. $8.00 per year. Articles of interest to public libraries and others in the nontheatrical film field. In-depth film reviews are indexed in MMRI.

Film News. Rohama Lee, ed. Film News, 1942–   . six times a year. $6.00 per year. Articles on the nontheatrical film, in-depth reviews of films, filmstrips, and other media, surveys of new books and periodical literature. Reviews indexed in MMRI.

Film Quarterly. Ernest Callenbach, ed. University of California, 1950– . quarterly. $5.00 per year. In-depth articles on motion pictures written for the scholar, plus reviews of new films and books. Film reviews indexed in MMRI.

Film Society Review. William A. Starr, ed. American Federation of Film Societies, 1965– . nine times a year. $5.00 per year. Reviews of new 16mm releases, plus book reviews and articles of interest especially to film societies. Reviews indexed in MMRI.

*Filmfacts. Ernest Parmentier. American Film Institute, 1958– . illus. $25.00 per year (loose-leaf in binder). Theatrical reviews are excerpted from well-known reviewers, together with a plot synopsis and full credits. Title and foreign-title indexes, plus an actor index. Reviews indexed in MMRI.

Filmmakers Newsletter. Suni Mallow, ed. Suni Mallow, 1968– . eleven times a year. $5.00 per year. Contains a calendar of cinema events in the coastal cities, a list of film festivals, special reports and articles on various aspects of contemporary personal film-making, and a calendar of underground film circuits.

Filmograph. Murray Summers, ed. Murray Summers, 1970– . quarterly. $7.00. Articles and filmographies on film personalities, plus letters and book reviews.

Films and Filming. Robin Bean, ed. Hansom Books (London), 1952– . monthly. $8.25 per year. Contains reviews of new theatrical films, articles, and interviews with stars, directors, and on film-making. Reviews indexed in MMRI.

Films in Review. Charles P. Reilly, ed. National Board of Review, 1948– . ten times a year. $7.00 per year. Career articles on actors and directors, 8mm film collectors column, film music column, films on TV, and other items of interest to film buffs. Indexed in MMRI.

Focus. Charles Flynn, ed. University of Chicago. quarterly. $2.00 per year. Film reviews, articles on films and interviews with film people are featured.

The Glass List. Paul Glass, ed. Glass Publishing Co. 1968– . bimonthly. $5.00. Articles, "top tape" charts, and master listing of 8-track and cassette tapes currently available, plus a selected list of new disc recordings.

Greater Amusements. Ray Gallo, ed. Greater Amusements, 1914– . monthly. $3.00 per year. Film reviews, news from distributors and exhibiters, and information on equipment. Combined with *International Projectionist Magazine.*

Harrison Tape Catalog. Molly Harrison, ed. M. and N. Harrison, 1970–   . six times a year. $3.50. A cumulative listing of 8-track, 4-track, open reel, and cassette tapes divided into popular, classical, spoken, and other categories.

High Fidelity/Musical America. Leonard Marcus, ed. Billboard Publications, 1905–   . monthly. $20.00. Articles, reviews and discographies of both popular and classical music, together with monthly concert news via *Musical America.* The annual *Concert Artists' Directory* is included each year. Indexed in *Reader's Guide* and MMRI.

The Hollywood Reporter. James Powers, ed. Hollywood Reporter, 1930–   . daily. $30.00 per year. Columns, news of the film industry, and film reviews are the highlights of this film periodical. Reviews indexed in MMRI.

Independent Film Journal. Morton Sunshine, ed. ITOA Independent, 1937–   . bimonthly. $3.00 per year. News and reviews of new theatrical films are highlighted, with a film shipping schedule, a calendar of feature releases, and a technical section. Reviews indexed in MMRI.

The Instructor. Elizabeth F. Noon, ed. The Instructor, 1891–   . ten times a year. $7.00 per year. Reviews of nontheatrical films are indexed in MMRI.

The Journal of the Popular Film. Sam L. Grogg, Jr., Michael T. Marsdon, and John G. Nachbar, eds. Bowling Green University Popular Press, 1972–   . quarterly. $4.00. A new journal on movies featuring interviews with film people, book and periodical reviews, bibliographies on specific film trends and occasional filmographies.

Journal of the Producers Guild of America. Lou Greenspan, ed. Producers Guild of America, 1959–   . monthly. (no price listed.) Book reviews and articles on film history and trends.

Journal of the Society of Motion Picture and Television Engineers. Victor H. Allen, ed. SMPTE, 1916–   . monthly. $21.00 per year. Technical information on the motion picture.

Journal of the University Film Association. Robert W. Wagner, ed. University Film Association, 1949–   . quarterly. $4.00 per year. Reviews of books and films, and articles on history, education, and production.

Landers Film Reviews. Bertha Landers, ed. Landers Associates, 1956–   . ten times a year. $30.00 per year. Loose-leaf format with reviews and evaluations of new nontheatrical films. Has title

and subject indexes, plus award section and other special information. Reviews indexed in MMRI.

Life. Thomas Griffith, ed. Time, 1936–   . weekly. $10.00
per year. Features one weekly in-depth theatrical film review in
almost every issue.

The Listening Post. Editor unlisted. Bro-Dart, 1970–   . Free.
nine times a year. An annotated index of new recordings (tape and
disc) plus a listing of nonreviewed releases, and printed order
forms. Cumulative issue available annually in September.

Marquee. Andrew Corsini, ed. Theater Historical Society, 1969–
    . bimonthly. $5.00 per year. Articles, statistics, and illustra-
tions of famous movie theaters of the past, the organs and organists
who played in them.

Mass Media Associates Newsletter. Ernest H. MacEwen and Clifford J. York, eds. Mass Media Associates, 1964–   . bimonthly.
$10.00 per year. Reviews of theatrical and nontheatrical films,
television programs, and recordings. Films and record reviews indexed in MMRI.

Media and Methods. Frank McLaughlin, ed. Media and Methods,
1967–   . nine times a year. $5.00 per year. Articles of interest
to English and film teachers featuring reviews of theatrical and
nontheatrical films. Reviews indexed in MMRI.

Monthly Film Bulletin. Jan Dawson, ed. British Film Institute
1934–   . monthly. $4.75. Reviews of new theatrical films
and shorts with complete credits. Annual index. In cases where
title varies on an American film, the British release title is usually
given.

Motion Picture Daily. Martin Quigley, Jr., ed. Quigley, 1918–
    . five days a week. $10.00 a year. Reviews of new feature
films and news of the film industry. Reviews indexed in MMRI.

Motion Picture Herald. Richard Gertner, ed. Quigley, 1915–
biweekly. $5.00 per year. Reviews of new feature films, short
subjects, and news of the film industry. Reviews indexed in
MMRI.

New York. Sheldon Zalaznick, ed. Aenid Equities, 1968–   .
weekly. $8.00 per year. Capsule reviews of films currently play-
ing in New York City and reviews of new films.

New Cinema Review. Editor unlisted. National Cinema Review,
1970–   . monthly. $4.00 per year. Reviews of films not in
theatrical or commercial release, underground films, a calendar of

special film events, interviews with film-makers, and independent film-making are features of this periodical.

New Yorker. William Shawn, ed. New Yorker, 1925–   . weekly. $10.00 per year. Features weekly film reviews. Reviews indexed in *Reader's Guide* and MMRI.

Newsweek. Editor unlisted. Newsweek, 1933–   . weekly. $12.00. Weekly film reviews. Reviews indexed in *Reader's Guide* and MMRI.

Notes. Frank C. Campbell, ed. Music Library Association, 1943–   . quarterly. $15.00 per year. Detailed reviews and announcements on music books, music, sheet music, recordings, and notes; articles on the record industry and music are important parts of this quarterly.

Opera News. Frank Merkling, ed. Metropolitan Opera Guild, 1935–   . weekly during opera season. $10.00. Biographies, articles on composers, singers, and conductors, obituaries, schedules, and reviews of operas in the United States and Europe, and book reviews are features of this periodical.

PTA Magazine. Eva H. Grant, ed. National Congress of Parents and Teachers, 1906–   . monthly. $150 per year. "Motion Picture Previews," rated by suitability for children and family viewing, is a feature.

Parents Magazine and Better Family Living. Mrs. Dorothy Cotton, ed. Parents, 1926–   . monthly. $4.00 per year. "Family Movie Guide" featured in each issue.

*Phonolog. Editor unlisted. Trade Service Publications, 1948–   . weekly. $132.00. A cumulative list of popular music (by song title and album title) and classical music on $33\frac{1}{3}$ and 45 rpm records. Classified by popular, theme songs, hillbilly music, show tunes, Hawaii, Latin America, film music, sacred, specialty, etc. There is a separate artist listing for classical and popular performers. In loose-leaf form. New sheets arrive each week and sections are constantly updated. Known as "The Encyclopedia of the Record Industry."

Photoplay. Patricia De Jager, ed. McFadden-Bartell, 1915–   . $5.00 per year. One page of short film reviews in each issue.

Playboy. Hugh Heffner, ed. HMH, 1953–   . monthly. $8.00 per year. Film reviews slanted toward the urban male viewer.

Pratfall! Larry Byrd. Hamlin, 1970–   . quarterly. $2.00 per year. Primarily devoted to stories and information on Laurel and Hardy, this magazine also covers material on other film comedians.

Previews. Phyllis Levy, ed. R. R. Bowker, 1972–   . nine times a year. $7.50 per year. News and reviews of nonprint media including 16mm and 8mm films, filmstrips, recordings, and other media. Reviews indexed in MMRI.

Reader's Guide to Periodical Literature. editor unlisted. H. W. Wilson, 1900–   . semimonthly. $32.00 per year. An index of material on films available in major general American periodicals. A complete "Motion Pictures" section includes an index to films reviewed. Supplements appear on a regular basis.

Record World. Sid Parnes, ed. Record World, 1947–   . weekly. $30.00 per year. The magazine of the music and record industry, concentrating on popular music with up-to-date charts, reviews, and articles on records and tapes.

Redbook. Sey Chassler, ed. McCall, 1903–   . monthly. $3.95 per year. "New Movies" column in each issue.

Roundsound. Edward F. Durbeck III, ed. Roundsound, 1972–   . every three weeks. $15.00 per year. An advertising journal for record collectors consisting of "want" lists and other information for collectors.

Saturday Review. Nicholas Charney and Jack Veronis, eds. W. D. Patterson, 1924–   . weekly. $8.00 per year. Weekly film reviews. Reviews indexed in *Reader's Guide* and MMRI.

Scholastic Teacher. Loretta Hunt Marion, ed. Scholastic Magazine, 1946–   . Weekly with monthly supplements. $5.00 per year. Reviews of nontheatrical films.

Schwann Record and Tape Guide. Editor unlisted. W. W. Schwann, 1949–   . monthly. $9.00 per year. A listing of all stereo records and tapes currently on the market. Formerly published as the *Schwann Long-Playing Catalog.*

Schwann Supplementary Record Guide. Editor unlisted. W. W. Schwann, 1968–   . semiannually. $1.20 per year. A listing of noncurrent popular records, monaural records, spoken, imports, religious, musical comedies, and film music.

Screen Facts. Alan G. Barbour, ed. Screen Facts Press, 1963–   . bimonthly. $7.00 per year. Career articles on film people with complete filmographies.

See. Sal Giarrizzo, ed. Film Education Resources, 1968–   . five times a year. $5.00 per year. A magazine which is valuable for the film teacher containing articles, interviews, nontheatrical and theatrical film reviews, book reviews, all lavishly illustrated.

Senior Scholastic. Roy Hemming, ed. Scholastic, 1920–   . weekly. $1.65 per year. One page of film reviews in each issue.

Seventeen. editor unlisted. Triangle, 1944–   . monthly. $6.00 per year. "At the Movies" and "Picture of the Month" in each issue.

Show. Huntington Hartford, ed. H and R Associates, 1970–   . monthly. $8.00 per year. Reviews of new theatrical films are a major feature of each issue.

Show Business. Leo Shull, ed. Leo Shull, 1941–   . weekly. $15.00 per year. Film reviews in each issue.

Sight and Sound. Penelope Houston, ed. Sight and Sound (London), 1932–   . quarterly. $4.00 per year. Film reviews and articles on actors, film-makers, and film history. Reviews indexed in MMRI.

Sightlines. Esme Dick, ed. Educational Film Library Association, 1967–   . five times a year. $8.00 per year. Contains articles on new films and film-makers, a Film Review Digest, news of EFLA, special features, but no reviews.

Soviet Film. Editor unlisted. Russian publication, available at newsstands only. monthly. $.35 per copy. Lavishly illustrated magazine on current Soviet productions and film personalities.

Stereo Review (formerly *HI-FI—Stereo Review*). William Anderson, ed. Ziff-Davis, 1944–   . monthly. $7.00. Articles on musicians, equipment, recordings, and reviews of classical and entertainment records, and stereo tapes are featured in this periodical. Reviews indexed in MMRI.

TV Guide. Marrill Panitt, ed. Triangle Publications, 1952–   . weekly. $7.00 per year. Critical commentary, stories on TV people and the television industry, reviews of feature films on television, and a complete listing of TV programs for each area of the United States. Not indexed.

Take One. Peter Lebensold, ed. Unicorn (Canada), 1966–   . bimonthly. $3.00 per year. Articles on film-makers and film-making plus film and book reviews.

Talking Book Topics. Editor unlisted. Talking Book Topics, 1934–   . bimonthly. free. Reviews, annotations of new recorded and taped books, and a plastic audio record appear in each issue of the magazine which informs readers (in large type) of developments and activities in library service for the blind and physically handicapped.

Tape Recording. Robert Angus, ed. A-TR Publications, 1954–
. seven times a year. $3.00 per year. Technical articles on
getting the most out of a tape recorder and player are the mainstay
of this periodical, which also has reviews on new tapes in each
issue. Reviews indexed in MMRI.

Those Enduring Matinee Idols. Robert Malcomson, ed. Malcomson, 1969–   . six times a year. $5.00 per year. A small maga-
zine devoted to movie serials.

Time. No editor listed. Time, 1923–   . weekly. $12.00 per
year. Film reviews in each issue under "Cinema." Reviews indexed in MMRI.

Variety. Abel Green, ed. Variety, 1905–   . weekly. $20.00
per year. Complete section on all aspects of the film with reviews
of current theatrical motion pictures. The most complete film
reviewing service of any publication. Concert reviews also appear.
Film reviews indexed in MMRI.

Views and Reviews. Jon Tuska, ed. Views and Reviews, 1969–
. quarterly. $4.00 per year. Filmographies on actors, de-
tectives, and western stars plus recordings and art.

The Village Voice. Daniel Wolf, ed. The Village Voice, 1955–
. weekly. $7.00. Detailed film reviews and criticism of new
theatrical films and special film programs in the New York City
area.

Vogue (Incorporating Vanity Fair). Diana Vreeland, ed. Conde
Nast, 1892–   . biweekly. $10.00 per year. Reviews of new
films in each issue.

Yesteryear. Ted Riggs, ed. Ted Riggs, 1971–   . semiannually.
$4.00 per year. A periodical featuring articles on old movies, early
radio-TV personalities, and other entertainers.

Reference Works Indexed by Subject

This subject index to the reference works included in this edition will lead the researcher directly to the books and periodicals containing the information needed to answer a particular reference question.

ACADEMY AWARDS—
  NOMINEES
Academy Awards Illustrated
American Movies Reference Book
Forty Years of Screen Credits

ACADEMY AWARDS—
  WINNERS
The Academy Awards: A Pictorial
  History
Academy Awards Illustrated
American Movies Reference Book
Film Daily Yearbook
Guidebook to Film
Hollywood and the Academy Awards
Information Please Almanac
World Almanac
World Book Encyclopedia

ACTORS—BIOGRAPHIES
American Movies Reference Book
The Bad Guys
Collier's Encyclopedia
Continued Next Week
Current Biography

Dames
Deadwood
Eastern Europe
L'Encyclopedie du Cinema
Film Fan Monthly
Filmgoer's Companion
Film Heritage
Filmograph
Films and Filming
Films in Review
France
Germany
Hall of Fame of Western Film Stars
The Heavies
A History of the Movies
Information Please Almanac
International Motion Picture Almanac
Introduction to the Egyptian Cinema
Motion Picture Performers
Outline of the Czechoslovakian
  Cinema
Screen Facts
Sight and Sound
Sweden
Theatre World

ACTORS—BIOGRAPHIES
(*Cont.*)
Whatever Became of . . . ?
Who's Who in TV
Winners of the West
Yesteryear
(See also COMEDIANS; VILLAINS;
  CHARACTER NAMES.)

ACTORS—CREDITS AND
FILMOGRAPHIES
Actor's Guide to the Talkies
All-Talking, All-Singing, All Dancing
The American Musical
Bogey
British Cinema
Burt Lancaster
Charles Laughton
The Cinema of Orson Welles
Clark Gable
Classics of the Silent Screen
Eastern Europe
L'Encyclopedie du Cinema
Errol Flynn
Film Daily Yearbook (1970)
Film Fan Monthly
Films of Alice Faye
Films of Bette Davis
Films of Clark Gable
Films of Errol Flynn
Films of Gary Cooper
Films of Greta Garbo
Films of Ingrid Bergman
Films of James Stewart
Films of Jean Harlow
Films of Joan Crawford
Films of John Wayne
Films of Katharine Hepburn
Films of Marilyn Monroe
Films of Marlene Dietrich
Films of Mary Pickford
Films of Nancy Carroll
Films of Spencer Tracy
The Fondas
Forty Years of Screen Credits

Fred Astaire
French Cinema
Gary Cooper Story
Germany
Gloria Swanson
The Great Movie Stars
Hollywood: The Golden Era
Hollywood Today
Humphrey Bogart
Immortals of the Screen
Japan
Judy
Karloff
Spencer Tracy
Starring John Wayne
The Stars
Sweden
Tarzan of the Movies
The Versatiles
Views and Reviews
Warner Brothers Presents
(See also COMEDIANS; VILLAINS;
  CHARACTER NAMES.)

ACTORS—PAST
Whatever Became of . . . ?
World Almanac

ACTORS—PHOTOGRAPHS
Academy Player's Directory
L'Encyclopedie du Cinema par
  L'Image
Guidebook to Film
New Pictorial History of the Talkies
New York Times Directory of the
  Film
New York Times Film Reviews
  (index volume)
Pictorial History of the Movies
Pictorial History of the Silent Screen
Pictorial History of the Western Film

ACTORS—REAL NAMES
Filmgoer's Companion
(See also PSEUDONYMS.)

ADDRESSES—FILM COMPANIES
Audiovisual Market Place
Audiovisual Source Directory
Feature Films on 8mm and 16mm
Film Daily Yearbook
International Motion Picture
  Almanac
International Television Almanac
Landers Film Reviews
NICEM Index to Producers and
  Distributors

ADDRESSES—RECORD COMPANIES
Billboard Buyer's Guide

ANIMATION
Animation in the Cinema
Art of Animation
Art of Walt Disney
Encyclopaedia Britannica
How to Make Animated Movies
Technique of Film Animation

ARTICLES
Motion Picture Performers

AUDIENCES
Collier's Encyclopedia
World Book Encyclopedia

AUDIOVISUAL EDUCATION
Audiovisual Instruction
Hope Reports

AWARDS (other than Academy Awards)
American Movies Reference Book
Emmy Awards: A Pictorial History
Encyclopaedia Britannica
Film Daily Yearbook
Foreign Films on American Screens
Guidebook to Film
Who Wrote the Movie—

BALLET MUSIC
Harvard Dictionary of Music
Schwann Record and Tape Guide

BIBLIOGRAPHY
A Basic Record Library
Compton's Encyclopedia and Fact
  Index
Current Film Periodicals in English
Facts on File
The Film Index
Film Review Index
Guidebook to Film
Guides for Newer Educational Media
Listening Bibliography
Motion Picture Performers
Multi-Media Reviews Index
Music Reference and Research
  Materials
99+ Films on Drugs

BIRTHDATES
Musician's Diary
World Almanac

BLACKS IN FILMS
Blacks in American Films
Guide to Films (16mm) about
  Negroes

BOOKS—BIBLIOGRAPHY
Books in Print
Current Film Periodicals in English
Film Daily Yearbook
Filmed Books and Plays
International Film Guide
Subject Guide to Books in Print

BOOKS—FILMS OF
Catalog of Copyright Entries—
  Motion Pictures
Filmed Books and Plays

BOOKS—MUSIC
Notes
Opera News

BOOKS—REVIEWS. See
REVIEWS—BOOKS.

BOOKSTORES
Guidebook to Film

BRITISH FILMS. See
FILMS—FOREIGN.

BROADCASTING. See
RADIO AND TELEVISION.

BURLESQUE
A Pictorial History of Burlesque

CANADA. See FILMS—
FOREIGN.

CARTOONS. See ANIMATION.

CAST NAMES. See
CHARACTER NAMES.

CASTS. See CREDITS.

CATALOGING
Code for Cataloging Music and
Phonorecords
Standards of Cataloging Nonprint
Materials

CENSORSHIP AND
CLASSIFICATION
Censorship and the Movies
Collier's Encyclopedia
Encyclopedia Americana
The Face on the Cutting Room Floor
Film Daily Yearbook
Foreign Films on American Screens
The Movie Industry Book
Movies and Censorship
New York Times Index
See No Evil

CHARACTER NAMES
American Film Institute Catalog of
Motion Pictures
Filmfacts
New York Times Film Reviews
Title Guide to the Talkies

CHILDREN'S FILMS. See
FILMS—CHILDREN AND
YOUNG ADULTS.

CINEMATOGRAPHY AND
CINEMATOGRAPHERS
The American Cinematographer
Film Daily Yearbook
Film Comment (8:27–57, Summer
1972)
New York Times Film Reviews
Wid's Year Book

COLLECTORS—FILM
Classic Film Collector
Collecting Classic Films
Film Collector's Registry
Film Collector's Yearbook
International Directory of 16mm
Film Collectors

COLLECTORS—RECORDS
AND TAPES
New Catalog of Historical Records
Round Sound
Sound Recordings Collections in the
United States of America and
Canada
World-Wide Record Collector's
Directory

COLOR FILMS
Encyclopaedia Britannica
Four Aspects of the Film
World Book Encyclopedia

COMEDIANS—BIOGRAPHIES AND FILMOGRAPHIES
Art of W. C. Fields
Buster Keaton
Clown Princes and Court Jesters
Films of Charlie Chaplin
Films of Laurel and Hardy
Films of W. C. Fields
4 Great Comedians
Laurel and Hardy
The Marx Brothers
Mr. Laurel and Mr. Hardy
Movie Comedy Teams
A Pictorial History of the Great
  Comedians
Pratfall
The Turned-On Hollywood 7
The World of Laughter

COMPOSERS
Film Music: From Violins to Video
(See also MUSIC AND MUSICIANS.)

CONCERTS
High Fidelity/Musical America

COPYRIGHTS
Catalog of Copyright Entries—
  Motion Pictures

CREDITS
Film Daily Yearbook
Film Index
Filmfacts
Films in America
The First 20 Years
Forty Years of Screen Credits
The Great Films
Monthly Film Bulletin
Motion Pictures
Motion Pictures from the Library of
  Congress Paper Print Collection
National Union Catalog: Motion
  Pictures and Filmstrips

New York Times Film Reviews
Published Screenplays: A Checklist
Science Fiction in the Cinema
Screen World
Selznick
Theatre World
Variety
Views and Reviews
What Did They Sing at the Met?

CZECHOSLOVAKIA. See FILMS—FOREIGN.

DANCE BANDS
Simon Says

DEAD END KIDS
Forty Years of Screen Credits

DICTIONARIES AND GLOSSARIES
Alphabetical Guide to Motion
  Picture, Television and Videotape
  Production
Dictionary of 1000 Best Films
A Dictionary of the Cinema
Glossary of Motion Picture
  Terminology
Grove's Dictionary of Music and
  Musicians
Guidebook to Film
Harvard Dictionary of Music
World Book Encyclopedia

DIRECTORIES
Audiovisual Market Place
Audiovisual Source Directory
Directory of Film Libraries in the
  USA
8mm Film Directory
Feature Films on 8mm and 16mm
Film Daily Yearbook
A Guide to Film Courses in Canada
IFIDA Film Directory

DIRECTORIES (*Cont.*)

International Directory of 16mm
Film Collectors
International Film Guide
International Motion Picture
Almanac
International Television Almanac
Library of Congress Catalog of
Motion Pictures and Filmstrips

DIRECTORS—AMERICAN

Action!
Allan Dwan
The American Cinema
American Movies Reference Book
Arthur Penn
Billy Wilder
Cinema of Alfred Hitchcock
Cinema of Fritz Lang
Cinema of Howard Hawks
Cinema of John Frankenheimer
Cinema of Joseph Losey
Cinema of Orson Welles
Collier's Encyclopedia
Compton's Encyclopedia and Fact
Index
Cukor and Co.
Current Biography
D. W. Griffith
Encyclopaedia Britannica
L'Encyclopedie du Cinema
Feature Films on 8mm and 16mm
Films and Filming
Films of Alfred Hitchcock
Films of Cecil B. DeMille
Films of Charlie Chaplin
Films of Hal Roach
Films of Josef von Sternberg
Films of Robert Rossen
Fritz Lang in America
George Stevens
Hitchcock's Films
Hollywood Today
Horizons West
Howard Hawks

John Ford
John Huston
The Lubitsch Touch
Losey on Losey
Mamoulian
Stanley Kubrick Directs
The World of the Film Director
World of Robert Flaherty
(See also PSEUDONYMS.)

DIRECTORS—FOREIGN

Antonioni
British Cinema
Bunuel
Cinema as Art
Cinema of Alain Resnais
Cinema of Francois Truffaut
Cinema of Fritz Lang
Eastern Europe
L'Encyclopedie du Cinema
Feature Films on 8mm and 16mm
Federico Fellini
Fellini
Films and Filming
Films of Akira Kurosawa
Films of Jean-Luc Godard
Films of Robert Bresson
Films of Roman Polanski
France
French Cinema
Germany
Godard
Ingmar Bergman
Introduction to the Egyptian Cinema
Japan
Jean-Luc Godard
Lindsay Anderson
Luis Bunuel
Michelangelo Antonioni
New Wave
Outline of Czechoslovakian Cinema
Second Wave
Sweden
Visconti
(See also PSEUDONYMS.)

DISCOGRAPHIES
American Record Guide
A Basic Record Library
Film Music: From Violins to Video
List-O-Tapes
Phonolog
Theatrical Events on Records and
  Tape
The World of Musical Comedy
(See also RECORDS AND TAPES.)

DISSERTATIONS. See THESES
AND DISSERTATIONS.

DISTRIBUTION
Catalog of Copyright Entries—
  Motion Pictures
Colliers's Encyclopedia
Encyclopaedia Britannica
Guidebook to Film
The Movie Industry Book
NICEM Index to Producers and
  Distributors

DOCUMENTARIES
Encyclopaedia Britannica
Film Comment
World of Robert Flaherty

EDUCATIONAL FILMS
Encyclopaedia Britannica
Film "Sneaks" Annual
(See also REVIEWS AND
  RATINGS—NONTHEATRICAL
  FILMS.)

EGYPT. See FILMS—FOREIGN.

8MM FILMS. See REVIEWS AND
RATINGS—NONTHEATRICAL
FILMS.

ENCYCLOPEDIAS
Collier's Encyclopedia
Compton's Encyclopedia and Fact
  Index

Encyclopedia Americana
Encyclopaedia Britannica
L'Encyclopedie du Cinema
Filmgoer's Companion
Focal Encyclopedia of Film and
  Television Techniques
World Book Encyclopedia

ENGLAND. See FILMS—
FOREIGN.

EQUIPMENT
Audio-Visual Equipment Directory
Greater Amusements
Guidebook to Film

EVALUATIONS. See REVIEWS
AND RATINGS.

EXHIBITION
Collier's Encyclopedia
Encyclopaedia Britannica
Greater Amusements

FAN MAGAZINES
Hollywood and the Great Fan
  Magazines
Photoplay

FESTIVALS
Cinema Canada
Encyclopaedia Britannica
Film and TV Festival Directory
Film News
Filmmaker's Newsletter
New Cinema Review
Screen Education News
Sightlines

FILING
ALA Rules for Filing Catalog Cards
Code for Cataloging Music and
  Phonorecords

FILM LIBRARIES. See
LIBRARIES.

FILM-MAKING
A-Z of Movie Making
Canyon Cinema News
Creative Film-Making
Experiment in the Film
Film Culture
Filmmaker's Newsletter
Films on the Campus
A Guide to Film Courses in Canada
New American Cinema
New Cinema Review
Sightlines

FILM SOCIETIES
Film Society Review
Filmviewer's Handbook
Handbook for Film Societies
Using Films

FILMOGRAPHIES
Canadian Feature Films
Filmograph
Shakespeare on Film
Take One

FILMS—BOX-OFFICE GROSSES
Variety (weekly)
Variety Anniversary Issue (all-time)

FILMS—CHILDREN AND YOUNG ADULTS
Films for Children
Films for Young Adults

FILMS—EXPERIMENTAL
See FILM-MAKING.

FILMS—FEATURE
The College Film Library Collection
Feature Films on 8mm and 16mm

FILMS—FOREIGN (NON-U.S.)
British Cinema
British Films

British National Film Catalog
CTVD
Canadian Feature Films
Classics of the Foreign Film
Film Canadiana
The Film Til Now
Foreign Films on American Screens
Foreign Language Audio-Visual Guide
France
French Cinema
The History of the British Film
IFIDA Film Directory
Introduction to the Egyptian Cinema
Japan
Outline of Czechoslovakian Cinema
Screen World
Soviet Film
Sweden

FILMS—FREE LOAN
Educator's Guide to Free Files
Guide to Free Loan Training Films
Guide to State-Loan Film
Guide to Foreign Government-Loan Films
Guide to Free Loan Films for Entertainment

FILMS—MUSICAL SCORES
Film Music: From Violins to Video

FILMS—PREHISTORY
Archaeology of the Cinema
Collier's Encyclopedia
Compton's Encyclopedia and Fact Index
The Eye of History
Magic Shadows

FILMS—SPONSORED
Business Screen
Educational Television
(see also FILMS—FREE LOAN.)

FILMS—SUBJECT AREAS
Guide to Films About Ecology, adaptation and Pollution

Guide to Films about the Use of Dangerous Drugs, Narcotics, Alcohol and Tobacco
99+ Films on Drugs

FILMSTRIPS
Educator's Guide to Free Filmstrips
Guide to Government-Loan Filmstrips, Slides and Audio Tapes
NICEM Index to 35mm Educational Filmstrips

FINANCES
Film Daily Yearbook

FRANCE. See FILMS—FOREIGN.

GENRES
Collier's Encyclopedia
Filmgoer's Companion
Films and Filming
The Gangster Film
A Half Century of American Film
Hollywood: The Golden Era
New York Times Index
Reference Guide to Fantastic Films
Science Fiction in the Cinema
(See also DOCUMENTARIES; HORROR FILMS; MUSICALS; WESTERNS.)

GLOSSARIES. See DICTIONARIES AND GLOSSARIES.

"GOLD RECORDS"
Variety Anniversary Issue

HISTORY
American Movies Reference Book
Behind the Screen
Cinema: The Arts of Man
Collier's Encyclopedia
Early American Cinema
Encyclopaedia Britannica
The Eye of History

The Fabulous Films of the 20's
Film Comment
The Film Till Now
The History of Motion Pictures
A History of the British Film
A History of the Movies
Hollywood
Hollywood in the Forties
Hollywood in the Thirties
Hollywood in the Twenties
In the Beginning
Journal of the University Film Association
The Liveliest Art
Lost Films
A Million and One Nights
Motion Pictures from the Library of Congress Paper Print Collection
Motion Pictures: The Development of an Art . . .
The Movies
A New Pictorial History of the Talkies
The Parade's Gone by
A Pictorial History of the Movies
A Picture History of the Cinema
The Real Tinsel
The Rise of the American Film
A Technological History of Motion Pictures and Television
World Book Encyclopedia
(See also FILMS—PREHISTORY.)

HORROR FILMS
Horror!
The Horror Film
Horror in the Cinema
An Illustrated History of the Horror Film
Karloff

INDEXES
Film Review Index
A Guide to Films About Famous People

INDEXES (*Cont.*)
An Index to Films in Review
Multi-Media Reviews Index
NICEM Index to 8mm Motion
  Cartridges
NICEM Index to 16mm Educational
  Films
NICEM Index to 35mm Filmstrips
New York Times Film Reviews
New York Times Index
Reader's Guide to Periodical Literature

JAPAN. See FILMS—FOREIGN.

LIBRARIES—FILMS
Directory of Film Libraries in the
  USA

LIBRARIES—RECORDS
Phonograph Record Libraries—Their
  Organization and Practice
Recordings in the Public Library

LITERARY SOURCES—
  FILMS
Catalog of Copyright Entries—Motion
  Pictures
Filmographic Dictionary of World
  Literature
A Title Guide to the Talkies
Who Wrote the Movie—

LITERARY WORKS. See
  BOOKS—FILMS OF.

MUSEUMS AND ARCHIVES
Guidebook to Film

MUSIC AND MUSICIANS
Baker's Biographical Dictionary of
  Musicians
Concise Biographical Dictionary of
  Singers

Encyclopedia of Music for Pictures
Film Music
Films in Review
Grove's Dictionary of Music and Musicians
A Handbook of Film, Theater and
  Television Music on Record
High Fidelity/Musical America
International Film Guide
Library of Congress Catalog—Music
  and Phonorecords
Marquee
Moonlight Serenade
Motion Picture Moods for Pianists
  and Organists
Music Reference and Research Materials
Music Since 1900
Musical Accompaniment of Moving
  Pictures
Musician's Diary
Notes
Opera News
Record World
Rock Encyclopedia
Simon Says
Sounds for Silents
Stereo Review
The Technique of Film Music
30 Years of Motion Picture Music

MUSICALS—FILM
All-Talking, All-Singing, All-Dancing
The American Musical
Blue Book of Hollywood Musicals
The Hollywood Musical
Judy: The Films and Career of Judy
  Garland
The Musical Film
Schwann Record and Tape Guide
30 Years of Motion Picture Music

MUSICALS—THEATRICAL
The Complete Book of the American
  Musical Theater
Ring Bells! Sing Songs!

Theatrical Events on Records and
Tapes
The World of Musical Comedy

NARRATORS
New York Times Film Reviews

NEGROES. See BLACKS.

OBITUARIES
Classic Film Collector
New York Times Index
Opera News
Variety
Variety Anniversary Issues
World Almanac

OPERA SINGERS—PRONUN-
CIATION
Opera News (December 18, 1971
p. 28)

OPERAS
Harvard Dictionary of Music
Opera News
Schwann Record and Tape Guide
What Did They Sing at the Met?

OPERAS—PRONUNCIATION
Opera News (December 18, 1971
p. 28)

ORGANIZATIONS
Film Daily Yearbook
International Motion Picture
Almanac

OUR GANG
Forty Years of Screen Credits
The Turned-On Hollywood 7

PERIODICALS
Ulrich's International Periodicals
Directory

PHOTOGRAPHY. See CINEMA-
TOGRAPHY.

PLAYS INTO FILMS
Filmed Books and Plays

PLOT SYNOPSES
American Film Institute Catalog of
Motion Pictures
Dialogue with the World
Filmfacts
Japan
TV Feature Film Source Book
TV Movies
Warner Brothers Presents

POSTERS-FILM
Guidebook to Film

PRODUCERS
American Movies Reference Book
Compton's Encyclopedia and Fact
Index
Films of Cecil B. DeMille
Films of Hal Roach
Journal of the Producer's Guild of
America
Samuel Goldwyn: The Producer and
His Films
Selznick

PRODUCTION
Alphabetical Guide to Motion Pic-
tures, Television and Videotape
Production
Collier's Encyclopedia
Compton's Encyclopedia and Fact
Index
Encyclopaedia Britannica
Encyclopedia Americana
Films on the Campus
International Motion Picture Alma-
nac
Journal of the University Film Asso-
ciation
Low Budget Features

REVIEWS AND RATINGS—
   THEATRICAL FILMS
   (*Cont.*)
Ebony
Esquire
Film
Film Information
Film Quarterly
Film "Sneaks" Annual
Filmfacts
Films
Films and Filming
Films in Review
Focus
Greater Amusements
The Hollywood Reporter
I Lost It at the Movies
Independent Film Journal
Life
Mass Media Associates Newsletter
Media and Methods
Monthly Film Bulletin
Motion Picture Daily
Motion Picture Herald
Movies for TV
Movies on TV
Multi-Media Reviews Index
New York
New Yorker
New York Times Directory of the
   Film
New York Times Film Reviews
New York Times Guide to Movies on
   TV
Newsweek
PTA Magazine
Parents Magazine
Photoplay
Playboy
The Private Eye, the Cowboy and
   the Very Naked Girl
Redbook
Saturday Review
See
Senior Scholastic

Seventeen
Show
Show Business
Sight and Sound
TV Guide
TV Movies
Take One
Time
Variety
The Village Voice
Vogue

REVUES
Revue
Ring Bells! Sing Songs!

RUNNING TIMES—NONTHE-
   ATRICAL FILMS
NICEM Index to 16mm Educational
   Films

RUNNING TIMES—THEATRI-
   CAL FILMS
Cue
Feature Films on 8mm and 16mm

RUSSIA.   See FILMS—FOREIGN.

SCREENPLAYS
Films and Filming (October 1971)
Published Screenplays: A Checklist
Who Wrote the Movie . . .

SERIALS—FILM, SILENT
Bound and Gagged
Continued Next Week
Film Daily Yearbook (before 1950)
The Serials: Suspense and Drama by
   Installment
Those Enduring Matinee Idols

SERIALS—RADIO
Radio's Golden Age
The Serials: Suspense and Drama by
   Installment
Tune in Tomorrow

SERIES
Filmgoer's Companion
The Great Movie Series

SHAKESPEARE ON FILM
Films in Review (June–July 1956,
  and August–September 1969)
Shakespeare on Film

SHEET MUSIC
Notes

SHORT SUBJECTS
Film Daily Yearbook
A Guide to Films for Discussion and
  Study
Motion Picture Herald (Product
  Digest)
The World of Laughter

SILENT FILMS
The Birth of a Nation Story
Classics of the Silent Screen
Clown Princes and Court Jesters
A Pictorial History of the Silent
  Screen
Spellbound in Darkness
Twenty Years of Silents
Wid's Year Book
Winners of the West

SINGERS
Concise Biographical Dictionary of
  Singers
Rock Encyclopedia

SLIDE FILMS. See FILM-
  STRIPS.

SLIDES
Guide to Government-Loan Filmstrips, Slides and Audio Tapes

SONGS—FILM
Blue Book of Hollywood Musicals
30 Years of Motion Picture Music

SONGS—POPULAR
Rock Encyclopedia
Variety Musical Cavalcade

SOUND
Encyclopaedia Britannica
Four Aspects of the Film
Information Please Almanac
A New Pictorial History of the
  Talkies
Wide-Screen Cinema and Stereo-
  phonic Sound
The World Almanac
World Book Encyclopedia

SPECIAL EFFECTS
The American Cinematographer
The Technique of Special Effects
  Cinematography

STATISTICS
Film Daily Yearbook
Films
International Film Guide
Wid's Year Book

STUDIOS
Compton's Encyclopedia and Fact
  Index
Film Daily Yearbook
Next Time, Drive Off the Cliff
Warner Brothers Presents

STUDY GUIDES
Dialogue with the World
800 Films for Film Study
Film Notes
A Guide to Films for Discussion and
  Study
Media One and Two
Short Films in Religious Education

STUNTS
Falling for Stars Newsletter
The Greatest Stunts Ever
Next Time, Drive Off the Cliff

SUBJECTS OF PLOTS
American Film Institute Catalog of
  Motion Pictures

SWEDEN. See FILMS—FOREIGN.

SYNOPSES. See PLOT SYN-
  OPSES.

TAPES
American Record Guide
Billboard
Educator's Guide to Free Tapes,
  Scripts and Transcriptions
Foreign Language Audio-Visual
  Guide
The Glass List
Guide to Government-Loan Film-
  strips, Slides and Audio Tape
Harrison Tape Catalog
High Fidelity/Musical America
List-O-Tapes
The Listening Post
Record World
Schwann Record and Tape Guide
Stereo Review
Tape Recording
(See also RECORDINGS.)

TEACHING THE FILM
800 Films for Film Study
Exploring the Film
A Film Course Manual
The Filmviewer's Handbook
Guidebook to Film
Human Adventure Through Film
Journal of the University Film Asso-
  ciation
Media and Methods
Media One and Two
The Motion Picture and the Teaching
  of English
Rediscovering the American Cinema
The School and the Art of the Mo-
  tion Picture

Screen Education News
See
Short Films in Religious Education
Themes—Short Films for Discussion

TECHNIQUES
Alphabetical Guide to Motion Pic-
  tures, Television and Videotape
  Production
American Cinematographer
Collier's Encyclopedia
Creative Film Making
Encyclopedia Americana
L'Encyclopedie du Cinema
Filmgoer's Companion
Focal Encyclopedia of Film and Tele-
  vision Technique
Glossary of Motion Picture Terminol-
  ogy
Independent Film Journal
Journal of the Society of Motion Pic-
  ture and Television Engineers
Short Films in Religious Education
Technique of Film Editing
Technique of Film Music
Technique of Special Effects Cinema-
  tography
The Work of the Film Director

TELEVISION
Collier's Encyclopedia
Compton's Encyclopedia and Fact
  Index
Educational Television
Encyclopaedia Britannica
Encyclopedia Americana
Films in Review
Focal Encyclopedia of Film and Tele-
  vision Technique
How Sweet It Was
International Television Almanac
Media Mix Newsletter
Movies for TV
Movies on TV
Pictorial History of Television
TV

TV Feature Film Source Book
TV Movies
Who's Who in TV
World Book Encyclopedia
World Radio TV Handbook

TERMS AND TERMINOL-
OGY. See DICTIONARIES AND
GLOSSARIES.

THEATER—LEGITIMATE
Theatre World

THEATERS—BUILDINGS
The Best Remaining Seats
Encyclopaedia Britannica
Film Daily Yearbook
Foreign Films on American Screens
Information Please Almanac
Marquee
Variety (Vol. 265, January 5, 1972,
p. 54)

THEMES—FILM. See SUBJECTS
OF PLOTS.

THESES AND DISSERTA-
TIONS—FILM
Guidebook to Films

3-D FILMS
Four Aspects of the Film

TIMES. See RUNNING TIMES.

TITLE CHANGES
Filmgoer's Companion
Monthly Film Bulletin

TITLES—FILM
American Movies Reference Book
The American Musical
British Cinema
British National Film Catalog
Catalog of Copyright Entries—
Motion Pictures

Classic Motion Pictures
Classics of the Silent Screen
Continued Next Week
Eastern Europe
L'Encyclopedie du Cinema
Film Canadiana
Filmfacts
Filmgoer's Companion
Films for Children
Films for Adults
Films in America
The First 20 Years
Four Aspects of the Film
French Cinema
Germany
The Great Films
IFIDA Film Directory
International Motion Picture
Almanac
Japan
Library of Congress Catalog of Mo-
tion Pictures and Filmstrips
New Cinema in the USA
Sweden
A Title Guide to the Talkies

TRICK SHOTS. See SPECIAL
EFFECTS.

UNDERGROUND FILMS. See
FILM-MAKING.

VAUDEVILLE
A Pictorial History of Vaudeville

VIDEOTAPING
Alphabetical Guide to Motion Pic-
tures, Television and Videotape
Production

VILLAINS
The Bad Guys
The Heavies

WAMPAS BABY STARS
Forty Years of Screen Credits

WESTERNS
The Bad Guys
Cinema Trails
Deadwood
Hall of Fame of Western Film Stars
Horizons West
Pictorial History of the Western
  Film
Starring John Wayne
The Western: An Illustrated Guide
The Western: From Silents to
  Cinerama
Winners of the West

WIDESCREEN FILMS
Collier's Encyclopedia
Encyclopaedia Britannica
Four Aspects of the Film
Wide-Screen Cinema and Stereo-
  phonic Sound

WRITERS
Hollywood Today
New York Times Film Reviews
Published Screenplays: A Checklist
A Title Guide to the Talkies
Who Wrote the Movie . . .

Audiovisual Terms and Their Definitions

ALA. The American Library Association is the major organization for librarians in the United States and Canada, with headquarters in Chicago. Several committees within the ALA are concerned with the audiovisual field and a marathon film preview session is held each year at the annual conference.

AECT. The Association for Educational Communications and Technology (formerly Department of Audiovisual Instruction) is a national organization which deals in audiovisual instruction, its materials, and those who use them. Its efforts are basically for schools and universities.

ACADEMY LEADER. See LEADER.

ACETATE FILM BASE. See BASE.

ACCESSION. The act of acquiring materials for a collection.

ACCESSION NUMBER. A number or code assigned to an item for filing or shelving.

ACOUSTICAL RECORDING. Disc recordings made before electrical recording in which the music or speech was channeled through an inverted megaphone rather than a microphone.

ADVERTISING FILM. See SPONSORED FILM.

ALBUM. A cardboard sleeve for a record or a cardboard box for more than on record.

ALBUM COVER. The design, artwork, and liner notes appearing on a record album.

ALTERNATE TITLE. A former title or second title of a film, filmstrip, or recording, such as *The Story of Peter and the Potter* being usually called *Peter and the Potter* (its alternate title).

AMPLIFIER. An electronic component which raises the sound on a projector or phonograph to the desired listening level.

83

ANALYTICAL ENTRY. A card catalog entry for part of a film or recording, usually a compilation or anthology, which breaks down the various parts of the contents as cross-references.

ANAMORPHIC LENS. A lens composed of elements which, when used as a "taking" lens, compresses a wide image onto a standard frame of film. When used as a projection lens, it spreads the "squeezed" image out to its proper width. The best-known anamorphic process is "CinemaScope."

ANAMORPHIC PRINT. A film photographed with a "squeeze" lens which must be shown through another such lens.

ANGLE. The slant or position of the camera in relation to the subject.

ANIMATION. The process which gives life to inanimate objects or drawings by shooting them one frame at a time. The best examples of this type of film are cartoons and "puppetoons."

ANSWER PRINT. The first projectable copy of a new film which may be altered before final prints are made.

ANTHOLOGY. A film or recording which contains a collection of different stories, styles, or footage. Film such as *The Golden Age of Comedy* and records such as *The Stories of Saki* fall into this category. Also known as a "compilation" film or record.

ANTISTATICS. Liquids or treated cloths which eliminate static electricity and dirt particles from discs, tapes, and films.

APERTURE. The opening of a lens, each lens opening being known as a "stop."

ARC LIGHT. An exceptionally bright nonelectric light made by the coming together of two sticks of tungsten. Used for theater projectors and for searchlights, as well as some 16mm auditorium projectors.

AUTEUR. Authorship. The "auteur" theory of filmmaking insists that directors are the "authors" of each of their films and that each has a discernible style.

AUDIO. The sound portion of a film or recording.

AUDIOVISUAL. A general term for nonbook items which can be seen and/or heard: sound films, recordings, filmstrips, etc.

AUDITIONING. The trial listening for a recording to determine content, sound quality, appropriateness for the collection, etc. (See also PREVIEWING)

AUTOMATIC CHANGER. A phonograph on which more than one disc may be played without interruption.

AUTOMATIC CHANGEOVER. A device, when hooked up to two projectors, which will automatically switch one projector off and the other one on to provide continuous projection, especially with multiple-reel films.

AUTOMATIC SEQUENCE. Albums of disc recordings in which

each disc may be played in order without turning it over. A 3-record album would have sides 1 and 6 pressed on the same disc, then 2 and 5, and 3 and 4.

BACKGROUND PROJECTION. An almost obsolete effect consisting of putting actors in front of a translucent screen and projecting a filmed background on it. Now somewhat replaced in recent years by "Matte Shots."

BAND. Each unit on a disc recording, separated by a small amount of space which moves the stylus to the next unit. Recordings which have more than one item or movement per side are said to be "banded." Banding aids the listener in selecting the desired band on the disc if he wishes to hear only one portion of the disc.

BASE. A supporting material which aids in the adherence of emulsion to motion picture film. As clear film, it is composed of acetate of cellulose, which is noninflammable.

BEGINNING TITLE. The introductory section of a film giving the title, credits, and other related information.

BIBLIOGRAPHY. A list of readings on a particular subject or area of information. (See also DISCOGRAPHY and FILMOGRAPHY.)

BILLING. See CREDITS.

BINDER. A fixative material which holds the emulsion to the film base.

BLOOP. A noise on a film soundtrack or tape recording which occurs when two ends are spliced together.

BLOW-UP. (1) A process used in making larger prints of smaller-gauged film, such as "blowing up" 16mm prints to 35mm for theatrical showings. (2) Enlarging a shot from a movie to give it more impact or enlarging a frame of a movie to use for display purposes.

BOOKING. The act of scheduling a particular media item for use at a specific time and place.

BOOM. (1) A moving crane on which the camera can move freely. (2) a moving crane for the microphone which can move the instrument above the heads of the actors and out of camera range while recording.

CAMERAMAN. See CINEMATOGRAPHER.

CAPTION. A title at the bottom of a filmstrip frame or superimposed at the bottom of movies for the deaf. (See also SUBTITLES.)

CARD CATALOG. See CATALOG.

CARTOON. See ANIMATION.

CARTRIDGE. A self-enclosed tape recording or motion picture film which moves in a continuous loop while being played or projected.

CASSETTE. A miniature self-contained reel-to-reel tape recording or movie enclosed in a plastic box.

CATALOG. (1) A list of audiovisual holdings put on 3 by 5 cards and filed by subject, title, and any other important information. (2) A printed listing of any one library's audiovisual holdings, usually bound and indexed.

CEMENT. An acetate liquid used to splice and hold two pieces of film together.

CINCH MARKS. See RAIN.

CINEMASCOPE. See ANAMORPHIC LENS.

CINEMATOGRAPHER. A motion picture cameraman.

CINERAMA. An obsolete camera and projection technique using three different films projected on a wide screen. It caused the "widescreen revolution" of the early 1950s in motion picture theaters. Replaced today by 70mm film.

CIRCULATION. A total distribution of audiovisual materials during a given length of time.

CIRCULATION DESK. The area where audiovisual materials are given out and returned.

CLAPPER BOARD. Two hinged pieces of wood which are "slapped" together to serve as a synchronization mark on the soundtrack of each shot of a motion picture production.

CLASSIFIED CATALOG. A card or printed catalog arranged in classified order according to a predetermined scheme.

CLAW. The pull-down mechanism on a movie camera or projector which pulls down one frame of film at a time while a shutter covers the movement. The result is an illusion of motion.

CLEANING. (1) The cleaning out of dirt and oils on recordings by an antistatic liquid, damp chamois cloth, or chemically treated cloth. (2) The cleaning out of dirt and oils in films by soft brushes, treated cloths, or application of film cleaning liquids, either by hand or machine.

CLIPPINGS. See STOCK SHOTS.

CLOSE-UP. A camera shot taken at extremely close range.

COLLECTION. The totality of recordings, films, filmstrips, and other audiovisual media in any given place.

COLOR FILM. Motion pictures with three layers of emulsion which are sensitive to all the colors of the spectrum.

COMMENTARY. See NARRATION.

COMPILATION FILM. See ANTHOLOGY.

CONTINUITY. The logical order of shots in a motion picture.

COPYRIGHT. The exclusive right, granted by the United States Copyright Office, to offer copies of a film or recording for public use. Material not copyrighted is said to be in the "public domain."

CRANE SHOT. A moving shot taken by a camera on a specially constructed crane.

CREDITS. Titles placed at the beginning or end of a film, giving names of the cast, technicians, and distributor.

CREEPING TITLE. A title which moves in a slow vertical direction on the screen as it is being read.

CUE DOTS. A circle appearing in the upper right-hand corner of a film to signify the coming to the end of a reel. On multiple-reel films, the cue dot tells the projectionist when to switch to the other projector to simulate a continuous showing.

CUT. (1) A cut is defined as "each time the camera changes position or a new shot appears on the screen." (2) When a director calls "cut," he is indicating that the camera should be stopped and the "take" is over. (3) A rough cut is the preliminary splicing together of all the shots taken for a given film so it can be projected, analyzed, and tightened. (4) The final trim (fine cut) of a film has each shot trimmed exactly to the desired length. This is usually the final version of the film.

CUTAWAY SHOT. See REACTION SHOT.

CUT-OUT RECORDS. See OUT-OF-PRINT RECORDS.

DAILIES. See RUSHES.

DAMAGE CARD. A file card on which damage to a given recording or film is written.

DEFINITION. Sharpness of the focus of an image.

DIRECTOR. The person mainly responsible for the final result of a film or a recording and who controls all phases of production.

DISC RECORDING. A phonograph record which is recorded by means of a cutting stylus and pressed onto vinyl plastic.

DISCOGRAPHY. A list of recordings on a specific subject or area of information. (See also BIBLIOGRAPHY and FILMO-GRAPHY.)

DISSOLVE. The slow fading out of one shot in a film and its replacement with another shot fading in. Used to indicate a change of setting or a lapse of time.

DOCUMENTARY. A factual film shot, many times without a script, with real people in actual settings.

DOLBY SYSTEM. A method of recording which reduces noise in tapes and discs.

DOLLY SHOT. A shot in a film in which the camera moves in or out on a stationary object and in the process changes the relative size of the object. The camera is said to "dolly" in and out. It may also "dolly" up and down, such as from the trunk of a tree to its highest branch.

DOUBLE TRACK TAPE. A tape recording in which one track is recorded to the end of the reel, after which it is turned over and the second track is played as it returns to the first reel. In stereo recordings, both tracks are played together, but recorded from different microphones to give a stereophonic effect.

DUBBING. (1) A process by which actors put new words on to the soundtrack of a motion picture made in a foreign language, such as "dubbing" an Italian film into English. (2) Adding sound of any kind to a film which was not recorded at the time of the shooting. This is also known as "post-dubbing."

DUPE. A copy of a tape recording or a motion picture. Short for "duplicate."

DUPE NEGATIVE. A duplicate copy of a master negative of a film used in case of loss or theft of the original. (See also SECOND GENERATION NEGATIVE.)

DUPING. The act of making additional copies of a film or recording, usually illegally in the case of copyrighted material.

DUST DISPELLERS. See ANTISTATICS.

DYNAMIC EDITING. See EDITING.

EFLA. The Educational Film Library Association, the nation's largest clearinghouse for nontheatrical film information, founded in 1943. It sponsors the annual American Film Festival.

EFLA CARDS. Film evaluations distributed to members of the Educational Film Library Association in the form of 3 by 5 file cards.

ERIC. The Education Resources Information Center, which provides reference publications through various centers in the United States.

EVR. Electronic Video Recording, developed by Dr. Peter Goldmark for CBS. The film is translated into a television picture by any TV set. The process was discontinued in 1972.

EARPHONES. Devices used for individual listening of recordings (and sometimes films and filmstrips) in libraries.

EDITING. (1) Splicing pieces of film together to form a unified whole. (2) DYNAMIC EDITING places shots and sequences into related form, but not necessarily matching from one shot to the next. (3) MATCHED EDITING arranges shots so each action from the preceding shot is carried over to the following shot, giving a continuous flow of action.

EDITING MACHINE. A device for running film by hand in order to determine the exact place for editing. Also known as a "movieola."

EDITOR. The person who edits film into its final form.

8MM FILMS. (1) Regular 8: The original smallgauge film with large sprocket holes and a small picture area (taken from split

16mm stock). (2) Super 8: A newer development with smaller sprocket holes and almost twice as much picture area per frame.

8-TRACK TAPE. A tape in cartridge form featuring eight separate tracks.

EMULSION. The image-bearing layer of a film.

END TITLE. The section of the film which announces the end of a production.

ESTABLISHING SHOT. A long shot usually introduced at the beginning of a sequence to orient the viewer to subsequent closer shots of the same area. Also known as a "key shot."

EXCHANGE. A theatrical film "library" located in a key geographical area to furnish theaters with films. Usually each major production company maintains a series of film exchanges throughout the United States.

EXCITER LAMP. An unfrosted light bulb which scans the sound track of a film and translates it into electrical energy which comes through the loudspeakers as music, sound effects and/or dialogue. Also called a photoelectric cell.

EXPERIMENTAL FILM. A production which uses film techniques in an unconventional and creative manner.

EXPOSURE. The amount of light allowed through the lens to register on the light-sensitive film.

EXTERIOR SHOT. A shot or scene filmed out of doors away from the studio.

FLIC. The Film Library Information Council, an organization for public library film librarians.

FADE IN—FADE OUT. A gradual appearance of a projected image from total darkness to full screen brilliancy, followed by the reverse to signify the end of a sequence, or the film itself.

FAST MOTION. A film device used to accelerate action in a shot or scene by shooting less frames per second. When projected, the scene moves faster, usually for comical or satirical effect.

FEATURE FILM. A film which runs over 48 minutes or which is on more than one reel. Sometimes loosely used to describe any fictional film.

FEED REEL. See REEL.

FICTIONAL FILM. A film which is not based on actual locations or real people, but rather, scripted, acted, and dramatized. The opposite of a documentary film.

FILMOGRAPHY. A bibliography of film titles, usually on a specified subject area, genre, director, or film personality. (See also BIBLIOGRAPHY and DISCOGRAPHY.)

FILMSTRIP. A strip of 35mm film in which each frame is projected separately as a still picture. It may be accompanied by a record or tape.

FILTER. (1) A device put over a lens to vary the light values on a film. (2) An electronic device used to clear up static and extraneous noises in a phonograph or tape player.

FIRST GENERATION PRINT. A positive print made directly from the original negative.

FLASH FORWARD. A shot or sequence inserted into a film to show something which might happen in the future.

FLASHBACK. A filmic device used to show a shot or sequence which happened in the past.

FLICKER. A flickering of the screen image when the speed of the projector is going too slowly, revealing the intermittent action of the claw and shutter. This was a failing of many early movies which were hand-cranked and many early moviegoers used the term "flickers" to refer to all movies.

FLIPOVER. A type of visual transition device in which the last frame of a scene freezes, then flips over to reveal the first frame of the next scene on the back of it.

FLUTTER. An audio problem in which the soundtrack does not come through the speakers clearly, usually due to the misthreading of the film around the sound drum.

FOCUS. A situation which occurs when a subject is the proper distance from the lens to produce a sharp picture. Also the act of sharpening a picture on the screen by manipulating the lens barrel.

FOLK MUSIC. A style of music reflecting the feelings of a group of people in a certain section of the country or the world.

FOOTAGE. The length of a film expressed in feet. Also sometimes used to refer to a strip of film.

FOREIGN VERSION. A film to which a foreign-language soundtrack has been added.

45 RPM RECORDS. A 7-inch disc recording developed by RCA featuring a large center hole and a speed of 45 rpm. Used mostly as a medium for popular "single" releases.

4-TRACK TAPE. A form of tape cartridge, featuring four separate tracks, which is almost obsolete today, being replaced by the 8-track stereo tape cartridge.

FRAME. A single picture, one of a series on a strip of motion picture film or filmstrip, placed between the sprocket holes on each side.

FRAMING. Moving the film gate aperture so that the frame of a film is correctly centered on the screen. When the top or bottom of the preceding frame is visible on the screen, the image is said to be poorly "framed" and must be corrected by the framing knob on the projector.

FREEZE FRAME. A filmic technique which uses the last frame of a scene as a still picture for an effect.

GAFFER. The chief electrician on a movie set.

GAIN. Volume. To increase the volume of a sound track or recording, one is said to "turn up the gain." When volume varies, one is said to "ride gain" to see that the volume remains constant.

GATE. The channel through which a film travels when it is projected on the screen. The gate is located between the light source and the lens and keeps the film flat so it can always remain in proper focus.

GAUGE. The measurement of the width of a film—16mm gauge, 35 mm gauge, etc.

GENRE. A specific kind or style of artistic achievements which can be grouped together: western films, contemporary opera, gangster movies of the 1930s, etc.

GREEN FILM. Any film which is new and has not yet been treated with the proper coating. Green film is usually difficult to project because it does not flow smoothly through the gate.

GROOVE. The V-shaped rut on a disc recording on which the stylus rests when being played.

GROOVE DAMAGE. Scratches or other damage done to the grooves of a disc recording.

HAND-HELD CAMERA. A camera which records a shot without resting on a tripod or otherwise anchored. Used in many amateur films and sometimes in documentaries.

HARDWARE. The items used to play or project audiovisual materials—phonographs, projectors, etc.

HEAD. The beginning of a film or reel. A film ready for projection (rewound) is said to be "heads up."

HI-FI. See HIGH FIDELITY.

HIGH FIDELITY. An improvement in the system of recording and pressing disc recordings, now used to describe any recording without surface noise and a wide sound range.

HILL AND DALE RECORDING. An early form of acoustical recording in which the stylus moved up and down in the groove, rather than from side to side as in present-day disc recordings.

IPS. An indication of the speed of a given tape recording in inches per second.

INFORMATION. (1) The amount of visual material on a given frame of film. (2) The amount of audio material on a given record groove or a piece of recording tape.

INSPECTION. The act of checking a film or recording for damage before putting it back into circulation.

INSPECTION MACHINE. An automatic machine for detecting damage, poor splices, etc., in movie film.

INSTRUCTIONAL FILMS. Motion pictures made to teach the viewer.

INTERCUTTING. The editing of two different sequences by alternating shots between the two.

INTERIOR SHOT. Any shot filmed indoors under artificial light.

INTERNEGATIVE. A color duplicate negative.

IRIS IN—IRIS OUT. A filmic effect in which a small hole grows slowly larger until the new scene covers the entire frame and the opposite effect of slowly closing until the screen is black. Often used by D. W. Griffith, but now relegated to cartoon films.

JACKETS. See RECORD JACKETS.

JUMP CUT. An awkward visual effect which occurs when some frames are cut out of the middle of a shot, causing the actors to "jump" suddenly to new positions.

JUNKING. Disposal of unwanted films or recordings.

KEY SHOT. See ESTABLISHING SHOT.

KINESCOPE RECORDINGS. A film made from a television program taken directly from the picture tube.

LABEL. The round identifying piece on a disc recording.

LABEL NUMBER. The individual number assigned by each record company to distinguish one recording from another.

LABORATORY. The area where films are developed and prints made.

LEADER. (1) A protective length of film, either white or colored, which is used to thread the projector so none of the actual picture is lost in threading. Many times this plain leader will have pertinent information on it, such as the title, laboratory information, and name of distributor. (2) A length of film which has "count-down" cue numbers used at the beginning of most reels. Two such leaders, developed by the Society of Motion Picture and Television Engineers and by the Academy of Motion Picture Arts and Sciences, are denoted as SMPTE and Academy leader, respectively.

LENGTH. See FOOTAGE.

LENS. The tube or barrel consisting of various optical elements which take and project films. All films run through the projector with the image upside down and the lens elements change and correct the picture to its right-side-up status on the screen.

LIBRARY SHOTS. See STOCK SHOTS.

LIFE OF MATERIALS. (1) A motion picture may last, under normal wear, usage, and protection, from 10 to 20 years if inspected after each booking. (2) Disc recordings, under normal playing conditions and with proper cleaning, care, and inspection, may last from 5 to 15 years. (3) Tapes in libraries have not been in use long enough to predict their average life.

LIGHTING. The artificial illumination used in making a film in a studio. Exterior shots use sunlight with reflectors.

LISTENING FACILITIES. The earphone and turntable set-up in a library where recordings may be listened to on an individual basis.

LOAN CARD. The card in the pocket of a recording (and sometimes films) indicating who has borrowed the material and when it is due.

LOCATION NUMBER. The number given to a film or record to identify its place on the shelf. Also called SHELF NUMBER.

LOCATION SHOOTING. Filming scenes away from the studio to achieve authenticity in setting or terrain. Where close-ups of the actors are not involved, a "second unit" goes to the location and does its filming, which is later spliced into the studio footage during the editing process.

LOGO. The "trademark" or identification of a film studio or recording company which is shown at the beginning of a film or on the record label.

LONG-PLAYING RECORD. A $33\frac{1}{3}$ rpm disc recording which is the equivalent of eight sides of a 12-inch 78 rpm album.

LONG SHOT. A shot taken with the camera far enough away to show the entire subject or area. Also known as an ESTABLISHING SHOT.

LOOP. A small amount of film used to give leeway in the threading of a projector. Since the soundtrack is printed on the film ahead of the image, the loop must be of the proper size or the dialogue will not fit the lips, but be ahead or behind the image.

LOOP FILM. A length of film joined into an endless band to facilitate constant repetition. Also known as "looping."

LOOPING. See LOOP FILM.

MLA. The Music Librarian's Association, a national organization devoted to music in libraries. It is an arm of the ALA.

MAGNETIC SOUND. A soundtrack that is reproduced by means of a magnetic strip of iron oxide and electronic pickup heads (as on a tape player) rather than by an optical soundtrack with a sound drum and photoelectric cell. Used for multichannel sound and in some 8mm sound projectors.

MAIN ENTRY. The full or principal entry card, generally under the title or subject, containing the fullest particulars of a film or recording. This card sometimes bears notes of all other entries, known as tracings.

MAIN TITLE. See BEGINNING TITLE.

MANUAL SEQUENCE. An album of more than one disc in which side 1 must be turned over before playing side 2. Its opposite, "automatic sequence," allows the two discs to be played one after the other before turning over the discs to play sides 3 and 4.

MARRIED PRINT. A final print which combines both the image and the sound on the same piece of film.

MATCHING EDITING. See EDITING.

MATRIX NUMBER. The number etched at the center of a disc recording just below the label.

MATTE SHOT. A trick effect (process shot) in which actors appear against a black background while the background on another piece of film is superimposed on it. The two pieces of film combine to make it seem as if the actors are appearing against a genuine background.

MEDIUM SHOT. A shot midway between a "long shot" and a "close-up."

MICROPHONE. A sensitive instrument which picks up sounds for recording a record, tape, or film soundtrack.

MISE-EN-SCENE. The act or art of placing actors, scenery, and properties in a film.

MIXING. The electronic process of putting several sounds onto a single master track for a recording or film soundtrack.

MONAURAL RECORDS. A recording in which all the sounds are emitted through one speaker or source.

MONTAGE. (1) The theory of film editing which demands that each shot in a film be related to the shot preceding it and the shot following it. (2) A trick effect which uses multiple images in quick succession to indicate the passing of time or the rise or fall of a character.

MOTION PICTURE. A series of still pictures projected rapidly in succession so they appear to be in motion. Also called "film," "movies," "moving pictures," and "cinema."

MOVIEOLA. See EDITING MACHINE.

MUSIC APPRECIATION RECORDS. Recordings which teach the listener how to better appreciate music and its composers and performers.

NAVA. The National Audiovisual Association, an organization concerned mainly with commercial film distribution, film rentals, and equipment.

NARRATION. The commentary accompanying a film or the audio portion of a recording.

NEEDLE. See STYLUS.

NEGATIVE. An image in which the gray tones and/or colors are reversed. The film from which positive prints are made.

NICEM. The National Information Center for Educational Media is an organization which provides computerized lists of AV materials and publishes master lists of media for reference purposes.

NITRATE FILM. A highly volatile film used in movies from 1896 through the 1940s. Because it bursts into fire so easily, it often caused theater fires, resulting in laws requiring fireproof projection booths. Since the 1940s, most 35mm prints have been made on or converted to safety film. All 8mm and 16mm films have always been on safety film and will not burn. (See also SAFETY FILM.)

NONTHEATRICAL FILM. (1) Any film gauge under 35mm, usually describing 16mm or 8mm. (2) Film productions not made for theatrical showing, but for educational, cultural, promotional, or instructional purposes.

NORMAL MOTION. See SPEED.

OPTICAL EFFECTS. See MATTE SHOTS, PROCESS PHOTOGRAPHY.

OPTICAL ENLARGEMENT. See BLOW-UP.

OPTICAL REDUCTION. A negative or positive film directly reduced from a wider film gauge to a smaller one, such as the reduction of a 35mm print to 16mm.

OPTICAL SOUND. A photographic pattern put on the side of a 16mm film which produces a recorded sound when projected onto a photoelectric cell connected to an amplifier. (See also MAGNETIC SOUND.)

ORIGINAL. The initial visual or aural record of a motion picture or recording.

OUT-OF-PRINT RECORDS. Recordings which are no longer available from the distribution source and must be tracked down through an "out-of-print" record dealer, if copies still remain. Also called "cut-outs."

OUT-TAKES. Shots and scenes cut from a film before the final print is made. Any unused film.

PAN. (1) Short for "panorama," a shot in which the camera moves usually from left to right in a sweeping arc to take in a large area. (2) SWISH PAN. A fast pan which blurs the image, then stops sharply to reveal a new scene. Used for visual transitions in films.

PERFORATIONS. The sprocket holes in the sides of motion picture film which, together with the claw mechanism, aid the movement of the film through the camera or projector gate.

PERSISTENCE OF VISION. The visual phenomenon which allows one's eyes to perceive a sense of motion when still frames of film are projected at a rate fast enough to set them in motion.

PERSONAL INTEREST FILE. A card file which contains names, addresses, and telephone numbers of patrons who are interested in specific or special types of records or films in order to help hobbyists and interest groups to discover each other.

PHONOGRAPH. A turntable with a long center spike on which more than one disc recording may be played without reloading.

PHONORECORDS. A term used to describe disc recordings.

PHOTOELECTRIC CELL. See EXCITER LAMP.

PLASTIC COVERS. See RECORD COVERS.

POLICIES. The written down statements governing the audio-visual department and how it selects it materials.

POSITIVE. See NEGATIVE and PRINT.

PREAMPLIFIER. A device which increases the strength of the sound signal in a phonograph or projector.

PRERECORDING. Recording the musical portions of a film before production begins, to be later mimed by the singers during production. Also used on musical TV programs.

PREVIEWING. Screening a film or filmstrip for evaluation before purchasing to determine its value and usefulness in the collection.

PRINT. A positive copy of a film made from a negative.

PROCESS PHOTOGRAPHY. Trick photography, including "matte shots," "background projection," etc.

PROJECTION ROOM. A soundproof enclosure where films are projected and the sound of the projectors is not audible to the audience.

PROJECTOR. The machine which shows the film on the screen.

PROPS. Short for "properties," inanimate objects such as vases, guns, knives, which are used or handled by the actors in a film. Objects which are not handled are considered part of the setting.

PUBLIC DOMAIN. Any material which is not copyrighted or on which the copyright has expired.

PUBLICITY. Promotion material, written, visual or oral, used to inform potential borrowers of new releases.

PUPPET FILMS. Films involving the use of puppets animated by the single-frame method or moved by hands or strings.

QUADRASONIC. A disc or tape which emits four separate sound sources from four different speakers.

RIAA. The Record Industry Association of America, which sets recording standards for the industry.

RACKING. See SHELVING.

RAIN. Films which have been run too many times through a dirty projector gate and have long black lines running through the picture are known as "rainy" prints. When loosly wound film is "pulled tight," these same black lines result in "cinch markes" on the film.

RAW STOCK. Unexposed movie film.

REACTION SHOTS. Shots inserted into scenes to show the actor's reaction to the main action. Also known as a "cut-away" shot.

REAR PROJECTION. See BACKGROUND PROJECTION.

RECORD COLLECTORS. Those record fans whose interests lead them to the collecting of specific types of recordings of a certain performer, conductor, orchestra, or genre.

RECORD COVERS. The paper or plastic covers which protect the sensitive grooves of the disc recording while it is in its cardboard jacket.

RECORD JACKETS. The outer cardboard cover which houses the disc recording.

REELS. (1) A spool which holds movie film or recording tape. (2) "FEED REEL" The full reel of film or tape which is threaded into the machine for showing or playing. (3) TAKE-UP REEL. The reel which receives the film or tape after it has been shown or played.

REFERENCE. A direction from one subject heading to another.

REFLECTOR. A shiny surface used to increase the amount of light available on a film set.

REGULAR 8. See 8MM FILM.

RELEASE PRINT. The final print of a motion picture which is released to be projected.

RENTAL FEE. The charge for renting a film, filmstrip, recording, tape, or other media from a library or collection.

REVERSAL PRINT. A film produced by a process which renders a positive image directly without the use of an intervening negative.

REWIND. The act of returning film or tape to the feed reel in a "heads up" position or a machine designed for this purpose.

ROLLING TITLE. See CREEPING TITLE.

RUSHES. Daily printing of all scenes shot on a film production, used to select the best scenes for the final print. Also called "dailies."

SMPTE. The Society of Motion Picture and Television Engineers, an organization of film and television technicians.

SMPTE LEADER. See LEADER.

SAFETY FILM. Film which will not catch fire. (See also NITRATE FILM.)

SAMPLERS. A recording released by a company in order to promote a variety of different artists by presenting one number from an average of 12 different new albums.

SCENE. A group of shots combined to form one complete filmic idea and with continuous action in a given locale or setting.

SCRATCHES. See RAIN.

SCREEN. A sheet of reflective material on which motion pictures are shown. They come in both wall and tripod styles and with a variety of surfaces. As a verb, the word means to view films.

SCREENPLAY. See SHOOTING SCRIPT.

SCRIPT. See SHOOTING SCRIPT.

SECOND GENERATION NEGATIVE. A new negative made from a positive print rather than the original negative. There is usually a loss of sharpness and clarity in a second generation negative, if the process is repeated, say, a fifth generation negative, the print quality suffers noticably. Also called a "Dupe Negative."

SECOND UNIT. A group which films shots on location (battles, foreign locales, etc.) that do not require the presence of the stars.

"SEE" REFERENCE. A reference from a heading under which no entries are placed to the one which contains them.

"SEE ALSO" REFERENCE. A reference often found in catalogs from one entry with entries under it, to a related one.

SEQUENCE. A group of scenes from a film which form a larger unit unto itself. Also a portion of a film lifted from a longer unit and released as a separate film.

SERIES ENTRY. A catalog entry under the name of a series.

SERIES TITLE. A collective title for films related to each other in subject matter, style, or approach.

SET. The background for any given scene in a film. Also an especially constructed background for a scene.

70MM FILM. The widest film gauge in current use today, usually reserved for spectacular "roadshow" films such as *Lawrence of Arabia* and *Hello Dolly*.

78 RPM RECORD. An obsolete form of disc recording which ran at a very fast speed, allowing for only 3 or 4 minutes of playing time per side.

SHELFLIST. A list of all film or recording holdings in a given library.

SHELF NUMBER. A number or letter-number combination assigned to an individual film or recording and under which it is filed or shelved.

SHELVING. The shelves used to hold audiovisual materials. As a verb, the act of racking these materials.

SHELLAC RECORD. A 78 rpm recording.

SHOOTING SCRIPT. The orderly, written-down work plan of a film containing the visual elements in one column and the audio material in the other. Also known as the "screenplay."

SHOT. One single scene from the starting to the stopping of the camera.

SHRINKAGE. The degree to which a film or tape has decreased its dimensions from the standard. These materials which show shrinkage are deemed no longer useful.

SHUTTER. The device in the camera and projector which closes off the taking of the picture while a new frame comes into place for the next exposure.

SINGLE TRACK TAPE. A reel-to-reel tape which contains only one set of information on it and which runs from beginning to end, but not back again.

16MM FILMS. The standard nontheatrical film gauge, 16mm wide with sprocket holes down one side and a sound-track down the other.

16⅔ RPM RECORDS. A slow-speed record used mainly for recorded literature for use by the partially sighted and blind.

SLEEVE. See RECORD JACKETS.

SLIDE FILM. See FILMSTRIP.

SLIDES. Individual projectable pieces of 35mm film, usually mounted in cardboard frames.

SLOW MOTION. An effect achieved by running the camera at more frames per second than normal. When projected, the motion seems to slow down on the screen.

SOFTWARE. A term for audiovisual materials, as opposed to projectors and phonographs, which are termed "hardware."

SOUND DRUM. The device over which the film is threaded in order to translate the sound track from a film into electrical energy and in turn into sound.

SOUND EFFECTS. Almost any imaginable sound which might be needed for a film or recording is filed on tape in the studio sound department and used as needed for a specific sound cue.

SOUND STAGE. A large interior studio where films and recordings are made.

SOUND SYSTEM. The speakers used to amplify sound in a phonograph or film projector.

SOUND TRACK. (1) OPTICAL. A photographed strip of sound which is converted into sound energy in the projector. (2) MAGNETIC. An oxide strip on a film or tape which is translated into sound.

SPECIAL EFFECTS. See PROCESS PHOTOGRAPHY.

SPEED. (1) SILENT. A film shown at between 16 and 18 frames per second. (2) SOUND. A film shown at the steady rate of 24 frames per second.

SPEED CONTROL. A device on a projector or phonograph which varies the running speed.

SPLICER. A device used to join pieces of film or tape together.

SPLIT SCREEN. (1) A shot where two or more separate but related images appear on the screen at the same time. (2) A process by which two different settings can be combined into one film, such as a dirt road in India (in the foreground) and a mountain in Crete (in the background) thus giving the viewer a composite image.

SPONSORED FILM. A motion picture produced under the aegis of an industrial or commercial firm for the purpose of public relations and promotion of a product or a company.

SQUEEZE. See ANAMORPHIC PRINT.

STATISTICS. The collection and interpretation of audiovisual data, such as circulation, audience, etc.

STEREO RECORDINGS. Discs and tapes which provide two sources of sound through two separate speakers.

STILL. A photograph taken from a frame of a motion picture or any publicity photograph taken of a production.

STOCK SHOTS. Shots or sequences from previous films spliced into new productions to save re-shooting the same type of footage. Also known as "library shots."

STOP MOTION. Filming an animated scene one frame at a time. (See also ANIMATION.)

STYLUS. The needle in a phonograph which rides the record grooves and sends sound information to the amplifier.

SUBJECTIVE CAMERA. A filmic device in which the camera replaces the person in a scene.

SUBTITLES. Superimposed words of dialog, usually at the bottom of the film, which translates foreign language dialog into English.

SUPER 8. See 8MM FILMS.

SUPERIMPOSITION. A shot in which one image is overlaid on another.

SYNCHRONIZATION (SYNC). The matching of sound and image on a film. When they are not matched, the film is said to be "out of sync" and is usually the fault of the film loop in the projector.

TAIL. The end portion of a reel of film or tape. When the tail is at the beginning (not yet rewound), the reel is said to be "tails up."

TAKE. Any individual shot in a motion picture, usually shot more than once, so the best "take" can be selected for the final print.

TAKE-UP REEL. See REEL.

TALKING BOOKS. Discs or tapes, usually recorded at a very slow speed, which are used basically for the blind.

TAPE DECK. A tape player without amplifiers or other componets.

TAPE RECORDING. An audio medium consisting of a reel of plastic tape on which iron oxide or other material has been affixed. (See also MAGNETIC SOUND.)

TELEPHOTO LENS. A long-distance lens with many elements which bring distant objects "up close."

TEST RECORDS. Discs or tapes which contain sounds to aid in adjusting the audio of a phonograph or tape player.

33⅓ RPM RECORDS. The standard "long-playing" record introduced in 1948, running at a speed of $33\frac{1}{3}$ rpm.

35MM FILMS. The standard film gauge used in movie theaters throughout the world. It contains sprocket holes on both sides of the film with the soundtrack situated between the picture and the sprocket holes.

THREADING. The act of putting a film or tape through the playing channel.

THREE SHOT. A shot containing three people or objects.

TILT. A device on a camera tripod which allows the camera to be moved up or down.

TIME-LAPSE PHOTOGRAPHY. A form of frame-by-frame filming in which only one frame is exposed at a long interval. When projected, the results may show a plant growing, a flower opening, or other long-term actions and motions.

TINTING. The act of dyeing a film one single color.

TITLE. The name of any given film or recording.

TITLE ENTRY. The record of a film or recording in the card catalog under the title.

TITLE INSERTS. Frames of dialog inserted into silent films to replace the lack of dialog.

TONE ARM. The device which holds the stylus in a phonograph or turntable.

TONING. The act of chemically treating a film with a dye in which the opaque parts of the image become colored and the clear parts remain unaffected.

TRACINGS. Indications on the main entry card showing what added entries and references exist.

TRACK. See SOUND TRACK.

TRACKING. See TRUCK SHOT.

TRAILER. A preview film.

TREATMENT. An outline of a film script.

TRIPOD. A three-legged portable camera stand.

TRUCK SHOT. A moving shot, usually taken from a moving truck or on a track, which follows the moving objects at either a head-on angle or on the bias and keeps the subject in the same relative size throughout the shot. (See also DOLLY SHOT.)

TURNTABLE. The rotating disc on which a phonograph record sets. Does not have a "drop" mechanism for playing more than one record at a time.

TWO SHOT. A filmed shot of two people or objects.

UFA. The University Film Association, which covers the production of media in colleges and universities.

UNION CATALOG. An orderly compilation of the holdings of two or more libraries.

VARIABLE-AREA RECORDING. One of two compatible types of optical soundtracks in which a clear line appears over a black background.

VARIABLE-DENSITY RECORDING. One of two compatible types of optical soundtracks in which various shades of gray, black, and white make up the track.

VIDEOTAPE. A large, multiple-track tape recording which captures both the audio and video portions of a television presentation.

VOICE OVER. The narration on a sound track which may have sound or music in the background.

WARPAGE. The distortion of the shape of a disc recording when exposed to heat.

WEEDING. The clearing out of damaged, outdated, and poorly circulating films, recordings, and other media.

WIDE-ANGLE LENS. A short focal-length lens which takes in a large area of a subject.

WIDTH. See GAUGE.

WIPE. A visual transition device used to transport the eye from one scene to another by means of a line moving across the screen, bringing with it a new image of a new scene, slowly "wiping" off the old one.

WIRE RECORDING. An obsolete recording method superceded by tape recording.

WORK PRINT. A positive print used during the final stages of a film production which can be cut and recut, marked up, drawn on, and any items, such as optical effects, noted on the print. Since the negative itself is never projected, the work print substitutes for the negative in all but the final stage of making the release negative.

WOW. A variation in a film sound track, disc, or tape when it is not moving at a constant speed, resulting in uneven pitch in both music and dialogue.

ZOOM LENS. A lens with elements which cause a scene to be brought up into close-up by manipulating the lens and not the subject. Can also be used to "zoom out" from a close-up to a long shot.

Addresses
of Publishers

ASC Holding Corp.
American Cinematographer
P.O. Box 2230
Hollywood, Calif. 90028

A-TR Publications
145 E. 52nd St.
New York, N.Y. 10022

Academy of Motion Picture
  Arts and Sciences
8955 Beverly Blvd.
Los Angeles, Calif. 90048

Aenid Equities
New York Magazine
207 E. 32nd St.
New York, N.Y. 10016

George Allen and Unwin Ltd.
40 Museum St.
London, WC1A 1LU, England

American Federation of Film
  Societies
144 Bleecker St.
New York, N.Y. 10012

American Film Institute
John F. Kennedy Center for
  the Performing Arts
Washington, D.C. 20566

American Library Association
50 E. Huron St.
Chicago, Ill. 60611

American Record Guide
P.O. Box 319, Radio City
  Station
New York, N.Y. 10019

American Society of
  Composers, Arrangers and
  Publishers
1 Lincoln Square Plaza
New York, N.Y. 10023

Americana Corp.
Grolier, Inc.
575 Lexington Ave.
New York, N.Y. 10022

Arbor House Publishing Co.,
  Inc.
757 Third Ave.
New York, N.Y. 10017

Archon. See Shoestring.

Arco Publishing Co., Inc.
219 Park Ave. S.
New York, N.Y. 10003

Arlington House, Inc.
81 Centre Ave.
New Rochelle, N.Y. 10801

Arno Press, Inc.
New York Times
330 Madison Ave.
New York, N.Y. 10017

Associated Publishers, Inc.
1538 9th St., N.W.
Washington, D.C. 20001

Association for Educational
  Communications and
  Technology
201 16th St. N.W.
Washington, D.C. 20036

Association for Recorded
  Sound Collections
New York Public Library
New York, N.Y. 10036

Association Press
291 Broadway
New York, N.Y. 10007

Audio-Visual Associates
Film Review Index
P.O. Box 324
Monterey Park, Calif. 91754

Award Records and Film Co.
1000 E. Colorado Blvd.
Pasadena, Calif. 91101

Backstage
165 W. 46th St.
New York, N.Y. 10036

Bantam Books, Inc.
666 Fifth Ave.
New York, N.Y. 10019

A. S. Barnes and Co., Inc.
Forgate Dr.
Cranbury, N.J. 08512

Beacon Press
25 Beacon St.
Boston, Mass. 02108

Belknap Press
Harvard University Press
79 Garden St.
Cambridge, Mass. 02138

William Benton
Compton's Encyclopedia.
  See Encyclopaedia Britannica
  Corp.

Billboard Publications, Inc.
2160 Patterson St.
Cincinnati, Ohio 45214

The Bobbs-Merrill Co., Inc.
430 W. 62nd St.
Indianapolis, Ind. 46268

Boosey and Hawkes, Inc.
P.O. Box 130
Oceanside, N.Y. 11572

Bordas Publishing Co.
Editions Bordas S.A.R.L.
37, rue Boulard
Paris 14, France

R. R. Bowker Co.
1180 Ave. of the Americas
New York, N.Y. 10036

Bowling Green University
  Popular Press
University Hall 101
Bowling Green, Ohio, 43403

Boxoffice
825 Van Brunt Rd.
Kansas City, MO. 62124

Bramhall House
Clarkston N. Potter, Inc.
23 E. 67th St.
New York, N.Y. 10021

British Film Institute
81 Dean St.
London W.C.1, England

Broadcast Information Bureau
845 Third Ave.
New York, N.Y. 10022

Broadcasting Publications, Inc.
1735 DeSales St., N.W.
Washington, D.C. 20036

Bro-Dart Publishing Co.
P.O. Box 923
Williamsport, Pa. 17701

Brussel and Brussel
18 E. 12 th St.
New York, N.Y. 10003

Cadillac Publishing Co., Inc.
220 Fifth Ave.
New York, N.Y. 10001

Canadian Film Institute
1762 Carling Ave.
Ottawa K2A 2H7 Ontario,
  Canada

Canadian Society of
  Cinematologists
2533 Gerrard St. E.
Scarborough, Ontario, Canada

Canyon Cinema Filmmakers'
  Cooperative
Room 220, Industrial Center
  Bldg.
Sausalito, Calif. 94965

Century House, Inc.
Watkins Glen, N.Y. 14801

Chilton Book Co.
401 Walnut St.
Philadelphia, Pa. 19106

Christian Century Foundation
407 S. Dearborn St.
Chicago, Ill. 60605

Christopher Publishing House
53 Billings Rd.
North Quincy, Mass. 02171

Cinefax
Box 151
Kew Gardens, N.Y. 11415

Cinema Magazine
9667 Wilshire Blvd.
Beverly Hills, Calif. 90212

Cinememories Publishers
P.O. Box 3493
Cocoa, Fla. 32922

Citadel Press, Inc.
222 Park Ave. S.
New York, N.Y. 10003

Columbia University Press
562 W. 113th St.
New York, N.Y. 10025

Commonweal Publishing Co.
232 Madison Ave.
New York, N.Y. 10016

Communication Arts Press
159 Forest Ave. N.E.
Atlanta, Ga. 30303

Comprehensive Service
250 W. 64th St.
New York, N.Y. 10023

Conde-Nast Publications
420 Lexington Ave.
New York, N.Y. 10017

Consumer's Union of U.S., Inc.
256 Washington St.
Mount Vernon, N.Y. 10550

Cowles Book Co., Inc.
488 Madison Ave.
New York, N.Y. 10022

Gary Crowdus
90 E. Seventh Ave.
New York, N.Y. 10011

Crowell Collier and Macmillan,
  Inc.
866 Third Ave.
New York, N.Y. 10022

Crown Publishers, Inc.
419 Park Ave. S.
New York, N.Y. 10016

Cue
20 W. 43rd St.
New York, N.Y. 10036

Daily Variety
6404 Sunset Blvd.
Hollywood, Calif. 90028

The Delacorte Press.
  See Dell.

Dell Publishing Co., Inc.
750 Third Ave.
New York, N.Y. 10017

Deus
Paulist Press
Glen Rock, N.J. 07452

Dial Press, Inc. See Dell.

Director's Guild of America
165 W. 46th St.
New York, N.Y. 10036

Doubleday and Co., Inc.
277 Park Ave.
New York, N.Y. 10017

Drama Book Specialists/
  Publishers
150 W. 52nd St.
New York, N.Y. 10019

Duell, Little
440 Park Ave. S.
New York, N.Y. 10016

E. P. Dutton and Co., Inc.
201 Park Ave. S.
New York, N.Y. 10003

Easton Valley Press
P.O. Box 113, Ansonia Station
New York, N.Y. 10023

Educational Film Library
  Association, Inc.
17 W. 60th St.
New York, N.Y. 10023

Educational Screen and
  Audiovisual Guide
434 S. Wabash Ave.
Chicago, Ill. 60605

Educator's Progress Service
P.O. Box 497
Randolph, Wis. 53956

El-Jon
P.O. Box 64364
Los Angeles, Calif. 90064

Encyclopaedia Britannica, Inc.
425 N. Michigan Ave.
Chicago, Ill. 60611

Esquire, Inc.
488 Madison Ave.
New York, N.Y. 10022

Facts on File, Inc.
119 W. 57th St.
New York, N.Y. 10019

Falcon Press. See Crown.

Field Enterprises Educational
    Corp.
510 Merchandise Mart Pl.
Chicago, Ill. 60654

Film Comment
214 E. 11th St.
New York, N.Y. 10003

Film Education Resources
    Corp.
1825 Willow Rd.
Northfield, Ill. 60093

Film Fan Monthly
77 Grayson Pl.
Teaneck, N.J. 07666

Film Library Information
    Council
P.O. Box 348, Radio City
    Station
New York, N.Y. 10019

Film News
250 W. 57th St.
New York, N.Y. 10019

Filmboard
Screen Education News
Chelmsford, Mass.

Films Incorporated
1144 Wilmette Ave.
Wilmette, Ill. 60091

Fleet Press Corp.
156 Fifth Ave.
New York, N.Y. 10010

Free Press. See Crowell Collier
    and Macmillan.

Glass Publishing Co.
919 N. Michigan Ave.
Chicago, Ill. 60611

Golden Press
Western Publishing Co., Inc.
1220 Mound Ave.
Racine, Wis. 53404

Dan Golenpaul Associates
502 Park Ave.
New York, N.Y. 10022

Greater Amusements
1600 Broadway
New York, N.Y. 10019

Greenwood Press, Inc.
51 Riverside Ave.
Westport, Conn. 06880

Grosset and Dunlap, Inc.
51 Madison Ave.
New York, N.Y. 10010

H and R Associates
866 United Nations Plaza
New York, N.Y. 10017

HMH (Hugh M. Hefner)
919 N. Michigan Ave.
Chicago, Ill. 60611

John G. Hagner
Falling for Stars
37808 Rudall Ave.
Palmdale, Calif. 93550

Hamilton-Hampton Books
P.O. Box 76
Newberry, S.C. 29108

Hamlin Publishing Co.
14128 Hamlin St.
Van Nuys, Calif. 91401

Hansom Books
Artillery Mansions
75 Victoria St.
London S.W.1, England

Harcourt Brace Jovanovich, Inc.
757 Third Ave.
New York, N.Y. 10017

M. and N. Harrison
274 Madison Ave.
New York, N.Y. 10016

Hastings House Publishers, Inc.
10 E. 40th St.
New York, N.Y. 10016

Hill and Wang, Inc.
72 Fifth Ave.
New York, N.Y. 10011

Hollywood Premium Record
  Guide
1047 W. 97th St.
Los Angeles, Calif. 90044

Hollywood Reporter
6715 Sunset Blvd.
Hollywood, Calif. 90028

Holt, Rinehart and Winston,
  Inc.
383 Madison Ave.
New York, N.Y. 10017

Hope Reports
58 Carverdale Dr.
Rochester, N.Y. 14618

Humanities Press, Inc.
303 Park Ave. S.
New York, N.Y. 10010

I.F.I.D.A.
477 Madison Ave., 12th Floor
New York, N.Y. 10022

Independent Theater Owners
  of America
165 W. 46th St.
New York, N.Y. 10036

Indiana University Press
Indiana University
Tenth and Morton Sts.
Bloomington, Ind. 47401

Informatics
London, England

The Instructor
Instructor Park
Dansville, N.Y. 14437

Johnson Publishing Co.
  (Ebony)
1270 Ave. of the Americas
New York, N.Y. 10036

Kent State University Press
Kent, Ohio 44242

Alfred A. Knopf, Inc.
201 E. 50th St.
New York, N.Y. 10022

Landers Associates
P.O. Box 69760
Los Angeles, Calif. 90069

Walt Lee
P.O. Box 66273
Los Angeles, Calif. 90066

Library of Congress
Copyright Office
Washington, D.C. 20402

Locare Motion Picture
  Research Group
910 N. Fairfax
Los Angeles, Calif. 90046

London House and Maxwell
British Book Centre, Inc.
122 E. 55th St.
New York, N.Y. 10022

Low Budget Features
1054 N. Cahuenga (Dept. H)
Hollywood, Calif. 90028

McCalls Magazine
230 Park Ave.
New York, N.Y. 10017

McCutchan Publishing Corp.
2526 Grove St.
Berkeley, Calif. 94704

MacFadden-Bartell Corp.
205 E. 42nd St.
New York, N.Y. 10017

McGraw-Hill Book Co.
330 W. 42nd St.
New York, N.Y. 10036

Macmillan. See Crowell Collier
  and Macmillan.

Robert Malcomson
38559 Ashbury Park Dr.
Mount Clemens, Mich, 48043

Suni Mallow
Filmmaker's Newsletter
41 Union Square W.
New York, N.Y. 10003

Mass Media Associates, Inc.
2116 N. Charles St.
Baltimore, Md. 21218

Media and Methods
134 N. 13th St.
Philadelphia, Pa. 19107

Media Mix Newsletter
P.O. Box 5139
Chicago, Ill. 60680

Jonas Mekas
P.O. Box 1499
New York, N.Y. 10001

Mentor Press
150 Fifth Ave.
New York, N.Y. 10011

Metropolitan Opera Guild
1865 Broadway
New York, N.Y. 10023

Marvin Miller Enterprises
7046 Hollywood Blvd.
Hollywood, Calif. 90028

William Morrow and Co., Inc.
105 Madison Ave.
New York, N.Y. 10016

W. Franklyn Moshier
312 Teresita Blvd.
San Francisco, Calif. 90027

Motion Picture Enterprises
Tarrytown, N.Y. 10591

Museum of Modern Art
11 W. 53rd St.
New York, N.Y. 10019

Music Library Association
University of Michigan
Ann Arbor, Mich. 48105

National Archives and Record
  Service
General Services
  Administration
F St. bet. 18th and 19th St.
  N.W.
Washington, D.C. 20408

National Association of
  Independent Schools
4 Liberty Square
Boston, Mass. 02109

National Audio-Visual
  Association, Inc.
3150 Spring St.
Fairfax, Va. 22030

National Board of Review of
  Motion Pictures
210 E. 68th St.
New York, N.Y. 10021

National Catholic Office for
  Motion Pictures
405 Lexington Ave.
New York, N.Y. 10017

National Center for Film Study
1307 S. Wabash Ave.
Chicago, Ill. 60605

National Cinema Review
Box 34
New York, N.Y. 10012

National Congress of Parents
  and Teachers
700 N. Rush St.
Chicago, Ill. 60611

National Council of Churches
  of Christ in the U.S.A.
Dept. of Publication Services
475 Riverside Dr.
New York, N.Y. 10027

National Council of Teachers
  of English
1111 Kenyon Rd.
Urbana, Ill. 61801

Al Nelson
P.O. Box 275
Delafield, Wis. 53018

New York Times
229 W. 43rd St.
New York, N.Y. 10036

New Yorker
25 W. 43rd St.
New York, N.Y. 10036

Newspaper Enterprises
  Association
230 Park Ave.
New York, N.Y. 10017

Newsweek
444 Madison Ave.
New York, N.Y. 10022

Oxford University Press, Inc.
200 Madison Ave.
New York, N.Y. 10016

Pacific Coast Publishers
4085 Campbell Ave.
Menlo Park, Calif. 94025

Pacifica House, Inc., Publishers
P.O. Box 2131
Toluca Lake
North Hollywood, Calif. 91602

Parents' Magazine Press
52 Vanderbilt Ave.
New York, N.Y. 10017

W. L. Patterson
Saturday Review
380 Madison Ave.
New York, N.Y. 10017

Penguin Books, Inc.
7110 Ambassador Rd.
Baltimore, Md. 21207

Geo. A. Pflaum, Publisher
38 W. Fifth St.
Dayton, Ohio 45402

Pierian Press
P.O. Box 1808
Ann Arbor, Mich. 48108

Praeger Publishers, Inc.
111 Fourth Ave.
New York, N.Y. 10003

Prentice-Hall, Inc.
Rt. 9W
Englewood Cliffs, N.J. 07632

Price, Stern, Sloan, Inc.,
   Publishers
422 N. LaCienega Blvd.
Los Angeles, Calif. 90048

Producers Guild of America
141 El Camino Dr.
Beverly Hills, Calif. 90212

Public Affairs Committee
381 Park Ave. S.
New York, N.Y. 10016

G. P. Putnam's Sons
200 Madison Ave.
New York, N.Y. 10016

Pyramid Publications, Inc.
919 Third Ave.
New York, N.Y. 10022

Quadrangle Books, Inc.
175 Fifth Ave.
New York, N.Y. 10010

Quigley Publications
1270 Ave. of the Americas
New York, N.Y. 10020

Record Undertaker
P.O. Box 437
New York, N.Y. 10023

Record World
200 W. 57th St.
New York, N.Y. 10019

John Howard Reid
10-2e Mosman St.
Mosman Bay, Australia

Ted Riggs
805 Bridgewater Rd.
Knoxville, Tenn. 37919

RoundSound
P.O. Box 8743
Boston, Mass. 02114

Samuel K. Rubin
Classic Film Collector
734 Philadelphia St.
Indiana, Pa. 15701

St. Martin's Press, Inc.
175 Fifth Ave.
New York, N.Y. 10010

Scarecrow Press, Inc.
52 Liberty St.
Metuchen, N.J. 08840

Scholastic Magazines, Inc.
50 W. 44th St.
New York, N.Y. 10036

W. W. Schwann
137 Newbury St.
Boston, Mass. 02116

Screen Facts Press
Box 154
Kew Gardens, N.Y. 11415

Charles Scribner's Sons
597 Fifth Ave.
New York, N.Y. 10017

Serina Press
70 Kennedy St.
Alexandria, Va. 22305

Seven Arts Press, Inc.
6605 Hollywood Blvd.
Hollywood, Calif. 90028

Sherbourne Press
1640 S. La Cienega Blvd.
Los Angeles, Calif. 90035

G. Shirmer
609 Fifth Ave.
New York, N.Y. 10017

The Shoestring Press, Inc.
995 Sherman Ave.
Hamden, Conn. 06514

Shorecrest
724 Fifth Ave.
New York, N.Y. 10019

Leo Shull Publications, Inc.
136 W. 44th St.
New York, N.Y. 10036

Sight and Sound
155 W. 15th St.
New York, N.Y. 10011

Signet Books
1301 Ave. of the Americas
New York, N.Y. 10036

Simon and Schuster, Inc.
630 Fifth Ave.
New York, N.Y. 10020

Society for Cinema Studies
Broadcasting and Film Div.
University of Iowa
Iowa City, Iowa 52240

Society of Motion Picture and
Television Engineers, Inc.
9 E. 41st St.
New York, N.Y. 10017

Lyle Stuart, Inc.
239 Park Ave. S.
New York, N.Y. 10003

Murray Summers
7926 Ashboro Dr.
Alexandria, Va. 22309

Talking Book Topics
15 W. 16th St.
New York, N.Y. 10011

C. S. Tepfer Publishing Co.
607 Main St.
Ridgefield, Conn. 06877

Theater Historical Society
P.O. Box 4445
Washington, D.C. 20017

Time Inc.
Time-Life Bldg.
Rockefeller Center
New York, N.Y. 10020

Trade Service Publications
2720 Beverly Blvd.
Los Angeles, Calif. 90057

Triangle Publications
250 King of Prussia St.
Radnor, Pa. 19088

Twayne Publications
31 Union Square W.
New York, N.Y. 10003

Unicorn Publishing Corp.
P.O. Box 2778, Station B.
Montreal 110, Canada

University Film Association
Dept. of Photography and
  Cinema
Ohio State University
156 W. 19th Ave.
Columbus, Ohio. 43210

University of California Press
2223 Fulton St.
Berkeley, Calif. 94720

University of Chicago Press
5801 Ellis Ave.
Chicago, Ill. 60637

University of Dayton Press
300 College Park Ave.
Dayton, Ohio. 45409

University of Oklahoma Press
1005 Asp Ave.
Norman, Okla. 73069

University of Rochester
School of Liberal and Applied
  Studies
Rochester, N.Y. 14627

University of Southern
  California Press
University Park
Los Angeles, Calif. 90007

University of Wisconsin Press
P.O. Box 1379
Madison, Wis. 53701

Variety
154 W. 46th St.
New York, N.Y. 10036

Views and Reviews Magazine
633 W. Wisconsin, Suite 1700
Milwaukee, Wis. 53203

Viking Press, Inc.
625 Madison Ave.
New York, N.Y. 10022

Village Voice
80 University Pl.
New York, N.Y. 10003

Wayner Publications
P.O. Box 871, Ansonia Station
New York, N.Y. 10023

Wayside Press, Inc.
1501 Washington Rd.
Mendota, Ill. 61342

The H. W. Wilson Co.
950 University Ave.
New York, N.Y. 10003

World Publishing Co.
110 E. 59th St.
New York, N.Y. 10022

World Radio-TV Handbook Co.
Hellerup, Denmark

Ziff-Davis Publishing Co.
1 Park Ave.
New York, N.Y. 10016

Selected Bibliography of Other Audiovisual Books

Books not primarily for reference use, but valuable for background and enrichment, are included in this section. All books are now in print, and they cover film, music, radio, recordings, and television. They are listed by subject area according to the listings in *Books in Print* and *Book Publishers' Record*.

New editions of some of this supplementary material may eventually become more important in subsequent editions of *A Reference Guide to Audiovisual Information*.

MOVING PICTURE ACTORS AND ACTRESSES
Faces, Forms, Films: The Artistry of Lon Chaney. Robert G. Anderson. Cranbury, N.J.: A. S. Barnes and Company. $8.50.

Famous Stars of Filmdom: Men (Essay Index Reprint Series). Elinor Hughes. Freeport, N.Y.: Books for Libraries, 1932. $12.50.

Famous Stars of Filmdom: Women (Essay Index Reprint Series). Elinor Hughes. Freeport, N.Y.: Books for Libraries, 1931. $12.50.

Films of Cary Grant. Donald Deschner. New York: Citadel Press, 1971. illus. $9.95.

Films of Fredric March. Lawrence J. Quirk. New York: Citadel Press, 1971. illus. $9.95.

Films of Paul Newman. Lawrence J. Quirk. New York: Citadel Press, 1971. illus. $9.95.

Fred Astaire–Ginger Rogers Movie Book. Arlene Croce. New York: Outerbridge and Dienstfrey, 1971. illus. $10.00.

Ladies in Distress. Kalton C. Lahue. Cranbury, N.J.: A. S. Barnes and Company, 1971. illus. $10.00.

Lana Turner. Joe Morella and Edward Z. Epstein. New York: Citadel Press, 1971. illus. $6.95.

Photoplay Treasury. Barbara Gelman. New York: Crown Publishers, 1971. illus. $9.95.

Rebel in Films. Joseph Morella and Edward Z. Epstein. New York: Citadel Press, 1971. $9.95.

Seventeen Interviews: Film Stars and Superstars of the Sixties. Edwin Miller. New York: Macmillan Company, 1970. $6.95.

Stardom. Alexander Walker. New York: Stein and Day, 1970. illus. $10.00.

MOVING PICTURE AUDIENCES
Great Audience. Gilbert V. Seldes. Westport, Conn.: Greenwood Press, 1950. $11.00.

Social Conduct and Attitudes of Movie Fans (Payne Fund Studies). Frank K. Shuttleworth and Mark A. May. New York: Arno Press, 1970. $8.00.

MOVING PICTURE CAMERAS
Collecting Vintage Cameras, Vol. 1, The American 35mm. Kalton C. Lahue and Joseph C. Bailey. New York: American Photographic Book Publishing Company, 1971. $4.50.

Technique of the Motion Picture Camera (rev. ed.) (Library of Communication Series). H. Mario Souto. Philadelphia: Hastings Books, 1967. illus. $16.00.

MOVING PICTURE CARTOONS
Animated Photography: The ABC of the Cinematograph (Literature of Cinema Series). Cecil M. Hepworth. New York: Arno Press. $5.00.

Art in Movement: New Frontiers in Animation. John Halas and Roger Manvell. Philadelphia: Hastings Books, 1970. $17.50.

Film and TV Graphics (Visual Communication Books Series). John Halas. Walter Herdeg, ed. Philadelphia: Hastings Books, 1967. illus. $17.95.

Make Your Own Animated Movies. Yvonne Andersen. Boston: Little, Brown and Company, 1970. illus. $5.95.

Teaching Film Animation. Yvonne Andersen. New York: Van Nostrand-Reinhold Books, 1970. $8.95.

MOVING PICTURE CRITICISM
Dwight MacDonald on Movies. Dwight MacDonald. New York: Berkley Publishing Corporation, 1971. $1.50 (paperbound).

Figures of Light: Film Criticism and Comment. Stanley Kauffmann. New York: Harper and Row, 1971. $8.95.

Film Masters: An Anthology of Criticism on Thirty-Two Film Directors. Jonathan Rosenbaum, ed. New York: Grosset and Dunlap, 1971. illus. $12.95.

Focus on Blow-Up (Film Focus Series). Roy Huss, ed. Englewood Cliffs, N.J.: Prentice-Hall, 1971. illus. $5.95 ($2.45 paperbound).

Focus On Citizen Kane (Film Focus Series). R. Gottesman, ed. Englewood Cliffs, N.J.: Prentice-Hall, 1971. $5.95 ($2.45 paperbound).

Going Steady. Pauline Kael. New York: Bantam Books, 1971. reprint. $1.95 (paperbound).

Kiss Kiss Bang Bang. Pauline Kael. Boston: Little, Brown and Company, 1968. $8.95.

Movies: A Psychological Study. Martha Wolfenstein and Nathan Leites. New York: Hafner Publishing Company. illus. $13.95.

Responses to Drama: An Introduction to Plays and Movies. Thelma Altshuler and Richard P. Janaro. Boston: Houghton Mifflin, 1967. $4.25 (paperbound).

Return of Mad Look at Old Movies. Dick De Bartolo et al. New York: New American Library. $.60 (paperbound).

Sunday Night at the Movies. G. William Jones. Richmond, Va.: John Knox Press, 1967. illus. $1.95 (paperbound).

Theory of the Film (rev. ed.). Bela Balazs, tr. by Edith Bone. New York: British Book Centre, 1971. $12.95.

Year in the Dark. Renata Adler. New York: Random House, 1970. $7.95.

MOVING PICTURE FILM COLLECTIONS
Bibliography of Film Librarianship. Sam Kula. Portland, Ore.: International Scholarly Book Services. $3.00.

Classical Movie Shorts. Leonard Maltin. New York: Crown Publishers, 1971. $9.95.

Screen Monographs One (Literature of Cinema Series). New York: Arno Press, 1970. $5.00.

Screen Monographs Two (Literature of Cinema Series). New York: Arno Press, 1970. $7.00.

World Dictionary of Stockshot and Film Production Libraries. J. Chittock. Elmsford, N.Y.: Pergamon Publishing Company. $12.50.

MOVING PICTURE INDUSTRY
Competitive Cinema. Terence Kelly. New York: International Publications Service, 1966. $7.50.

Dreams for Sale: The Rise and Fall of the Triangle Film Corporation. Kalton C. Lahue. Cranbury, N.J.: A. S. Barnes and Company, 1971. illus. $8.50.

Hollywood: The Movie Colony, the Movie Makers (Literature of Cinema Series). Leo C. Rosten. New York: Arno Press. reprint of 1941 ed. $13.50.

International Film Industry: Western Europe and America Since 1945 (International Studies). Thomas H. Guback. Bloomington, Ind.: Indiana University Press, 1969. $10.00.

Japanese Film: Art and Industry. Joseph L. Anderson and Donald Ritchie. New York: Grove Press, 1960. $3.95 (paperbound).

Motion Picture Empire. Gertrude Jobes. Hamden, Conn.: Shoe String Press, 1966. illus. $10.00.

Movie Moguls: An Informal History of the Hollywood Tycoons. Philip French. Chicago: Henry Regnery Company, 1971. illus. $5.95.

Movie Reader. Ian Cameron. New York: Frederick A. Praeger, 1971. illus. $12.50 ($4.50 paperbound).

Moving Picture World, 1907–1911. New York: Arno Press. 10 vols. illus. $750.00.

Real Tinsel: The Story of Hollywood Told by the Men and Women Who Lived It. Bernard Rosenberg and Harry Silverstein. New York: Macmillan Company, 1970. illus. $9.95.

Twenty-Four Times a Second: Films and Film-Makers. William S. Pechter. New York: Harper and Row, 1971. $7.95.

Upton Sinclair Presents William Fox (Literature of Cinema Series). New York: Arno Press. reprint of 1933 ed. $12.50.

MOVING PICTURE MUSIC
Bachrach–David Songbook. Burt Bachrach and Hal David. New York: Simon and Schuster, 1970. $7.50.

The Cinema Organ. Reginald Foort. Vestal, N.Y.: Vestal Press. $6.00.

Cole Porter Song Book. Cole Porter. New York: Simon and Schuster, 1959. illus. $12.50.

Composing for the Films (Select Bibliographies Reprint Series). Hanns Eisler. Freeport, N.Y.: Books for Libraries. facsimile ed. reprint of 1947 ed. $9.75.

Fred Astaire–Ginger Rogers Movie Book. Arlene Croce. New York: Outerbridge and Dienstfrey, 1971. illus. $10.00.

George and Ira Gershwin Songbook. George Gershwin and Ira Gershwin. New York: Simon and Schuster, 1960. $10.00.

Great Songs of the Sixties. Milton Okun, ed. Chicago: Quadrangle Books, 1970. illus. $17.50.

Underscore. Frank Skinner. Hackensack, N.J.: Wehman Brothers. $6.00.

MOVING PICTURE PLAYS
Antonioni: Four Screenplays. Michelangelo Antonioni. New York: Grossman Publishers, 1971. $3.95 (paperbound).

Audiovisual Script Writing. Norton S. Parker. New Brunswick, N.J.: Rutgers University Press, 1968. $12.50.

Bunuel: Three Screenplays. Luis Bunuel, tr. from French by Piergiuseppi Bozzetti. New York: Grossman Publishers, 1970. illus. $6.95 ($3.50 paperbound).

Cabinet of Dr. Caligari (Film Scripts—Modern Series). Robert Weine. New York: Simon and Schuster, 1970. $1.95 (paperbound).

Clair: Four Screenplays. Rene Clair, tr. from French by Piergiuseppi Bozzetti. New York: Grossman Publishers, 1970. illus. $10.00 ($4.95 paperbound).

Complete Works of S. M. Eisenstein. Marcel Martin et al., eds. New York: Grove Press, 1971. illus. $50.00.

David Holzman's Diary. L. Kit Carson and Jim McBride. New York: Farrar, Straus and Giroux, 1970. $4.95 ($2.25 paperbound).

Duet for Cannibals. Susan Sontag. New York: Farrar, Straus and Giroux, 1970. illus. $4.95 ($2.25 paperbound).

Fellini: Early Screenplays. Federico Fellini, tr. from Italian by Judith Green. New York: Grossman Publishers, 1971. $6.95 ($2.95 paperbound).

Film Script. Irwin R. Blacker. Los Angeles: Nash Publishing Corporation, 1971. $5.95 ($2.95 paperbound).

Five Film Scripts. Incl. Noa Noa; African Queen; Night of the Hunter; Bride Comes to Yellow Sky; Blue Hotel. James Agee. Boston: Beacon Press, 1964. $2.75 (paperbound).

Four Screenplays. Carl T. Dreyer, tr. by Oliver Stallybrass. Bloomington, Ind.: Indiana University Press, 1971. text ed. illus. $3.95 (paperbound).

Greed (Film Scripts—Classic Series). Erich Von Stroheim. New York: Simon and Schuster, 1970. $4.95.

Jean Renoir Films. 1924-1939. Claude Beylie, ed., tr. by Helen R. Lane. New York: Grove Press, 1971. $50.00.

Jour Se Leve (Film Scripts—Classic Series). Jacques Prevert and Marcel Carne. New York: Simon and Schuster, 1970. $1.95 (paperbound).

Little Fauss and Big Halsy. Charles Eastman. New York: Farrar, Straus and Giroux, 1970. $4.95 ($2.25 paperbound).

Man and a Woman (Film Scripts—Modern Series). Claude Lelouche. New York: Simon and Schuster, 1970. $1.95 (paperbound).

A Nous La Liberte/Entr'Acte (Film Scripts—Classic Series). Rene Clair. New York: Simon and Schuster, 1970. $1.95 (paperbound).

Oedipus Rex (Film Scripts—Modern Series). Pier P. Pasolini. New York: Simon and Schuster, 1970. $1.95 (paperbound).

Pandora's Box (Film Scripts—Classic Series). G. W. Pabst. New York: Simon and Schuster, 1970. $1.95 (paperbound).

Photodrama (Literature of Cinema Series). Henry A. Phillips. New York: Arno Press. reprint of 1914 ed. $7.00.

Practical Manual of Screen Playwriting for Theater and Television Films. Lewis Herman. Cleveland: World Publishing Company. $3.95 (paperbound).

Seven Samurai (Film Scripts—Modern Series). Akira Kurosawa. New York: Simon and Schuster, 1970. $2.95.

Trial (Film Scripts—Modern Series). Orson Welles. New York: Simon and Schuster, 1970. $1.95 (paperbound).

Visconti, Five Screenplays: Vol. 1 Terra Trema and Senso, Vol. 2 *White Nights, Rocco and His Brothers, Job.* Luchino Visconti, tr. by Judith Green. New York: Grossman Publishers, 1969. illus. Vol. 1, $6.95; Vol. 2, $7.95 ($3.50 each, paperbound).

MOVING PICTURE PLAYS—HISTORY AND CRITICISM
Best Film Plays, 1970-1971. Irwin R. Blacker. Los Angeles: Nash Publishing Corporation, 1971. $8.50.

Film As Film: Critical Responses to Film Art. Joy G. Boyum and Adrienne Scott. Boston: Allyn and Bacon, 1971. $4.95 (paperbound).

Film Experience. Roy Huss and Norman Silverstein. New York: Dell Publishing Company. $1.95 (paperbound).

From Caligari to Hitler: A Psychological History of the German Film. Siegfried Kracauer. Princeton, N.J.: Princeton University Press. $9.00 ($2.95 paperbound).

Journeys. Gunter Eich, tr. from German by Michael Hamburger. (Cap Editions.) New York: Grossman Publishers, 1970. $3.50 ($1.50 paperbound).

Man and the Movies: Essays on the Art of Our Time. William R. Robinson, ed. Baton Rouge: Louisiana State University Press, 1967. illus. $7.95.

Moving Image: A Guide to Cinematic Literacy. Robert Gessner. New York: E. P. Dutton and Company, 1968. illus. $8.95 ($3.95 paperbound).

New American Cinema: A Critical Anthology. Gregory Battcock, ed. New York: E. P. Dutton and Company, 1967. orig. text. illus. $1.95 (paperbound).

World on Film. Stanley Kauffmann. New York: Harper and Row, 1966. $7.95.

MOVING PICTURE THEATERS
Architecture for the Theatre. Roberto Aloi. New York: William Heinman, 1958. illus. $30.00.

Motion-Picture Work (Literature of Cinema Series). David Hulfish. New York: Arno Press. reprint of 1915 ed. $25.00.

Picture Palace and Other Buildings for the Movies. Dennis Sharp. New York: Frederick A. Praeger, 1969. illus. $12.50.

MOVING PICTURES
America at the Movies (Literature of Cinema Series). Margaret Thorp. New York: Arno Press. reprint of 1939 ed. $11.00.

Art in Cinema: A Symposium of Avant-Garde Film (Contemporary Art Series). Frank Stauffacher, ed. New York: Arno Press, 1968. reprint of 1947 ed. $7.50.

Art of the Film (rev. ed). Ernest Lindgren. New York: Macmillan Company, 1963, 1970. illus. $7.50 ($2.95 paperbound).

Art of the Motion Picture (Literature of Cinema Series). Jean Benoit-Levy. New York: Arno Press. reprint of 1946 ed. $9.00.

Art of the Moving Picture. Vachel Lindsay. New York: Liveright Publishing Corporation, 1970. reprint of 1922 ed. $7.95 ($2.95 paperbound).

Art of Photoplay Making (Literature of Cinema Series). Victor O. Freeburg. New York: Arno Press. reprint of 1918 ed. $9.00.

Basic Motion Picture Technology. I. Bernard Hoppe. New York: Hastings House Publishers, 1970. $10.00.

Behind the Scenes: Theater and Film Interviews from the Trans-atlantic Review. Joseph F. McCrindle, ed. New York: Holt, Rinehart and Winston, 1971. $7.95 ($3.45 paperbound).

Casebook on Film. Charles T. Samuels. New York: Van Nostrand-Reinhold Books, 1970. $3.50 (paperbound).

Celluloid and Symbols. John C. Cooper and Carl Skrade, eds. Philadelphia: Fortress Press, 1970. $2.95 (paperbound).

Cinema As a Graphic Art. Vladimir Nilsen. New York: Hill and Wang, 1959. illus. $6.95.

Cinema Eye, Cinema Ear: Some Key Film-Makers of the Sixties. John R. Taylor. New York: Hill and Wang, 1964. illus. $5.95 ($2.25 paperbound).

Close-Up: A Magazine Devoted to the Art of Films, Vols. 1–10 (Contemporary Art Series). Kenneth MacPherson and Winifred Bryher, eds. New York: Arno Press, 1968. reprint of 1927 ed. $245.00.

Contemporary Cinema. Penelope Houston. Baltimore: Penguin Books, 1963. illus. $1.45 (paperbound).

Dramatic Art of the Film. Alan Casty. New York: Harper and Row, 1971. $3.50 (paperbound).

Elements of Film. Lee Bobker. New York: Harcourt Brace Jovanovich, 1969. illus. $4.75 (paperbound).

Expanded Cinema. Gene Youngblood. New York: E. P. Dutton and Company, 1970. illus. $9.95.

Experimental Cinema. David Curtis. New York: Universe Books, 1971. illus. $6.95.

Experimental Cinema, Nos. 1–5 (Contemporary Art Series). Seymour Stern and Lewis Jacobs, eds. New York: Arno Press, 1971. reprint of 1934 ed. illus. $20.00.

Fifty-Year Decline and Fall of Hollywood. Ezra Goodman. New York: Simon and Schuster, 1961. $5.95.

Film: A Montage of Theories. Richard D. MacCann, ed. New York: E. P. Dutton and Company. illus. $2.45 (paperbound).

Film: A Psychological Study (Film Series). Hugo Munsterberg. New York: Dover Publications, 1969. reprint of 1916 ed. orig. title: *Photoplay: A Psychological Study.* $2.00 (paperbound).

Film: An Anthology (2nd ed.). Daniel Talbot, ed. Berkeley, Calif.: University of California Press, 1966. $2.45 (paperbound).

Film As Art (abr. ed.). Rudolf Arnheim. Berkeley, Calif: University of California Press, 1957. $1.95 (paperbound).

Film, Book 2. Films of Peace and War. Robert Hughes, ed. New York: Grove Press, 1962. illus. $2.45 (paperbound).

Film Course Manual. Charles Sweeting. Berkeley, Calif.: McCutchan Publishing Corporation, 1971. $2.25 (paperbound).

Film Essays and a Lecture. Sergei Eisenstein, tr. by Jay Leyda. New York: Frederick A. Praeger, 1970. $6.95 ($2.95 paperbound).

Film Form. Sergei Eisenstein. New York: Harcourt Brace Jovanovich, 1969. reprint of 1949 ed. $2.45 (paperbound).

Film in a Manipulated World. Ivan Svitak. New York: Atheneum Publishers, 1971. $6.95.

Film Readings in the Mass Media. Allen Kirschner and Linda Kirschner. New York: Odyssey Press. $4.35 (paperbound).

Film Sense. Sergei Eisenstein. New York: Harcourt Brace Jovanovich, 1969. reprint of 1947 ed. $2.45 (paperbound).

Film and Society (Research Anthology Series). Richard D. MacCann. New York: Charles Scribner's Sons, 1964. $2.95 (paperbound).

Film Techniques and Film Acting. V. I. Pudovkin. New York: Crown Publishers, 1959. $3.75.

Film: The Creative Process (2nd ed.). John Howard Lawson. New York: Hill and Wang, 1967. illus. $7.95 ($2.95 paperbound).

Film World. Ivor Montagu. Baltimore: Penguin Books, 1964. illus. $1.75 (paperbound).

Films and Feelings. Raymond Durgnat. Cambridge, Mass.: M.I.T. Press, 1967, 1971. $1.95 (paperbound).

Films in Focus. Louis Reile. Meinrad, Ind.: Abbey Press, 1970. $1.25 (paperbound).

Films No. One-Four (Contemporary Art Series). Lincoln Kirstein et al., eds. New York: Arno Press, 1968. reprint of 1940 ed. $25.00.

Footnotes to the Film (Literature of Cinema Series). Charles Davy. New York: Arno Press. reprint of 1938 ed. $12.00.

Foreign Films on American Screens. Michael F. Mayer. New York: Arco Publishing Company, 1965. illus. $4.50 ($2.00 paperbound).

Gangsters and Hoodlums: The Underworld in the Cinema. Raymond Lee and B. C. Van Hecke. Cranbury, N.J.: A. S. Barnes and Company, 1970. illus. $8.95.

Hollywood Cage. Charles Hamblett. New York: Hart Publishing Company, 1970. $7.95 ($2.95 paperbound).

Hollywood Hallucination. Parker Tyler. New York: Simon and Schuster, 1970. $5.95 ($1.95 paperbound).

Hollywood—the Haunted House. Paul Mayersberg. New York: Ballantine Books, 1969. reprint of 1967 ed. $.95 (paperbound).

Hollywood Panorama. Bob Harman. New York: E. P. Dutton and Company, 1971. illus. $3.95 (paperbound).

Introduction to the American Underground Film. Sheldon Renan. New York: E. P. Dutton and Company, 1967. illus. $2.25 (paperbound).

Introduction to the Art of the Movies. Lewis Jacobs. New York: Octagon Books, 1970. $9.00 ($2.25 paperbound).

It's Only a Movie. Clark McKowen and William Sparke. Englewood Cliffs, N.J.: Prentice-Hall, 1971. $8.95 ($3.95 paperbound).

Literature and Film. Robert Richardson. Bloomington, Ind.: Indiana University Press, 1969. $4.95.

Living Pictures: Their History, Photo-Production and Practical Working (Literature of Cinema Series). Henry V. Hopwood. New York: Arno Press. reprint of 1899 ed. $10.00.

Magic and Myth of the Movies. Parker Tyler. New York: Simon and Schuster, 1970. $5.95 ($1.95 paperbound).

Media for Our Time: An Anthology. D. De Nitto. New York: Holt, Rinehart and Winston, 1971. $6.95 (paperbound).

Mobile Image: Movies (Media Probes Series). William Kuhns. New York: Herder and Herder, 1970. $1.25 (paperbound).

Motion-Picture Work (Literature of Cinema Series). David Hulfish. New York: Arno Press. reprint of 1915 ed. $25.00.

Movie Man. David Thomson. New York: Stein and Day, 1969. $2.95 (paperbound).

Movie Quiz Book (Film Reference Series). Malcolm F. Vance. New York: Paperback Library, 1970. illus. $1.25 (paperbound).

Movies: An American Idiom. Arthur F. McClure. Rutherford, N.J.: Fairleigh Dickinson University Press. $15.00.

Movies, Delinquency, and Crime (2nd ed.). Herbert Blumer et al. Montclair, N.J.: Patterson Smith Publishing Corporation. $8.00.

Movies as Medium. Lewis Jacobs, ed. New York: Farrar, Straus and Giroux, 1970. illus. $8.50 ($3.65 paperbound).

Movies and Society. I. C. Jarvie. New York: Basic Books, 1970. $10.00.

Movies in Society. Mark Koenigil. New York: Robert Speller and Sons, Publishers, 1962. $5.95.

Negative Space: Manny Farber on the Movies. Manny Farber. New York: Frederick A. Praeger, 1971. illus. $7.95.

New American Cinema: A Critical Anthology. Gregory Battcock, ed. New York: E. P. Dutton and Company, 1967. illus. $1.95 (paperbound).

Notes of a Film Director (rev. ed.) (Film Series). Sergei Eisenstein, tr. by X. Danko. New York: Dover Publications, 1970. reprint of 1959 ed. $3.00 (paperbound).

Novels into Film. George Bluestone. Berkeley, Calif.: University of California Press, 1957. $2.45 (paperbound).

On Film (Dover Film Series). Jean Cocteau. New York: Dover Publications, 1971. $2.00 (paperbound).

Photoplay: A Psychological Study (Literature of Cinema Series). Hugo Munsterberg. New York: Arno Press. reprint of 1916 ed. $7.50.

Photoplay: An Anthology (Dover Film Series). Richard Griffith, ed. New York: Dover Publications, 1971. $3.50 (paperbound).

Pictorial Beauty on the Screen (Literature of Cinema Series). Victor O. Freeburg. New York: Arno Press. reprint of 1923 ed. $7.00.

Politics and Film (Praeger Film Library Series). Leif Furhammar and Folke Isaksson. New York: Frederick A. Praeger, 1971. illus. $12.50.

Private Screenings. John Simon. New York: Macmillan Company, 1967. $6.95.

Public Arts. Gilbert Seldes. New York: Simon and Schuster, 1957. $1.95 (paperbound).

Reflections on the Screen. George W. Linden. Belmont, Calif.: Wadsworth Publishing Company, 1970. $10.60.

Renaissance of the Film. Julius Bellone. New York: Macmillan Company, 1970. illus. $2.95 (paperbound).

Screen Arts: A Guide to Film and Television Appreciation (Search Series). Edward Fischer. New York: Sheed and Ward, 1969. reprint of 1960 ed. orig. title: *Screen Arts.* $1.95 (paperbound).

Seven Lively Arts. Gilbert Seldes. Cranbury, N.J.: A. S. Barnes and Company, 1962. $2.45 (paperbound).

Sex, Psyche, Etcetera in the Film. Parker Tyler. New York: Horizon Press, 1969. $7.50.

Sight and Sound, and Society. David M. White and Richard Averson, eds. Boston: Beacon Press, 1968. $7.50.

Signs and Meaning in the Cinema (Cinema One Series, No. 9). Peter Wollen. Bloomington, Ind.: Indiana University Press, 1969. illus. $5.95 ($1.95 paperbound).

So You Think You Know Movies. Donald Kennedy. New York: Ace Books, 1970. $.60 (paperbound).

Stars and Strikes: Unionization in Hollywood. Murray Ross. New York: AMS Press, 1941. $9.50.

Suspense in the Cinema. Gordon Gow. Cranbury, N.J.: A. S. Barnes and Company. $2.95 (paperbound).

Terrors of the Screen. F. Manchel. Englewood Cliffs, N.J.: Prentice-Hall, 1970. $4.25.

Theory of Film: Character and Growth of a New Art. Bela Balazs. New York: Dover Publications, 1971. $2.75 (paperbound).

Theory of Film: The Redemption of Physical Reality. Siegfried Kracauer. New York: Oxford University Press, 1960. $12.50 ($2.75 paperbound).

Tower of Babel: Speculations on the Cinema. Eric Rhode. Philadelphia: Chilton Books, 1967. $5.95.

Underground Film: A Critical History. Parker Tyler. New York: Grove Press, 1970. illus. $7.50.

What is Cinema. Andre Bazin, tr. by Hugh Gray. Berkeley, Calif.: University of California Press, 1967. $5.75 ($2.25 paperbound).

What is Cinema, Vol. 2. Andre Bazin, tr. by Hugh Gray. Berkeley, Calif.: University of California Press. $7.95.

When the Movies Were Young. Mrs. D. W. Griffith. Bronx, N.Y.: Benjamin Blom, 1968. reprint of 1925 ed. illus. $9.75.

MOVING PICTURES—BIBLIOGRAPHY

Documentary Film (3rd ed.) (Communication Arts Books Series). Paul Rotha et al., New York: Hastings House Publishers, 1964. illus. $10.00.

General Bibliography of Motion Pictures (Contemporary Art Series). Carl Vincent et al., eds. New York: Arno Press, 1971. reprint of 1953 ed. $15.00.

To Be Continued. Ken Weiss and Ed Goodgold. New York: Crown Publishers, 1971. $9.95.

MOVING PICTURES—BIOGRAPHY
Cinema Eye, Cinema Ear: Some Key Film-Makers of the Sixties. John R. Taylor. New York: Hill and Wang. illus. $5.95 ($2.25 paperbound).

Garden of Allah. Sheilah Graham. New York: Crown Publishers, 1970. $5.95.

Hollywood Today (Hollywood Series). Allen Eyles and Pat Billings. Cranbury, N.J.: A. S. Barnes and Company, 1971. $2.95 (paperbound).

Jean Vigo. P. E. Salles Gomes, tr. by Allan Francovich. Berkeley, Calif.: University of California Press. $8.95.

Moguls. Norman Zierold. New York: Coward-McCann, 1969. $6.95.

Movies in the Age of Innocence. Edward Wagenknecht. Norman, Okla.: University of Oklahoma Press, 1962. illus. $7.95.

MOVING PICTURES—DIRECTORIES
Early American Cinema (International Film Guide Series). Anthony Slide. Cranbury, N.J.: A. S. Barnes and Company, 1970. $2.95 (paperbound).

Kemp's Film and Television Yearbook 1971 (16th ed.). New York: International Publications Service, 1971. $20.00.

The War-Peace Film Guide. Lucy Dougall. Berkeley, Calif.: World Without War Council Publications, 1970. $.75 (paperbound).

MOVING PICTURES—EDITING
Films Beget Films: A Study of the Compilation Film. Jay Leyda. New York: Hill and Wang, 1971. reprint of 1964 ed. $4.95 ($1.95 paperbound).

Technique of Editing 16mm Films (Library of Communication Techniques Series). John Burder. New York: Hastings House Publishers, 1968. illus. $9.50.

Technique of the Film Cutting Room (Library of Communication Techniques Series). Ernst Walter. New York: Hastings House Publishers, 1969. illus. $11.50.

MOVING PICTURES—EVALUATION
Film as Film: Critical Responses to Film Art. Joy G. Boyum and
Adrienne Scott. Boston: Allyn and Bacon, 1971. $4.95
(paperbound).

Three Faces of the Film. Parker Tyler. Cranbury, N.J.: A. S.
Barnes and Company, 1967. illus. $2.95.

World on Film. Stanley Kauffman. New York: Harper and Row,
1966. $7.95.

MOVING PICTURES—HISTORY
American Comedy Since Sound (International Film Guide Series).
Allen Eyles. Cranbury, N.J.: A. S. Barnes and Company, 1969.
illus. $3.50 (paperbound).

American Theater and the Motion Picture in America (English
Literary Reference, House Series). John Anderson and Rene
Fulop-Miller. New York: Johnson Reprint Corporation, 1970.
reprint of 1938 ed. $22.50.

Beauty and the Beast: Diary of a Film (Dover Film Series). Jean
Cocteau. New York: Dover Publications, 1971. $2.00
(paperbound).

Beginnings of the Biograph. Gordon Hendricks. New York:
Beginnings of the American Film, 1964. $6.00.

Behind the Screen. Kenneth MacGowan. New York: Delacorte,
1965. illus. $12.50.

Cinema. Thomas Wiseman. Cranbury, N.J.: A. S. Barnes and
Company, 1965. illus. $12.00.

Cinema Yesterday and Today (Dover Film Series). Rene Clair,
tr. by Stanley Appelbaum. New York: Dover Publications, 1971.
$3.00 (paperbound).

Concise History of the Cinema (International Film Guide Series).
Peter Cowie, ed. Cranbury, N.J.: A. S. Barnes and Company,
1970. 2 vols. illus. $3.50 ea. (paperbound).

Emergence of Film Art. Lewis Jacobs. New York: Lion Press,
1970. $10.00 ($4.95 paperbound).

Experimental Cinema, Nos. 1-5 (Contemporary Art Series). Seymour Stern and Lewis Jacobs, eds. New York: Arno Press, 1971.
reprint of 1934 ed. illus. $20.00.

Films in America. Martin Quigley and Richard Gertner. Racine,
Wis.: Western Publishing, 1970. illus. $12.95.

History of Motion Pictures (Literature of Cinema Series). Maurice Bardeche and Robert Brasillach. New York: Arno Press. reprint of 1938 ed. $14.00.

History of the American Film Industry from the Beginnings to 1931 (Film Series). Benjamin B. Hampton, ed. by Richard Griffith. New York: Dover Publications, 1970. orig. title: *History of the Movies.* illus. $4.00 (paperbound).

Hollywood: The Golden Era. Jack Spears. Cranbury, N.J.: A. S. Barnes and Company, 1970. $12.00.

Introduction to the Art of the Movies. Lewis Jacobs. New York: Farrar, Straus and Giroux, 1960. illus. $2.25 (paperbound).

Liveliest Art. Arthur Knight. New York: New American Library, 1971. $1.25 (paperbound).

Million and One Nights. Terry Ramsaye. New York: Simon and Schuster, 1964. illus. $10.00 ($3.95 paperbound).

Movie Going Fun in the Forties. A. Barbour. New York: Macmillan Company, 1971. $7.95.

Movie Serials: Their Sound and Fury. Jim Harmon and Donald F. Glut. New York: Doubleday and Company, 1971. $4.95.

Movies (rev. ed.). Richard Griffith and Arthur Mayer. New York: Simon and Schuster, 1970. $19.95.

Movies in the Age of Innocence. Edward Wagenknecht, ed. New York: Ballantine Books, 1971. reprint of 1962 ed. illus. $2.95 (paperbound).

Movies: The History of an Art and an Institution (Culture and Discovery Series). Richard Schickel. New York: Basic Books, 1964. illus. $5.95.

New Cinema in the U.S.A. Roger Manvell. New York: E. P. Dutton and Company, 1966. illus. $1.95 (paperbound).

New Spirit in the Cinema (Literature of Cinema Series). Huntly Carter. New York: Arno Press. reprint of 1930 ed. $14.00.

One Reel a Week. Fred J. Balshofer and Arthur C. Miller. Berkeley, Calif.: University of California Press, 1968. illus. $6.95.

Pictorial History of the Western Film. William K. Everson. New York: Citadel Press, 1971. reprint of 1969 ed. illus. $3.95.

Politics and Film (Praeger Film Library Series). Leif Furhammar and Folke Isaksson. New York: Frederick A. Praeger, 1971. illus. $12.50.

Reel Plastic Magic: A History of Films and Filmmaking in America. Lawrence Kardish. Boston: Little, Brown and Company, 1971. illus. $6.95.

Rise of the American Film (Studies in Culture and Communication Series). Lewis Jacobs. New York: Teachers College Press, 1968. reprint of 1938 ed. illus. $12.50 ($5.25 paperbound).

Running Away from Myself: A Dream Portrait of America Drawn from the Films of the Forties. Barbara Deming. New York: Grossman Publishers, 1969. illus. $6.95.

Seventy Years of Cinema. Peter Cowie. Cranbury, N.J.: A. S. Barnes and Company, 1968. illus. $15.00.

Shakespeare on Silent Film. Robert H. Ball. New York: Theatre Arts Books, 1968. illus. $12.50.

Short History of the Movies. Gerald Mast. New York: Pegasus, 1971. $4.95.

Silent Cinema. Liam O'Leary. New York: E. P. Dutton and Company, 1965. illus. $1.95 (paperbound).

Sociology of Film Art. George A. Huaco. New York: Basic Books, 1965. $5.50.

Stage to Screen: Theatrical Method from Garrick to Griffith. A. Nicholas Vardat. Bronx, N.Y.: Benjamin Blom, 1968. $12.50.

Violent America: The Movies, 1946-1964. Lawrence Alloway. Greenwich, Conn.: New York Graphic Society, 1971. illus. $7.95.

When Movies Began to Speak. Frank Manchel. Englewood Cliffs, N.J.: Prentice-Hall, 1969. $4.25.

When the Movies Were Young. D. W. Griffith. New York: Dover Publications, 1970. reprint of 1925 ed. $2.50 (paperbound).

Wit and Wisdom of Hollywood: From the Squaw Man to the Hatchet Man. Max Wilk. New York: Atheneum Publishers, 1971. $8.95.

MOVING PICTURES—MORAL AND RELIGIOUS ASPECTS
Celluloid and Symbols. John C. Cooper and Carl Skrade, eds. Philadelphia: Fortress Press, 1970. orig. text. $2.95 (paperbound).

Cinema: Its Present Position and Future Possibilities (Literature of Cinema Series). Cinema Commission of Inquiry. New York: Arno Press. reprint of 1917 ed. $15.00.

Content of Motion Pictures (Literature of Cinema Series: Payne Fund Studies of Motion Pictures and Social Values). Edgar Dale. New York: Arno Press. reprint of 1935 ed. $7.50.

Eros in the Cinema. Raymond Durgnat. New York: Fernhill House, 1966. $4.50.

Hollywood's Movie Commandments, a Handbook for Motion Picture Writers and Reviewers. Olga J. Martin. New York: Arno Press. reprint of 1937 ed. $9.00.

Homosexuality in the Movies. P. Tyler. New York: Holt, Rinehart and Winston, 1971. $8.50.

Motion Pictures and Standards of Morality (Payne Fund Studies). Charles C. Peters. New York: Arno Press. reprint of 1933 ed. $9.00.

Movies and Conduct (Literature of Cinema Series: Payne Fund Studies of Motion Pictures and Social Values). Herbert Blumer. New York: Arno Press. reprint of 1933 ed. $9.00.

Movies, Delinquency and Crime (Literature of Cinema Series: Payne Fund Studies of Motion Pictures and Social Values). Herbert Blumer and Philip M. Hauser. New York: Arno Press. reprint of 1933 ed. $7.50.

Movies in Society. Mark Koenigil. New York: Robert Speller and Sons, Publishers, 1962. $5.95.

Stag Movies. Larry Harris. Hollywood, Calif: Academy-Parliament, illus. $4.75.

Theology through Film. Neil P. Hurley. New York: Harper and Row, 1970. illus. $5.95.

MOVING PICTURES—PRODUCTION AND DIRECTION
Action Camera. Rich Carter and David C. Carroll. New York: Charles Scribner's Sons, 1971. illus. $5.95.

Behind the Scenes in a Film Studio. Elizabeth B. Grey. New York: Roy Publishers, 1968. illus. $3.50.

Breaking Through, Selling Out, Dropping Dead. William Bayer. New York: Macmillan Company, 1971. $6.95.

Celluloid Muse: Hollywood Directors Speak. Charles Higham and Joel Greenberg. Chicago: Henry Regnery Company, 1971. illus. $7.95.

Cinema As Art. Ralph Stephenson and J. R. Debrix. Baltimore: Penguin Books, 1965. illus. $1.65 (paperbound).

Cinema of Otto Preminger. Gerald Pratley. Cranbury, N.J.: A. S. Barnes and Company, 1971. illus. $2.95 (paperbound).

Directing Motion Pictures. Terence Marner, ed. Cranbury, N.J.: A. S. Barnes and Company. $2.95 (paperbound).

Directors at Work: Interviews with American Film Makers. Bernard Kantor et al. New York: Funk and Wagnalls, 1970. $10.00.

Director's Event: Interviews with Five American Film-Makers. Eric Sherman and Martin Rubin. New York: Atheneum Publishers, 1970. illus. $6.95.

Directors for the Seventies. Ian Cameron. New York: Frederick A. Praeger, 1971. illus. $6.95 ($2.95 paperbound).

Documentary in Action: A Casebook in Film Making. Alan Rosenthal. Berkeley, Calif.: University of California Press, 1971. $8.00.

Don't Say Yes Until I Finish Talking: A Biography of Darryl F. Zanuck. Mel Gussow. New York: Doubleday and Company, 1971. $7.95.

Film and the Director: A Handbook and Guide to Film Direction (Giant Series). Don Livingston. New York: G. P. Putnam's Sons, 1969. reprint of 1958 ed. illus. $1.95 (paperbound).

Film Director: A Practical Guide to Motion Pictures and Television Techniques. Richard L. Bare. New York: Macmillan Company, 1971. $8.95.

Film Director as Superstar. Joseph Gelmis. New York: Doubleday and Company, 1970. illus. $3.50 (paperbound).

Film Experience. Roy Huss and Norman Silverstein. New York: Harper and Row, 1968. illus. $6.95.

Film-Maker's Art. Haig P. Manoogian. New York: Basic Books, 1966. illus. $7.50.

Film Makers on Film Making. Harry M. Geduld, ed. Bloomington, Ind.: Indiana University Press, 1967. illus. $7.50 ($2.35 paperbound).

Film Scripts One. George P. Garrett et al., eds. New York: Appleton-Century-Crofts, 1971. $4.95 (paperbound).

Film Scripts Two. George P. Garrett et al., eds. New York: Appleton-Century-Crofts, 1971. $4.95 (paperbound).

Film Technique and Film Acting. V. Pudovkin, ed. by Ivor Montagu. New York: Grove Press, 1970. reprint. $1.95 (paperbound).

Five C's of Cinematography. Joseph U. Mascelli. Hollywood: Cine-Graphic, 1970. reprint of 1965 ed. $15.00.

Handbook of Film Production. J. Quick and T. Lebeau. New York: Macmillan Company, 1971. $12.95.

How to Make a Jewish Movie. Melville Shavelson. Englewood Cliffs, N.J.: Prentice-Hall, 1971. illus. $6.95.

How to Make Movie Magic. Julien Caunter. Philadephia: Chilton Book Company, 1971. illus. $8.95.

Jean Vigo (Film Library). John M. Smith. New York: Frederick A. Praeger, 1971. illus. $6.95 ($2.95 paperbound).

Jean Vigo. P. E. Salles Gomes, tr. by Allan Francovich. Berkeley, Calif.: University of California Press. $8.95.

Lessons with Eisenstein. Vladimir Nizhny. New York: Hill and Wang, 1969. reprint of 1962 ed. $5.75 ($1.95 paperbound).

Make Your Own Professional Movies. N. Goodwin and J. Manilla. New York: Macmillan Company, 1971. $5.95 ($1.50 paperbound).

Making of Feature Films: A Guide. Ivan Butler. Baltimore: Penguin Books, 1971. $1.75 (paperbound).

Making of One Day in the Life of Ivan Denisovich. Ronald Harwood, tr. from Russian by Gillon Aitken. New York: Ballantine Books, 1971. illus. $1.25 (paperbound).

Making Wildlife Movies: A Beginners Guide. Christopher Parsons. Harrisburg, Pa.: Stackpole Books, 1971. illus. $7.95.

Man and the Movies: Essays on the Art of Our Time. William R. Robinson, ed. Baton Rouge: Louisiana State University Press, 1967. illus. $7.95.

Movie Moguls: An Informal History of the Hollywood Tycoons. Philip French. Chicago: Henry Regnery Company, 1971. illus. $5.95.

Moving Pictures: How They Are Made and Worked (Literature of Cinema Series). Frederick A. Talbot. New York: Arno Press. reprint of 1912 ed. $14.00.

People Who Make Movies. Theodore Taylor. New York: Doubleday and Company, 1967. $3.95.

Primer for Film-Making: A Complete Guide to 16 and 35mm Film Production. Kenneth Roberts and Winston S. Sharples. Indianapolis: Bobbs-Merrill Company, 1971. illus. $15.00 ($6.75 paperbound).

Work of the Film Director. A. J. Reynertson. New York: Hastings House Publishers, 1970. $13.50 ($7.60 paperbound).

MOVING PICTURES—SOCIAL ASPECTS
Movies and Society. I. C. Jarvie. New York: Basic Books, 1970. $10.00.

MOVING PICTURES—STUDY AND TEACHING
Film Making in Schools. Douglas Lowndes. New York: Watson-Guptill Publications, 1969. illus. $8.95.

Films on the Campus. Thomas Fensch. Cranbury, N.J.: A. S. Barnes and Company, 1970. illus. $15.00.

MOVING PICTURES, DOCUMENTARY
Bellicho's China Is Near. Marco Bellocchio, tr. from Italian by Judith Green. New York: Grossman Publishers, 1970. orig. title: *Cine E Vicina.* illus. $1.95 (paperbound).

Documentary Film (3rd ed.) (Communication Arts Book Series). Paul Rotha et al. New York: Hastings House Publishers, 1964. illus. $10.00.

Film and Its Techniques. Raymond Spottiswoode. Berkeley, Calif.: University of California Press, 1951. illus. $9.50.

Grierson on Documentary. Forsyth Hardy. New York: Frederick A. Praeger, 1971. illus. $10.95 ($5.50 paperbound).

Long Look at Short Films: An A.C.T.T. Report on the Short Entertainment and Factual Film. Derrick Knight and Vincent Porter. Elmsford, N.Y.: Pergamon Publishing Company. $2.45 (paperbound).

Pare Lorentz and the Documentary Film. Robert L. Snyder. Norman, Okla.: University of Oklahoma Press, 1968. illus. $6.95.

Technique of Documentary Film Production (rev. ed.) (Library of Communication Techniques Series). W. Hugh Baddeley. New York: Hastings House Publishers, 1963. $10.00.

MOVING PICTURES AND RELIGION
Popcorn and Parable: A New Look at the Movies. Roger Kahle and Robert E. Lee. Minneapolis: Augsburg Publishing House, 1971. $2.95 (paperbound).

MOVING PICTURES AS A PROFESSION
Making Movies: Student Films to Features. Hila Colman.
Cleveland: World Publishing Company, 1971. $4.95.

*Opportunities in the Motion Picture Industry and How to
Qualify for Positions in Its Many Branches* (Literature of Cinema
Series). Photoplay Research Society. New York: Arno Press.
reprint of 1922 ed. $5.00.

Your Career in Film Making. (Career Book Series). George N.
Gordon and Irving A. Falk. New York: Julian Messner, 1969.
$3.95.

Your Career in Motion Pictures, Radio and Television. Charles R.
Jones. New York: Sheridan House. $5.00.

MOVING PICTURES IN CHURCH WORK
Sunday Night at the Movies. G. William Jones. Richmond, Va.:
John Knox Press, 1967. illus. $1.95 (paperbound).

Television-Radio-Film for Churchmen (Communication for
Churchmen Series, vol. 2). B. F. Jackson, Jr., ed. Nashville:
Abingdon Press, 1969. $6.50.

MOVING PICTURES IN EDUCATION
*Educational Films: Writing, Directing, Producing for Classroom,
Television and Industry.* Lewis Herman. New York: Crown
Publishers, 1965. $5.95.

Eight MM Sound Film and Education. Louis Forsdale. New
York: Teachers College Press, Columbia University, 1962.
$2.95 (paperbound).

Film in Higher Education and Research. Peter D. Groves, ed.
Elmsford, N.Y.: Pergamon Publishing Company, 1966. illus.
$7.00 ($4.95 paperbound).

Motion Pictures in Education: A Summary of the Literature
(Literature of Cinema Series). Edgar Dale et al. New York: Arno
Press. reprint of 1938 ed. $15.00.

One Hundred One Films for Character Growth. Jane Cushing.
Notre Dame, Ind.: Fides Publishers, 1969. $1.50 (paperbound).

MUSIC
Adventure in Music. Burnett James. Boston: Crescendo
Publishers. $7.95

Adventure in Music. Robert W. Mendl. Chester Springs, Pa.:
Dufour Editions, 1964. $4.50.

Backgrounds to Music. J. Scherek. Portland, Ore.: International Scholarly Book Service, 1947. $1.70.

Basic Music. Whitehall Company. Northbrook, Ill.: Whitehall Company. $6.50 ($2.95 paperbound).

Beethoven and His World. Erich Valentin. New York: Viking Press, 1969. illus. $6.95.

Black Music in Our Culture. Dominique-Rene De Lerma. Kent, Ohio: Kent State University Press, 1970. $7.50.

Blues: An Anthology. W. C. Handy. New York: Macmillan Company, 1971. $7.95 ($3.95 paperbound).

Classic and Romantic Music. Friedrich Blume, tr. by M. D. Norton. New York: W. W. Norton and Company, 1970. $6.00 text ed. $1.95 (paperbound).

Classical Themes for People Who Hate Classical Music. New York: Essandess Specials. $1.95 (paperbound).

Conductor's World. David Wooldridge. New York: Frederick A. Praeger, 1970. illus. $10.00.

Copland on Music. Aaron Copland. New York: W. W. Norton and Company, 1963. $1.95 (paperbound).

Critical Affairs: A Composer's Journal. Ned Rorem. New York: George Braziller, 1970. $5.95.

Electronic Music (rev. ed.). Washington, D. C.: Music Educators National Conference, 1968. $2.00 (paperbound; includes bound-in record).

Everyman and His Music (facsimile ed.) (Essay Index Reprint Series). Percy A. Scholes. Freeport, N.Y.: Books for Libraries, 1917. $7.50.

Heroes of Music (Heroes of Series). Renee Fisher. New York: Fleet Press Corporation, 1971. illus. $5.00.

Hindemith. Ian Kemp. New York: Oxford University Press, 1970. illus. $2.50 (paperbound).

Humor of Music. Laning Humphrey. Boston: Crescendo Publishers, 1970. $4.50.

Infinite Variety of Music. Leonard Bernstein. New York: New American Library. $2.95.

In Praise of Music. Richard Lewis, ed. New York: Grossman Publishers, 1963. illus. $4.95.

Introduction to Western Music. F. E. Kirby. New York: Free Press, 1969. $8.95.

Journey Towards Music, a Memoir. Victor Gollancz. New York: E. P. Dutton and Company, 1965. illus. $6.00.

Landowska on Music. Wanda Landowska, ed. by Denise Restout and Robert Hawkins. New York: Stein and Day, 1969. illus. $12.50; $25.00 deluxe ed; $3.95 (paperbound).

Learning to Listen: A Handbook for Music. Grosvenor Cooper. Chicago: University of Chicago Press, 1957. $4.75.

Listen: A Guide to the Pleasures of Music. Roland Nadeau and William Tesson. Boston: Allyn and Bacon, 1971. text ed. $8.95.

Listener's Handbook (3rd ed). Ira Schroeder. Ames, Iowa: Iowa State University Press, 1966. text ed. illus. $3.95.

Listening to Music. R. L. Crocker and A. P. Basart. New York: McGraw-Hill, 1971. $9.95.

Literary Style and Music. Herbert Spencer. Port Washington, N.Y.: Kennikat Press, 1970. reprint of 1951 ed. $6.00.

Ludwig Van Beethoven: Highlight Collection of His Best Loved Original Works. New York: Crown Publishers. $2.95 (paperbound).

Mind and Music (facsimile ed.) (Select Bibliographies Series). Frank S. Howes. Freeport, N.Y.: Books for Libraries. reprint of 1948 ed. $8.75.

Music and Its Masters. Otis B. Boise. New York: AMS Press. reprint of 1902 ed. $10.00.

Music and Poetry (Studies in Poetry Series, No. 38). Sidney Lanier. New York: Haskell House Publishers, 1969. reprint of 1898 ed. $8.95.

Music and Politics. Jazz and Pop, ed. Cleveland: World Publishing Company. $5.95.

Music and Sound. Llewelyn S. Lloyd. Westport, Conn.: Greenwood Press, 1937. $9.25.

Musical Memories. Camille Saint-Saens. New York: AMS Press, 1919. $15.00.

Music: Imaginative Listening. Louis Ferraro and Sam Adams. Baton Rouge: Claitors Book Store, 1969. $8.00.

Music, Its Secret Influence Throughout the Ages. Cyril Scott. New York: Samuel Weiser, 1969. reprint of 1933 ed. $5.00.

Music Makers (Concordia Music Education Series, Bk. 5). Victor Hildner et al. St. Louis: Concordia Publishing House, 1968, illus. $3.95 text ed.; $6.75 teacher's ed.

Music: Mirror of the Arts. Alan Rich. New York: Frederick A. Praeger, 1969. $15.00.

Music of Our Time. Nick Rossi and Robert Choate. Boston: Crescendo Publishers, 1970. illus. $12.50.

Music of the Spheres and the Dance of Death. Kathi Meyer-Baer. Princeton, N.J.: Princeton University Press, 1970. $13.50.

Nature of Music. Julius Klauser. New York: AMS Press. reprint of 1909 ed. $13.00.

Noise of Music. Alan R. Warwick. Boston: Crescendo Publishers, 1970. $6.95.

Norton Scores: An Anthology for Listening (2 vols., expanded ed.). Roger Kamien. New York: W. W. Norton and Company, 1970. $12.50 ea.

On Music and Musicians. Robert Schumann. New York: McGraw-Hill, 1946. $2.95 (paperbound).

Opera Guide. Gerhart Von Westerman, ed. by Harold Rosenthal, tr. by Anne Ross. New York: E. P. Dutton and Company, 1968. reprint of 1965 ed. illus. $2.95 (paperbound).

Outspoken Essays on Music (facsimile ed.) (Essay Index Reprint Series). Camille Saint-Saens, tr. by F. Rothwell. Freeport, N.Y.: Books for Libraries, 1922. $7.00.

Poetics of Music in the Form of Six Lessons. Igor Stravinsky. Cambridge, Mass.: Harvard University Press, 1970. $7.95.

Portrait of Carnegie Hall. Theodore O. Cron and B. Goldblatt. New York: Macmillan Company, 1966. $9.95.

Questions About Music (Charles Eliot Norton Lecture Series, 1968–1969). Roger Sessions. Cambridge, Mass.: Harvard University Press, 1970. $5.95.

Retrospectives and Conclusions. Igor Stravinsky and Robert Craft. New York: Alfred A. Knopf, 1969. $7.95.

Rudiments of Music. William Lovelock. New York: St. Martin's Press, 1971. illus. $2.95 (paperbound).

Serious Music and All That Jazz (Fireside Paperback Series). Henry Pleasants. New York: Simon and Schuster, 1971. $2.95 (paperbound).

Short Introduction to Music. Adelaide Hess. New York: G. Schirmer, 1954. $1.00 (paperbound).

Sounds of Music: Descending Intervals. C. Spohn and W. Poland. Englewood Cliffs, N.J.: Prentice-Hall, 1967. text ed. $4.95 (paperbound).

Sounds of Music: Harmonic Intervals. C. Spohn and W. Poland. Englewood Cliffs, N.J.: Prentice-Hall, 1967. text ed. $4.95 (paperbound).

Themes and Episodes. Igor Stravinsky and Robert Craft. New York: Alfred A. Knopf, 1966. $7.95.

They All Had Glamour: From the Swedish Nightingale to the Naked Lady. Edward B. Marks. Bronx, N.Y.: Benjamin Blom, 1944. $12.50.

A Thing or Two About Music. Nicolas Slonimsky. Westport, Conn.: Greenwood Press. reprint of 1948 ed. $13.25.

Treasury of Music. Rich. New York: Frederick A. Praeger. $15.00.

What Do You Know About Music. Henry V. Thomas. New York: Vantage Press. $7.50.

Zoltan Kodaly, His Life and Work. Laszlo Eosze. Boston: Crescendo Publishers, 1969. illus. $7.50.

MUSIC (GENERAL)

Book of Music. Jack Spicer. Berkeley, Calif.: White Rabbit/Open Space. $1.00 (paperbound).

Business of Modern Music. Nanry. New York: E. P. Dutton and Company. $6.95 ($2.95 paperbound).

Goldstein's Greatest Hits. Richard Goldstein. New York: Tower Publications, 1971. reprint. $.95 (paperbound).

Harmonization-Transposition at the Keyboard (rev. ed.). Alice M. Kern. Evanston, Ill.: Summy-Birchard Publishers, 1968. $5.00 (paperbound).

Music: Mirror of the Arts. Alan Rich. New York: Frederick A. Praeger, 1969. $15.00.

Music and Western Man (Canadian Broadcasting Corporation Series). Peter Garvie, ed. Chester Springs, Pa.: Dufour Editions, 1958. $6.50.

Music in American Life. Jacques Barzun. Magnolia, Mass.: Peter Smith Publisher. $4.00.

On Music & Musicians. Robert Schumann. New York: W. W. Norton and Company, 1969. $6.95.

Open Door to Beautiful Music. Thelma H. Jones. Alhambra, Calif.: Miller Books, 1970. $1.80 (paperbound).

Prelude to the Afternoon of a Faun (Critical Score Series). Claude Debussy, ed. by William W. Austin. New York: W. W. Norton and Company, 1971. $6.00 ($1.85 paperbound).

Sound and Hearing. Charles Gramet. New York: Abelard-Schuman, 1965. illus. $4.75.

Technique of Accompaniment. Philip Cranmer. Chester Springs, Pa.: Dufour Editions. $3.25.

The Other Side of the Record. Charles O'Connell. Westport, Conn.: Greenwood Press. reprint of 1947 ed. $13.25.

This Modern Music. Gerald Abraham. Chester Springs, Pa.: Dufour Editions, 1955. reprint of 1933 ed. $1.75.

MUSIC—ACOUSTICS AND PHYSICS

Acoustical Foundations of Music. John Backus. New York: W. W. Norton and Company, 1969. illus. $7.95.

Acoustics of Music. Wilmer T. Bartholomew. Englewood Cliffs, N.J.: Prentice-Hall, 1942. $9.95.

Art of Prolonging the Musical Tone. C. Brumby. Portland, Ore.: International Scholarly Book Services. $3.50.

Guide to Musical Acoustics. H. Lowery. New York: Dover Publications. $1.25 (paperbound).

Harmonics: Or the Philosophy of Musical Sounds (2nd ed.) (Music Series). Robert Smith. New York: Plenum Publications, 1966. $7.50.

Music, Acoustics and Architecture. Leo L. Beranek. New York: John Wiley and Sons, 1962. $19.95.

Music, Sound and Sensation: A Modern Exposition. Fritz Winckel, tr. by Thomas Binkley. New York: Dover Publications, 1967. illus. $2.50 (paperbound).

Music and Sound (Select Bibliographies Reprint Series). Llewelyn S. Lloyd. Freeport, N.Y.: Books for Libraries, 1937. $9.00.

Musical Acoustics (4th ed.). Charles A. Culver. New York: McGraw-Hill, 1956. $9.50.

Musical Instruments and Audio. G. A. Briggs. Boston: Cahners Publishers, 1966. illus. $7.95.

Observer's Book of Music (Observer's Pocket Series). Freda Dinn. New York: Warne Frederick and Company, 1953. illus. $1.95.

On the Sensations of Tone. Hermann L. Helmholtz. New York: Dover Publications, 1954. $4.00 (paperbound).

Pianos, Pianists and Sonics. Gilbert A. Briggs. Boston: Cahners Publishers, 1951. illus. $5.95.

Physics of Music (6th ed.). Alexander Wood, ed. by J. M. Bowsher. New York: Barnes and Noble, 1964. $5.75.

Physics of Musical Sounds. Charles A. Taylor. New York: American Elsevier Publishers, 1966. $9.50.

Science and Music. James Jeans. New York: Dover Publications, 1968. reprint of 1937 ed. $2.00 (paperbound).

Science of Vocal Pedagogy: Theory and Application. D. Ralph Appelman. Bloomington, Ind.: Indiana University Press, 1967. illus. $15.00 (companion album of 5 records $10.00).

Sound and Music: A Non-Mathematical Treatise on the Physical Constitution of Musical Sounds and Harmony. Sedley Taylor. New York: Johnson Reprint Corporation, 1873. illus. $10.50.

Tone: A Study in Musical Acoustics. Seigmund Levarie & Ernst Levy. Kent, Ohio: Kent State University Press. illus. $7.95 ($3.25 paperbound).

MUSIC—ANALYSIS, APPRECIATION

An Anthology of Musical Criticism. Norman Demuth, Westport, Conn.: Greenwood Press. reprint of 1947 ed. $15.75.

Appreciation of Music (Living Method Course). Abram Chasins. New York: Crown Publishers, 1966. $9.95 (with records).

Art of Judging Music. Virgil Thomson. Westport, Conn.: Greenwood Press, 1969. $13.50.

Art of Listening: Developing Musical Perception. Howard Brofsky and Jeanne Bamberger. New York: Harper and Row, 1969. orig. text. illus. $5.00 (paperbound) (7 records $13.00).

At Home with Music (facsimile ed.) (Essay Index Reprint Series). Sigmund G. Spaeth. Freeport, N.Y.: Books for Libraries, 1945. illus. $15.75.

Basic Studies in Music. William H. Baxter, Jr. Boston: Allyn and Bacon, 1968. $7.95.

Classic and Romantic Music. Friedrick Blume, tr. by Norton M. Herter. New York: W. W. Norton and Company, 1970. $1.95 (paperbound).

Complete Book of Classical Music. David Ewen. Englewood Cliffs, N.J.: Prentice-Hall, 1965. $14.95.

Complete Book of the Great Musicians, 3 Vols. in One. Percy A. Scholes. New York: Oxford University Press, 1949. illus. $7.00.

Continuity of Music. Irving Kolodin. New York: Alfred A. Knopf, 1969. $10.00.

Delights of Music: A Critic's Choice. Neville Cardus. New York: Fernhill House, Ltd., 1966. $4.00. International Publications Service, 1966. $5.25.

Design for Understanding Music. A. Verne Wilson. Evanston, Ill.: Summy-Birchard Company, 1966. illus. $9.75.

Discovering Music (4th ed.). Howard D. McKinney and W. R. Anderson. New York: Van Nostrand Reinhold Company, 1962. $8.95.

Elements of Musical Understanding. Allen Winold. Englewood Cliffs, N.J.: Prentice-Hall, 1966. illus. $9.95.

Enjoyment of Music (3rd ed.). Joseph Machlis. New York: W. W. Norton and Company, 1970. illus. $8.95; abridged ed. $7.95.

Ewen's Lighter Classics in Music. David Ewen. New York: Arco Publishing Company, 1961. $5.00.

Ewen's Musical Masterworks (2nd ed.). David Ewen. New York: Arco Publishing Company, 1967. $6.95.

Foundations of Music. Wayne Barlow. New York: Appleton-Century-Crofts, 1953. illus. $5.50.

Guide to Musical Styles: From Madrigal to Modern Music. Douglas Moore. New York: W. W. Norton and Company, 1963. illus. $1.95 (paperbound).

Hearing: Gateway to Music. Adele Katz and Ruth H. Rowen. Evanston, Ill.: Summy-Birchard Company, 1959. $6.25.

History of Music in Performance. Frederick Dorian. New York: W. W. Norton and Company, 1943. illus. $2.25 (paperbound).

History of Music in Sound, 10 Handbooks. Gerald Abraham, ed. New York: Oxford University Press, 1953–1959. $2.50 each.

History of Musical Thought (3rd ed.). Donald N. Ferguson. New York: Appleton-Century-Crofts, 1959. illus. $7.50.

Home Book of Musical Knowledge. David Ewen. Englewood Cliffs, N.J.: Prentice-Hall, 1954. $9.95.

How to Become a Musical Critic. George B. Shaw, ed. by Dan H. Laurence. New York: Hill and Wang, 1967. reprint. $2.45 (paperbound).

How to Understand Music: A Concise Course in Musical Culture by Object Lessons and Essays. William S. Mathews. New York: AMS Press, 1900–1901. 2 vols. $20.00.

Human Side of Music (Music Series). Charles W. Hughes. New York: Plenum Publishing Corporation, 1970. reprint of 1948 ed. $14.50.

Infinite Variety of Music. Leonard Bernstein. New York: Simon and Schuster, 1966. $6.50.

Interpretation of the Music of the Seventeenth and Eighteenth Centuries. Arnold Dolmetsch. Seattle: University of Washington Press, 1969. illus. $3.95 (paperbound).

Introduction to Contemporary Music. Joseph Machlis. New York: W. W. Norton and Company, 1961. illus. $9.50.

Introduction to Music. Hugh M. Miller. New York: Barnes and Noble, 1958. illus. $1.75 (paperbound).

Introduction to Music (3rd ed.). Martin Bernstein and M. Picker. Englewood Cliffs, N.J.: Prentice-Hall, 1966. illus. $9.95.

Introduction to Music (rev. 2nd ed.). David D. Boyden. New York: Alfred A. Knopf, 1970. $8.95.

Introduction to Music Appreciation: An Objective Approach to Listening (rev. ed.). William H. Miller. Philadelphia: Chilton Book Company, 1970. $6.00.

Invitation to Music. Elie Siegmeister. Irvington-on-Hudson, N.Y.: Harvey House, 1961. $5.95.

Language of Music. Klaus Liepmann. New York: Ronald Press Company, 1953. illus. $7.00.

Listener's Guide to Music: With a Concert-Goer's Glossary (10th ed.). Percy A. Scholes. New York: Oxford University Press, 1961. illus. $1.75 (paperbound).

Listener's Guide to Musical Understanding (3rd ed.). Leon Dallin. Dubuque, Iowa: William C. Brown and Company, 1968. $5.50.

The Listener's History of Music. Percy A. Scholes. New York: Oxford University Press, 1954. Vol. 1: *To Beethoven* (7th ed.), Vol. 2: *The Romantic and Nationalist Schools of the Nineteenth Century* (4th ed.), Vol. 3: *To the Composers of Today* (5th ed.). $3.00 ea. $7.20 3 vol. ed.

Listener's Music Book. Olga S. Stokowski. New York: W. W. Norton and Company, 1935. illus. $3.95.

Listening to Music: A Guide to Enjoyment (2nd rev. ed.). Roger Fiske. Mystic, Conn.: Lawrence Verry, 1966. $3.00.

Listening to Music Creatively (2nd ed.). Edwin J. Stringham. Englewood Cliffs, N.J.: Prentice-Hall, 1959. $9.50.

Making Friends with Music: An Introduction to Musical Appreciation (Making Friends Series). James Glennon. Boston: Crescendo Publishers, 1970. illus. $1.50 (paperbound).

Meaning and Magic of Music. Peter Gammond. Racine, Wis.: Western Publishing Company, 1970. $3.95.

Miniature History of Music for the General Reader and the Student (4th ed.). Percy A. Scholes. New York: Oxford University Press, 1955. $.65.

Music: Adventures in Listening. Joseph Machlis. New York: W. W. Norton and Company, 1968. $5.36.

Music from Inside Out. Ned Rorem. New York: George Braziller, 1967. $4.00.

Music Lover's Pocket Book. Harry Dexter and Raymond Tobin. Boston: Crescendo Publishers, 1969. $2.50.

Music of the Classical Era: Twenty Examples for Analysis. Owen Jander, ed. New York: Thomas Y. Crowell Company, 1967. $6.95 (paperbound).

Music Right and Left. Virgil Thomson. Westport, Conn.: Greenwood Press, 1968. reprint of 1945 ed. illus. $10.50.

Music: The Listener's Art (2nd ed.). Leonard G. Ratner. New York: McGraw-Hill, 1966. illus. $8.95.

Music Tells the Tale. Geoffrey Palmer and Lloyd Noel. New York: Frederick Warne and Company, 1967. illus. $4.95.

Music Throughout the World (rev. ed.). Marian Cotton and Adelaide Bradburn. Evanston, Ill.: Summy-Birchard Publishing Company, 1960. illus. $6.40.

Musical Experience of Composer, Performer, Listener. Roger Sessions. Princeton, N.J.: Princeton University Press. $4.50 ($1.95 paperbound).

Musical Scene. Virgil Thomson. Westport, Conn.: Greenwood Press, 1945. $13.75.

New Listener's Companion and Record Guide (3rd ed.). B. H. Haggin. New York: Horizon Press, 1970. $3.95 (paperbound).

New Musical Companion. A. L. Bacharach, ed. New York: International Publications Service, 1964. $6.25.

Norton Scores: An Anthology for Listening. Roger Kamien, ed. New York: W. W. Norton and Company, 1970. 2 vols. $3.95 ea. ($4.95 paperbound).

Olin Downes on Music: A Selection from His Writings During the Half-Century: 1906-1955. Olin Downes, ed. by Irene Downes. Westport, Conn.: Greenwood Press, 1957. $17.50.

One Hundred One Masterpieces of Music and Their Composers. Martin Bookspan. New York: Doubleday and Company, 1968. $8.95.

Scored for Listening: A Guide to Music. Guy A. Bockmon and William J. Starr. New York: Harcourt Brace Jovanovich. illus. $4.25 (paperbound).

Sense of Music. Victor Zuckerkandl. Princeton, N.J.: Princeton University Press. illus. $9.00 ($2.95 paperbound).

Spell of Music: An Attempt to Analyze the Enjoyment of Music (Select Bibliographies Reprint Series). John A. Fuller-Maitland. Freeport, N.Y.: Books for Libraries, 1926. $8.50.

Story of One Hundred Symphonic Favorites. Paul Grabbe. New York: Grosset and Dunlap, 1960. $2.50.

Structure of Music. Robert Erickson. New York: Farrar, Straus and Giroux, 1963. illus. $2.45 (paperbound).

Study in Musical Analysis. A. Walker. New York: Free Press, 1963. $6.00.

This Is Music. David Randolph. New York: McGraw-Hill, 1964. $6.50.

Treatise on Good Taste in the Art of Music (2nd ed.) (Music Reprint Series). Francesco Geminiani. New York: Plenum Publishing Corporation, 1969. $15.00.

Twentieth Century Music (rev. ed.). Marion Bauer and Ethel Peyser. New York: G. P. Putnam's Sons, 1947. illus. $6.00.

Understanding Music (2nd rev. and enlarged ed.). William S. Newman. New York: Harper and Row. illus. $2.25 (paperbound).

Understanding Music: Style, Structure, & History. William Fleming and Abraham Veinus. New York: Holt, Rinehart and Winston, 1958. $10.50.

The Well Tempered Listener. Deems Taylor. Westport, Conn.: Greenwood Press. reprint of 1940 ed. $13.75.

What Music Is. Herbert Weinstock. New York: Doubleday and Company, 1968. illus. $1.45 (paperbound).

What to Listen for in Music (rev. ed.). Aaron Copland. New York: McGraw-Hill, 1957. illus. $6.95.

Why of Music: Dialogues in an Unexplored Region of Appreciation. Donald N. Ferguson. Minneapolis: University of Minnesota Press, 1969. illus. $7.95.

Workbook for a Listener's Guide to Musical Understanding. Leon Dallin. Dubuque, Iowa: William C. Brown and Company, 1968. $5.25 (paperbound).

World of Music. Leroy Ostransky. Englewood Cliffs, N.J.: Prentice-Hall, 1969. $3.50 (paperbound).

World of Twentieth Century Music. David Ewen. Englewood Cliffs, N.J.: Prentice-Hall, 1968. $14.95.

MUSIC—BIBLIOGRAPHY

Book of World-Famous Music: Classical, Folk and Popular (rev. ed.). James J. Fuld. New York: Crown Publishers, 1971. $12.50.

Breitkopf Thematic Catalogues: The Six Parts and Sixteen Supplements, 1762-1787. Johann G. Breitkopf, ed. by B. Brook. New York: Dover Publications, 1966. $20.00.

Fundamental Music Reference Books. D. North. Littleton, Colo.: Libraries Unlimited, 1971. $8.00.

General Bibliography for Music Research. K. E. Mixter. Detroit: Information Coordinators, 1962. $2.00.

General Index to Modern Musical Literature in the English Language Including Periodicals for the Years 1915-1926 (Music Series). Eric Blom. New York: Plenum Publishing Corporation, 1970. reprint of 1927 ed. $8.50.

Handbook of American Sheet Music (2 series ed.). H. Dichter. Philadelphia: Alfred Saiper Publisher. illus. $2.00 ea.

Handbook of Music Bibliography. Sydney R. Charles. New York: Free Press, 1971. $12.95.

Music and Drama (Besterman World Bibliographies Series). Theodore Besterman. New York: Rowman and Littlefield, 1971. $15.00.

Music Librarianship. Eric T. Bryant. New York: Hafner Publishing Company, 1963. reprint of 1959 ed. illus. $8.95.

Music Reference and Research Materials (2nd ed.). Vincent Duckles. New York: Free Press, 1967. $8.50.

Musicalia: Sources of Information in Music (2nd ed.). J. H. Davies. Elmsford, N.Y.: Pergamon Publishing Company, 1966. illus. $4.50 ($2.95 paperbound).

Outline of Musical Bibliography. Andrew Deakin. New York: Adler's Foreign Books. reprint of 1899 ed. $16.50.

Popular Titles and Subtitles of Musical Compositions. Freda P. Berkowitz. Metuchen, N.J.: Scarecrow Press, 1962. $4.50.

Standard Musical Repertoire with Accurate Timings. William J. Reddick. Westport, Conn.: Greenwood Press, 1947. $8.50.

MUSIC—DICTIONARIES

Complete Dictionary of Music (2nd ed.). William Waring. New York: AMS Press. reprint of 1779 ed. $25.00.

Concise Dictionary of Music. Jack M. Watson and Corinne Watson. New York: Apollo Editions. illus. $2.75 (paperbound).

Concise Oxford Dictionary of Music (2nd ed.). Percy Scholes, ed. by John O. Ward. New York: Oxford University Press, 1964. $2.95 (paperbound).

Dictionary of Cinema, Sound and Music (Polyglot). W. E. Clason. New York: American Elsevier Publishing Company, 1956. $27.25.

Dictionary of Modern Music and Musicians. Arthur E. Hull, ed. New York: AMS Press. reprint of 1924 ed. $22.50.

Dictionary of Music (Music Series). Hugo Riemann. New York: Plenum Publishing Corporation, 1970. reprint of 1908 ed. $37.50.

Dictionary of Music. Eric Blom. New York: E. P. Dutton and Company. $5.50.

Dictionary of Musical Terms. Theodore Baker. New York: AMS Press, 1970. reprint of 1923 ed. $8.00.

Everyman's Dictionary of Music. Eric Blom, ed. by Jack Westrup. New York: E. P. Dutton and Company, 1971. $5.50.

Harper's Dictionary of Music. Christine Amer. New York: Harper and Row, 1971. $7.95.

International Cyclopedia of Music and Musicians (9th ed.). Oscar Thompson, ed. New York: Dodd, Mead and Company, 1964. $35.00.

Larousse Encyclopedia of Music. Larousse. Cleveland: World Publishing Company. illus. $29.95.

Music: A to Z. Jack Sacher, ed. New York: Grosset and Dunlap. $4.75 ($2.95 paperbound).

Music Dictionary. Arnold Broido and Marilyn K. Davis. New York: Doubleday and Company, 1956. illus. $4.25.

Music Lovers' Encyclopedia. Rupert Hughes et al., eds. New York: Doubleday and Company, 1957. $5.95.

New College Encyclopedia of Music. J. A. Westrup and F. L. Harrison, eds. New York: W. W. Norton and Company, 1960. $10.00.

New Dictionary of Music. Arthur Jacobs. Baltimore: Penguin Books, 1958. $1.75 (paperbound).

Observer's Book of Music (Observer's Pocket Series). Freda Dinn. New York: Frederick Warne and Company, 1953. illus. $1.95.

Pergamon Dictionary of Musicians and Music: Vol. 1, Musicians, Vol. 2, Music. Robert Illing. Elmsford, N.Y.: Pergamon Publishing Company. $3.75 ea. ($2.95 ea. paperbound).

Pronouncing and Defining Dictionary of Music. William S. Mathews, tr. by Emil Liebling. New York: AMS Press, 1896. $10.00.

Student's Dictionary of Music. William Lovelock. New York: Frederick Ungar Publishing Company. $3.50.

MUSIC—DISCOGRAPHY

Ewen's Musical Masterworks (2nd ed.). David Ewen. New York: Arco Publishing Company, 1967. $6.95.

Guide to Low-Priced Classical Records. Herbert Russcol. New York: Hart Publishing Company, 1969. $10.00 ($2.95 paperbound).

Introduction to Contemporary Music. Joseph Machlis. New York: W. W. Norton and Company, 1961. illus. $9.50.

Milton Cross New Encyclopedia of the Great Composers and Their Music. Milton Cross and David Ewen. New York: Doubleday and Company. 2 vols. $11.95.

Negro and His Music, including *Negro Art: Past and Present* (American Negro—His History and Literature Series). Alain Locke. New York: Arno Press, 1969. reprint of 1936 ed. $8.00 ($2.95 paperbound).

New Listener's Companion and Record Guide (3rd ed.). B. H. Haggin. New York: Horizon Press, 1970. $3.95 (paperbound).

One Hundred One Masterpieces of Music and Their Composers. Martin Bookspan. New York: Doubleday and Company, 1968. $8.95.

Our American Music: A Comprehensive History from 1620 to the Present (4th ed.). John T. Howard. New York: Thomas Y. Crowell, 1965. illus. $12.95.

This Modern Music (facsimile ed.) (Essay Index Reprint Series). John T. Howard. Freeport, N.Y.: Books for Libraries, 1942. $8.50.

MUSIC—ECONOMIC ASPECTS
Careers and Opportunities in Music (Dutton Career Books). Alan Rich. New York: E. P. Dutton and Company, 1964. illus. $4.95.

Music Industry Book (Entertainment Industry Series, Vol. 2). Walter E. Hurst and William S. Hale. Hollywood, Calif.: Seven Arts Press, 1963. $25.00.

Music Machine: The Shocking Inside Story of the Record and Music Industry. Roger Karshner. Los Angeles: Nash Publishing Corporation, 1971. $7.95.

Music Publishers Office Manual (Entertainment Industry Series, Vol. 3). Walter E. Hurst and William S. Hale. Hollywood, Calif.: Seven Arts Press, 1966. $25.00.

MUSIC—HISTORY AND CRITICISM
A History of Music. 2 vols., incl. Vol. 1: *Ancient Forms to Polyphony;* Vol. 2: *Renaissance and Baroque.* Alec Robertson and Denis Stevens, eds. New York: Barnes and Noble, 1962 (vol. 1), 1965 (vol. 2). $6.00 (vol. 1), $6.75 (vol. 2).

Art and Times of the Guitar: From the Hitties to the Hippies. Frederick V. Grunfeld. New York: Macmillan Company, 1969. $9.95.

Beethoven and His Forerunners. Daniel G. Mason. New York: AMS Press, 1930. $13.50.

Beethoven Letters in America (Music Series). Oscar G. Sonneck. New York: Plenum Publishing Corporation, 1927. $12.50.

Book of World-Famous Music: Classical, Folk, and Popular (rev. ed.). James J. Fuld. New York: Crown Publishers, 1971. $12.50.

Boulez on Music Today. Pierre Boulez. Cambridge, Mass.: Harvard University Press, 1970. orig. title: *Thoughts on Music.* $6.95.

Classical Style: Haydn, Mozart, Beethoven. Charles Rosen. New York: Viking Press, 1971. illus. $12.50.

Composers on Music: An Anthology of Composers' Writings. Sam Morgenstern, ed. New York: Hillary House Publishers, 1958. $6.50.

Composers on Music: An Anthology of Composers' Writings from Palestrino to Copland. Sam Morgenstern, ed. Westport, Conn.: Greenwood Press, 1956. $20.75.

Concert Tradition. Percy M. Young. New York: Roy Publishers, 1969. illus. $6.95.

Concise History of Music. William Lovelock. New York: Frederick Ungar Publishing Company, 1962. illus. $3.95.

Critical Composer (Essay Index Reprint Series). Irving Kolodin, ed. Freeport, N.Y.: Books for Libraries, 1940. $9.75.

Dictionary of Musicians from the Earliest Time (2nd ed.) (Music Series). John F. Sainsbury. New York: Plenum Publishing Corporation, 1969. 2 vols. $27.50.

Essence of Opera (Library Series). Ulrich Weisstein, ed. New York: W. W. Norton and Company, 1969. reprint of 1964 ed. $2.95 (paperbound).

Evolution of the Art of Music. Charles H. Parry, ed. by Henry C. Colles. Westport, Conn.: Greenwood Press, 1930. $15.00.

Five Centuries of Keyboard Music. John Gillespie. New York: Dover Publications, 1965. $4.50 (paperbound).

Forty Thousand Years of Music. Jacques Chailley, tr. by R. Meyers. New York: Farrar, Straus, and Giroux, 1965. illus. $10.00.

Four Ages of Music. Walter Wiora, tr. by M. Herter Norton. New York: W. W. Norton and Company, 1965. illus. $2.35 (paperbound).

From Bach to Stravinsky: The History of Music by Its Foremost Critics. David Ewen, ed. Westport, Conn.: Greenwood Press, 1968. reprint of 1933 ed. illus. $12.75.

From the Renaissance to Romanticism: Trends in Style in Art, Literature and Music 1300-1830. Frederick B. Artz. Chicago: University of Chicago Press, 1962. $6.50 ($2.45 paperbound).

General History of Music. Charles Burney. New York: Dover Publications, 1935. 2 vols. $10.00 ea.

General History of Music from the Earliest Times (Music Series). Thomas Busby. New York: Plenum Publishing Corporation, 1968. 2 vols. $37.50.

Golden Guitars: The Story of Country Music. Irwin Stambler and Grelun Landon. New York: Scholastic Book Services, 1971. illus. $5.95.

Great Concert Music. Philip Hale, ed. by John N. Burk. Westport, Conn.: Greenwood Press. reprint of 1939 ed. $15.00.

The Growth of Music: A Study in Musical History. H. C. Colles, rev. by Eric Blom. New York: Oxford University Press, 1956. in 3 parts: Pt. 1: *From the Troubadours to J. S. Bach* (3rd ed.); Pt. 2: *The Age of the Sonata from C.P.E. Bach to Beethoven* (2nd ed.); Pt. 3: *The Ideals of the Nineteenth Century; The Twentieth Century* (2nd ed.). $2.25 ea. ($5.60 3 vols. in one).

Gustave Mahler (Music Series). Bruno Walter, tr. by James Galston. New York: Plenum Publishing Corporation, 1970. reprint of 1941 ed. $9.50.

Henry Purcell. Dennis D. Arundell. Westport, Conn.: Greenwood Press, 1971. reprint of 1927 ed. illus. $7.75.

Heritage of Music (Essay Index Reprint Series). R. R. Terry et al., ed. by Hubert J. Foss. Freeport, N.Y.: Books for Libraries, 1927. $9.50.

Historical Anthology of Music, Vol. 1: *Oriental, Medieval, and Renaissance Music* (rev. ed.). Vol. 2: *Baroque, Rococo, and Pre-Classical Music.* Archibald T. Davison and Willi Apel, eds. Cambridge, Mass.: Harvard University Press, 1949 (vol. 1), 1950 (vol. 2). illus. $11.00 ea.

History of American Music. Louis C. Elson. New York: Burt Franklin, Publisher, 1971. reprint. $15.00.

History of Music. Cecil Gray. New York: Barnes and Noble, 1968. $6.50.

History of Music to the Death of Schubert (Music Series). John K. Paine. New York: Plenum Publishing Corporation, 1970. reprint of 1907 ed. illus. $12.50.

History of Music and Musical Style. Homer Ulrich and Paul A. Pisk. New York: Harcourt Brace Jovanovich, 1963. illus. $9.95.

History of Pianoforte Music (Music Series). Herbert Westerby. New York: Plenum Publishing Corporation, 1970. reprint of 1924 ed. $15.00.

History of Western Music. Donald J. Grout. New York: W. W. Norton and Company, 1960. illus. $9.50.

How Music Grew. Marion Bauer and Ethel Peyser. New York: G. P. Putnam's Sons, 1939. $6.50.

Illustrated History of Music. Marc Pincherle, ed. by Georges Bernier and Rosamond Bernier. New York: Reynal and Company, 1959. $22.50.

Introduction to Music (rev. 2nd ed.). David D. Boyden. New York: Alfred A. Knopf, 1970. $8.95.

Introduction to Musical History (Hutchinson University Library—Fine Arts). Jack Westrup. New York: Hutchinson University Library, 1970. $4.00 ($1.75 paperbound).

Jazz Piano: Early Blues to Contemporary Modern Jazz. Win Stormen. New York: Arco Publishing Corporation, 1958. $1.95 (paperbound).

Listen Here. Vernon Duke. Stamford, Conn.: Astor-Honor, 1963. $5.95 ($2.45 paperbound).

The Listener's History of Music. 3 vols., incl. Vol. 1: *To Beethoven* (7th ed.); Vol 2: *The Romantic and Nationalist Schools of the Nineteenth Century* (4th ed.); Vol 3: *To the Composers of Today* (5th ed.). Percy A. Scholes. New York: Oxford University Press, 1954. $3.00 ea. ($7.20 3 vol. ed.).

Man and His Music: The Story of Musical Experience in the West. Alec Harman et al. New York: Oxford University Press, 1962. $12.50.

Masterpieces of Music before 1750. Carl Parrish and John F. Ohl. New York: W. W. Norton and Company, 1951. illus. $5.95.

Men of Music (rev. ed.). Wallace Brockway and Herbert Weinstock. New York: Simon and Schuster, 1950. $8.95. 1958. $3.45 (paperbound).

Miscellaneous Studies in History of Music. Oscar G. Sonneck. New York: AMS Press, 1971. reprint of 1921 ed. $12.00.

Modern Music: Composers and Music of Our Time (Essay and General Literature Index Reprint Series). Max Graf. Port Washington, N.Y.: Kennikat Press, 1969. reprint of 1946 ed. $12.50.

Music: A Design for Listening (2nd ed.). Homer Ulrich. New York: Harcourt Brace Jovanovich, 1962. $8.50.

Music and the Culture of Man. S. Scholl and S. White. New York: Holt, Rinehart and Winston, 1970. $5.25 (paperbound).

Music in Europe and the United States: A History. Edith Borroff. Englewood Cliffs, N.J.: Prentice-Hall, 1971. illus. $11.95.

Music and Its Story. Percy M. Young. New York: Roy Publishers, 1971. illus. $4.25.

Music of Our Time. Nick Rossi and Robert Choate. Boston: Crescendo Publishers, 1970. illus. $12.50.

Music through the Ages (2nd ed.). Marion Bauer and Ethel Peyser, ed. by E. E. Rogers. New York: G. P. Putnam's Sons, 1967. illus. $8.95.

Music through the Centuries. Sadie Rafferty and Nick Rossi. Somerville, Mass.: Bruce Humphries, Publishers. $12.50.

Music through the Renaissance (Music Horizons Series). James C. Thomson. Dubuque, Iowa: William C. Brown Company, 1968. $3.25 (paperbound).

Music in the United States: A Historical Introduction. H. Wiley Hitchcock. Englewood Cliffs, N.J.: Prentice-Hall, 1969. $6.50 ($3.50 paperbound).

Musical History, Biography, and Criticism (Music Reprint Series). George Hogarth. New York: Plenum Publishing Company, 1969. reprint of 1848 ed. $15.00.

Musicians in English Society from Elizabeth to Charles First (Music Series). Walter L. Woodfill. New York: Plenum Publishing Corporation, 1969. reprint of 1953 ed. illus. $15.00.

National Music of America and Its Sources. Louis C. Elson. Detroit, Mich.: Gale Research Company. reprint of 1924 ed. $15.00.

New Musical Companion. A. L. Bacharach, ed. New York: International Publications Service, 1964. $6.25.

Outline History of Music (rev. ed.) (Studies in Musicology, No. 1). Karl Nef, tr. by Carl F. Pfatteicher. New York: Columbia University Press, 1957. $6.00.

Outline History of Music. Milo A. Wold and Edmund Cykler. Dubuque, Iowa: William C. Brown Company, 1966. $5.75 (paperbound).

Pantheon Story of Music. Joseph Wechsberg. New York: Pantheon Books, 1968. illus. $4.95.

Pelican History of Music, Vol. 3, Classical and Romantic. Hugh Ottaway and Arthur Hutchings, ed. by Denis Stevens and Alec Robertson. Baltimore: Penguin Books, 1968. $1.65 (paperbound).

Pictorial History of Music. Paul H. Lang and Otto L. Bettmann. New York: W. W. Norton and Company, 1960. illus. $15.00.

Popular History of the Art of Music from the Earliest Times until the Present (rev. ed.). William S. Mathews. New York: AMS Press, 1906–1910. $30.00.

Popular History of Music (rev. ed.). Carter Harman. New York: Dell Publishing Company, 1969. $.95 (paperbound).

Progress of Music (Essay Index Reprint Ser.). George Dyson. Freeport, N.Y.: Books for Libraries, 1932. $8.75.

Questions about Music. Roger Sessions. New York: W. W. Norton and Company, 1971. reprint of 1970 ed. $1.75 (paperbound).

Rock Revolution (rev. ed.). Arnold Shaw. New York: Paperback Library, 1971. reprint of 1969 ed. illus. $.95 (paperbound).

Segovia Technique. V. Bobri. New York: Macmillan Company, 1971. $6.95.

Shakespeare in Music. Phyllis Hartnoll, ed. New York: St. Martin's Press, 1964. $10.50.

Short History of Keyboard Music. F. E. Kirby. New York: Free Press, 1966. $10.95.

Short History of Music. Alfred Einstein. New York: Alfred A. Knopf, 1954. $6.95.

Sketches of the Origin, Process and Effects of Music (Music Series). R. Eastcott. New York: Plenum Publishing Corporation, 1971. reprint of 1793 ed. $15.00.

Studies in Music Literature: Classical Period to Present Day. Verne W. Thompson and Eugene J. Selhorst. Dubuque, Iowa: William C. Brown Company, 1968. $5.25 (paperbound).

Teach Yourself History of Music. Allen Percival. New York: Dover Publications. $2.50.

Treasury of Early Music. Carl Parrish. New York: W. W. Norton and Company, 1958. illus. $8.50 ($3.95 paperbound).

Way of Music (2nd ed.). William E. Brandt. Boston: Allyn and Bacon, 1968. illus. $8.95.

Wonderful World of Music (rev. ed.) (Wonderful World Series). Benjamin Britten and Imogen Holst. New York: Doubleday and Company, 1968. illus. $3.95.

Zoltan Kodaly: His Life and Work. Laszlo Eosze. Boston, Mass.: Crescendo Publishers, 1969. illus. $7.50.

MUSIC—HISTORY AND CRITICISM—ANCIENT
Ancient and Oriental Music (History of Music Series, Vol. 1). Romain Goldron, tr. by Stella S. Sterman. New York: Doubleday and Company, 1968. $4.95.

Ancient and Oriental Music. Egon Wellesz, ed. New York: Oxford University Press, 1957. $12.50.

Music of the Most Ancient Nations, Particularly of the Assyrians, Egyptians, and Hebrews, with Special Reference to Recent Discoveries in Western Asia and in Egypt (Select Bibliographies Reprint Series). Carl Engel. Freeport, N.Y.: Books for Libraries, 1909. $11.50.

Rise of Music in the Ancient World. Curt Sachs. New York: W. W. Norton and Company, 1943. illus. $10.00.

MUSIC—HISTORY AND CRITICISM—MEDIEVAL
Ars Nova and the Renaissance, c. 1300-1540. Anselm Hughes and Gerald Abraham, eds. New York: Oxford University Press, 1953. $2.50.

Byzantine and Medieval Music: St. Sophia to Notre Dame (History of Music Series, Vol. 2). Romain Goldron, tr. by Doris C. Dunning. New York: Doubleday and Company, 1968. illus. $4.95.

Early Medieval Music up to 1300. Anselm Hughes, ed. New York: Oxford University Press, 1953. $2.50.

Music in Medieval and Renaissance Life. Andrew C. Minor. Columbia, Mo.: University of Missouri Press, 1964. $4.50 (paperbound). $4.95 12 in. monaural record. $8.50 book and record.

Music in the Medieval World. Albert Seay. Englewood Cliffs, N.J.: Prentice-Hall, 1965. illus. $6.50 ($3.50 paperbound).

Music in the Middle Ages. Gustave Reese. New York: W. W. Norton and Company, 1940. illus. $8.95.

Music in the Renaissance (rev. ed.). Gustave Reese. New York: W. W. Norton and Company, 1959. illus. $15.00.

Studies in Medieval and Renaissance Music. Manfred F. Bukofyer. New York: W. W. Norton and Company, 1950. $8.50.

Trouveres and Troubadours: A Popular Treatise. Pierre Aubry, tr. by Claude Aveling. New York: Cooper Square Publishers, 1914. $6.00.

MUSIC—HISTORY AND CRITICISM—16th CENTURY

Late Renaissance and Baroque Music—Man and His Music, Pt. 2 (Man and His Music Series, Vol. 2). Alec Harman and Anthony Milner. New York: Schocken Books, 1969. $2.95 (paperbound).

Mediaeval and Early Renaissance Music—Man and His Music, Pt. 1 (Man and His Music Series, Vol. 1). Alec Harman. New York: Schocken Books, 1969. $2.75 (paperbound).

Music in Elizabethan England (Folger Booklet on Tudor and Stuart Civilization Series). Dorothy E. Mason. Charlottesville, Va.: University Press of Virginia, 1958. illus. $1.50 (paperbound).

Music in English Renaissance Drama. John H. Long, ed. Lexington, Ky.: University Press of Kentucky, 1968. illus. $7.50.

Music of the Italian Renaissance (Music Series). Nesta De Robeck. New York: Plenum Publishing Corporation, 1928. $8.50.

Music in Medieval and Renaissance Life. Andrew C. Minor. Columbia, Mo.: University of Missouri Press; 1964. $4.50 (paperbound). $4.95 12 in. monaural record. $8.50 book and record.

Music and the Reformation in England, 1549–1660. Peter Le Huray. New York: Oxford University Press, 1967. $12.50.

Music in the Renaissance (rev. ed). Gustave Reese. New York. W. W. Norton and Company, 1959. illus. $15.00.

Music of the Renaissance: The Link with Humanism (Music of History Series, Vol. 4). Romain Goldron, tr. by Doris Dunning. New York: Doubleday and Company, 1968. illus. $4.95.

Music in Shakespearean Tragedy. F. W. Sternfeld. New York: Dover Publications, 1963. illus. $10.00.

Music on the Shakespearian Stage. George H. Cowling. New York: Russell and Russell Publishers, 1964. reprint of 1913 ed. illus. $5.00.

New Oxford History of Music Vol. 4: The Age of Humanism, 1540–1630. Gerald Abraham, ed. New York: Oxford University Press, 1968. illus. $22.50.

Renaissance and Baroque Music, a Comprehensive Survey. Friedrich Blume, tr. by M. Herter Norton. New York: W. W. Norton and Company, 1967. illus. $1.95 (paperbound).

Shakespeare and Music (Music Ser.). Edward W. Naylor. New York: Plenum Publishing Corporation, 1965. $7.50.

MUSIC—HISTORY AND CRITICISM—17TH CENTURY
Baroque Music (Prentice-Hall History of the Music Series). Claude V. Palisca. Englewood Cliffs, N.J.: Prentice-Hall, 1968. $6.50 ($3.50 paperbound).

Music of the Baroque. Edith Borroff. Dubuque, Iowa: William C. Brown Company, 1970. illus. $2.75 (paperbound).

Music in the Baroque Era. Manfred F. Bukofzer. New York: W. W. Norton and Company, 1947. illus. $8.95.

Sonata in the Baroque Era (rev. ed.). William S. Newman. Chapel Hill, N.C.: University of North Carolina Press, 1966. illus. $10.00.

MUSIC—HISTORY AND CRITICISM—18TH CENTURY
Basic Principles of Technique of the Eighteenth and Nineteenth Century Composition. Allen I. McHose. New York: Appleton-Century Crofts, 1951. illus. $7.50.

Contrapuntal Harmonic Technique of the Eighteenth Century. Allen I. McHose. New York: Appleton-Century Crofts, 1947. $7.75.

Music in the Classic Period. Reinhard G. Pauly. Englewood Cliffs, N.J.: Prentice-Hall, 1965. illus. $6.50 ($3.50 paperbound).

Music in the Classic Period (Music Horizons Series). Theodore E. Heger. Dubuque, Iowa: William C. Brown Company, 1969. $2.50 (paperbound).

Musical Tour Through the Land of the Past (facsimile ed.) (Essay Index Reprint Series). Romain Rolland, tr. by B. Miall. Freeport, N.Y.: Books for Libraries, 1922. $9.00.

MUSIC—HISTORY AND CRITICISM—19TH CENTURY
Church Music in the Nineteenth Century. Arthur Hutchings. New York: Oxford University Press, 1967. $5.00.

Critical Composer: The Musical Writings of Berlioz, Wagner, Shumann, Tchaikovsky and Others (Essay and General Literature Index Reprint Series). Irving Kolodin, ed. Port Washington, N.Y.: Kennikat Press, 1969. reprint of 1940 ed. $9.00.

Basic Principles of Technique of the Eighteenth and Nineteenth Century Composition. Allen I. McHose. New York: Appleton-Century Crofts, 1951. illus. $7.50.

From Grieg to Brahms (new ed.). Daniel G. Mason. New York: AMS Press, 1927. $9.00.

Hundred Years of Music (3rd ed.). Gerald Abraham. Chicago: Aldine Publishing Company, 1964. $6.95.

Music Dramas of Richard Wagner. Albert Lavignac, tr. by Esther Singleton. New York: AMS Press, 1970. reprint of 1904 ed. $12.50.

Music in Our Time: Trends in Music Since the Romantic Era. Adolfo Salazar, tr. by Isabel Pope. Westport, Conn.: Greenwood Press, 1946. $12.75.

Music in the Romantic Era. Alfred Einstein. New York: W. W. Norton and Company, 1947. illus. $8.00.

Music of the Romantic Period (Music Horizons Series). Johannes Riedel. Dubuque, Iowa: William C. Brown Company, 1969. illus. $2.50 (paperbound).

Musical Impressions: Selections from Paul Rosenfeld's Criticism. Paul Rosenfeld, ed. by Herbert A. Leibowitz. New York: Hill and Wang, 1969. $7.95.

Musical Portraits: Interpretations of Twenty Modern Composers (facsimile ed.) (Essay Index Reprint Series). Paul Rosenfeld. Freeport, N.Y.: Books for Libraries, 1920. $9.75.

Nineteenth Century Romanticism in Music. R. M. Longyear. Englewood Cliffs, N.J.: Prentice-Hall, 1969. $6.50 ($3.50 paperbound).

Romantic Period in Music. Kenneth B. Klaus. Boston: Allyn and Bacon, 1970. illus. $9.75.

Sidelights on a Century of Music 1825-1924. Gervase Hughes. New York: St. Martin's Press, 1970. $5.95.

Slavonic and Romantic Music. Gerald Abraham. New York: St. Martin's Press, 1968. $17.50.

MUSIC—HISTORY AND CRITICISM—20TH CENTURY
Agony of Modern Music. Henry Pleasants. New York: Simon and Schuster, 1962. $1.45 (paperbound).

Black Nationalism and the Revolution in Music. Frank Kofsky. New York: Pathfinder Press, 1970. illus. $7.95 ($2.75 paperbound).

Business of Music. Ernst Roth. New York: Oxford University Press, 1969. $7.50.

Changing Forms in Modern Music (2nd ed.). K. Eschman. Boston: E. C. Schirmer Music Company, 1967. $5.00.

Composers of Tomorrow's Music. David Ewen. New York: Dodd, Mead and Company, 1971. $5.00.

Contemporary Composers on Contemporary Music. E. Schwartz and B. Childs, eds. New York: Holt, Rinehart and Winston, 1967. $9.50.

Contemporary Music in Europe: A Comprehensive Survey. Paul H. Lang and Nathan Broder, eds. New York: W. W. Norton and Company, 1967. reprint of 1965 ed. illus. $2.65 (paperbound).

David Ewen Introduces Modern Music: A History and Appreciation from Wagner to the Avant-Garde (rev. and enlarged ed.). David Ewen. Philadelphia: Chilton Book Company, 1969. illus. $5.50.

Dilemma of American Music, and Other Essays. Daniel G. Mason. Westport, Conn.: Greenwood Press, 1928. $12.75.

Exploring Twentieth-Century Music. Otto Deri. New York: Holt, Rinehart and Winston, 1968. $9.50.

Harmonic Materials of Modern Music. Howard Hanson. New York: Appleton-Century Crofts, 1960. illus. $6.95.

History of Modern Music. Paul Collaer, tr. by Sally Abeles. New York: Grosset and Dunlap, 1963. $2.95 (paperbound).

Introduction to Contemporary Music. Joseph Machlis. New York: W. W. Norton and Company, 1961. illus. $9.50.

Introduction to Twentieth Century Music (3rd ed.). Peter S. Hansen. Boston: Allyn and Bacon, 1971. $9.50.

Language of Modern Music (3rd ed.) (St. Martin's Paperbacks Series). Donald Mitchell. New York: St. Martin's Press, 1970. $2.50 (paperbound).

Modern Composer and His World. John Beckwith and Udo Kasemets, eds. Toronto: University of Toronto Press, 1961. $6.00.

Modern Composers (Essay Index Reprint Series). Guido Pannain. Freeport, N.Y.: Books for Libraries. $11.50.

Modern Music. John T. Howard and James Lyons. New York: New American Library. $.95 (paperbound).

Music, Here and Now. Ernst Krenek, tr. by Barthold Fles. New York: Russell and Russell Publishers, 1967. reprint of 1939 ed. $7.50.

Music and Imagination. Aaron Copland. New York: New American Library, 1959. $.75 (paperbound).

Music of Our Day (Essay Index Reprint Series). Lazare Saminsky. Freeport, N.Y.: Books for Libraries. $11.50.

Music in Our Time: Trends in Music Since the Romantic Era. Adolfo Salazar, tr. by Isabel Pope. Westport, Conn.: Greenwood Press, 1946. $12.75.

Music in the Twentieth Century. William Austin. New York: W. W. Norton and Company, 1966. illus. $11.00.

Music since 1900 (4th ed.). Nicholas Slonimsky. New York: Charles Scribner's Sons, 1971. $30.00.

Musical Impressions: Selections from Paul Rosenfeld's Criticism. Paul Rosenfeld, ed. by Herbert A. Leibowitz. New York: Hill and Wang, 1969. $7.95.

Musical Portraits: Interpretations of Twenty Modern Composers (facsimile ed.) (Essay Index Reprint Series). Paul Rosenfeld. Freeport, N.Y.: Books for Libraries, 1920. $9.75.

New Book of Modern Composers (rev. ed.). David Ewen, ed. New York: Alfred A. Knopf. $10.00.

New Directions in Music—1950-1970. David H. Cope. Dubuque, Iowa: William C. Brown Company, 1970. $2.50 (paperbound).

New Music (Select Bibliographies Reprint Series). George Dyson. Freeport, N.Y.: Books for Libraries, 1924. $7.50.

New Music: Breaking the Sound Barrier. Gregory Battcock. New York: E. P. Dutton and Company, 1971. illus. $2.95 (paperbound).

New Music: 1900-1960 (enlarged ed.). Aaron Copland. New York: W. W. Norton and Company, 1969. reprint of 1968 ed. orig. title: *Our New Music, Il.* $1.95 (paperbound).

Paths to Modern Music. Laurence Davies. New York: Charles Scribner's Sons, 1971. $10.00.

Post-Victorian Music. Charles L. Graves. Port Washington, N.Y.: Kennikat Press, 1970. reprint of 1911 ed. $12.50.

Problems of Modern Music. Paul H. Lang, ed. New York: W. W. Norton and Company, 1962. $1.45 (paperbound).

Rock Folk. Michael Lydon. New York: Dial Press, 1971. illus. $6.95.

Romanticism and the Twentieth Century—Man and His Music, Part 4 (Man and His Music Series, Vol. 4). Wilfrid Mellers. New York: Schocken Books, 1969. $2.75 (paperbound).

Schoenberg and His School: The Contemporary Stage of the Language of Music (Music Series). Rene Leibowitz, tr. from French by Dika Newlin. New York: Plenum Publishing Corporation, 1970. reprint of 1949 ed. $9.50.

Serious Music and All That Jazz. Henry Pleasants. New York: Simon and Schuster, 1969. $5.95.

Sidelights on a Century of Music 1825-1924. Gervase Hughes. New York: St. Martin's Press, 1970. $5.95.

Sound of Our Time. Dave Laing. Chicago: Quadrangle Books, 1970. $5.95.

This Modern Music (facsimile ed.) (Essay Index Reprint Series). John T. Howard. Freeport, N.Y.: Books for Libraries, 1942. $8.50.

Tonality in Modern Music. Rudolph Reti. New York: Macmillan Company, 1962. orig. title: *Tonality-Atonality-Pantonality.* $1.50 (paperbound).

Twentieth Century Church Music. Erik Routley. New York: Oxford University Press, 1964. $5.75.

Twentieth Century Composers (facsimile ed.) (*Essay Index Reprint Series*). David Ewen. Freeport, N.Y.: Books for Libraries, 1937. $10.75.

Twentieth Century Music (rev. ed.). Marion Bauer and Ethel Peyser. New York: G. P. Putnam's Sons, 1947. illus. $6.00.

Twentieth Century Music. H. H. Stuckenschmidt. New York: McGraw-Hill, 1969. $4.95 ($2.45 paperbound).

Twentieth Century Music (*Music Horizons Series*). Robert D. Wilder. Dubuque, Iowa: William C. Brown Company, 1969. $2.50 (paperbound).

Twentieth Century Music. Peter Yates. New York: Funk and Wagnalls Company. $2.95 (paperbound).

Twentieth-Century Music: An Introduction. Eric Salzman. Englewood Cliffs, N.J.: Prentice-Hall, 1967. $6.50 ($3.50 paperbound).

Twentieth Century Music: Its Forms, Trends and Interpretations Throughout the World. Leonard Buskin. New York: Grossman Publishers, 1968. $7.50.

World of Music. George W. Woodworth. Cambridge, Mass.: Harvard University Press, 1964. $5.75.

World of Twentieth Century Music. David Ewen. Englewood Cliffs, N.J.: Prentice-Hall, 1968. $14.95.

MUSIC—NEGROES

Black Music. LeRoi Jones. New York: William Morrow and Company, 1971. $7.95 ($1.95 paperbound).

Black Music in America (*Culture and Discovery Books*). John Rublowsky. New York: Basic Books, 1971. illus. $6.95.

Black Music in Our Culture. Dominique-Rene De Lerma. Kent, Ohio: Kent State University Press, 1970. $7.50.

Black Song: The Forge and the Flame. John Lovell, Jr. New York: Macmillan Company, 1971. illus. $10.00.

Blues People: Negro Music in White America. LeRoi Jones. New York: William Morrow and Company, 1963. $7.95 ($1.95 paperbound).

Introduction to the Music of Black Americans. William Cole. Boston: Crescendo Publishers, 1971. $6.00.

Music of Black Americans: A History. Eileen Southern. New York: W. W. Norton and Company, 1971. illus. $10.00 ($4.45 paperbound).

Negro Folk Music, U.S.A. Harold Courlander. New York: Columbia University Press, 1970. reprint of 1963 ed. $12.50 ($3.25 paperbound).

Negro and His Songs: A Study of Typical Negro Songs in the South. Howard W. Odum and Guy B. Johnson. New York: New American Library, 1925. $3.95.

Negro in Music and Art (International Library of Negro Life and History Series). Patterson. Washington, D.C.: United Publishing Corporation, 1970. $13.88.

Slave Songs of the Georgia Sea Islands. Lydia Parrish. Detroit: Folklore Associates, 1965. reprint of 1942 ed. $10.00.

Social Implications of Early Negro Music in the United States (American Negro: His History and Literature Series, No. 2). Bernard Katz, ed. New York: Arno Press, 1968. reprint of 1969 ed. $7.50 ($2.45 paperbound).

Songs for a Kingdom. Edwin Mumford. Jericho, N.Y.: Exposition Press, 1965. $4.00.

Songs of Our Years. Clyde O. Jackson. Jericho, N.Y.: Exposition Press, 1968. $4.00.

Sound of Soul. Phyl Garland. New York: Pocket Books, 1971. reprint. $.95 (paperbound).

Urban Blues. Charles Keil. Chicago: University of Chicago Press, 1966. illus. $6.50 ($2.45 paperbound).

World of Soul (rev. ed.). Arnold Shaw. New York: Paperback Library, 1971. reprint of 1970 ed. illus. $1.25 (paperbound).

MUSIC—PERFORMANCE
Concert Theatre (Theatre Student Series). Clayton E. Liggett. New York: Richards Rosen Press, 1970. illus. $5.97.

Form and Performance. Erwin Stein. New York: Alfred A. Knopf, 1962. illus. $6.95.

History of Music in Performance. Frederick Dorian. New York: W. W. Norton and Company, 1943. illus. $2.25 (paperbound).

History of Musical Style. Richard L. Crocker. New York: Mc-Graw-Hill, 1966. $9.50.

Interpretation of Early Music (2nd ed.). Robert Donington. New York: St. Martin's Press, 1965. illus. $27.50.

Interpretation of Music. Thurston Dart. New York: Harper and Row. $1.45 (paperbound).

Interpretation of Music. Thurston Dart. New York: Hutchinson University Publishers, 1964. $5.00.

Lost Tradition in Music, Vol. 2: Musical Performance in the Time of Mozart and Beethoven. Fritz Rothschild. New York: Oxford University Press, 1961. $4.80.

Music and the Line of Most Resistance (Music Series). Artur Schnabel. New York: Plenum Publishing Corporation, 1969. reprint of 1942 ed. $8.50.

Musical Form and Musical Performance. Edward T. Cone. New York: W. W. Norton and Company, 1968. $4.00.

Rudiments of Music. Robert W. Ottman and Frank D. Mainous. Englewood Cliffs, N.J.: Prentice-Hall, 1970. $4.95 (paperbound).

Toscanini Legacy (2nd ed.). Spike Hughes. New York: Dover Publications, 1969. reprint of 1959 ed. $3.00 (paperbound).

MUSIC—PERIODICALS—INDEXES
General Index to Modern Musical Literature in the English Language Including Periodicals for the Years 1915–1926 (Music Series). Eric Blom. New York: Plenum Publishing Corporation, 1970. reprint of 1927 ed. $8.50.

MUSIC—TERMINOLOGY
Handbook of Music Terms. W. Parks Grant. Metuchen, N.J.: Scarecrow Press, 1967. $16.50.

Introduction to the Language of Music. Stephanie Barach. New York: Robert B. Luce, 1962. illus. $3.89.

Listener's Dictionary of Musical Terms. Helen L. Kaufmann. New York: Grosset and Dunlap, 1960. $2.50.

Observer's Book of Music (Observer's Pocket Series). Freda Dinn. New York: Frederick Warne and Company, 1953. illus. $1.95.

MUSIC—YEARBOOKS
Memorable Days in Music. Marion E. Cullen, ed. Metuchen, N.J.: Scarecrow Press, 1970. $5.00.

Yearbook of the International Folk Music Council Vol. 1: 1969.
Alexander L. Ringer, ed. Urbana, Ill.: University of Illinois Press,
1971. illus. $8.95.

MUSIC, AFRICAN
African Music on LP. An Annotated Discography. Alan P.
Merriam. Evanston, Ill.: Northwestern University Press, 1970.
$20.00.

African Native Music, an Annotated Bibliography. Douglas H.
Varley. New York: Humanities Press, 1970. Reprint of 1936 ed.
$5.00 (paperbound).

African Rhythm. A. M. Jones. New York: International Publications Service, 1965. $1.25.

Essays on Music and History in Africa. Klaus P. Wachsmann, ed.
Evanston, Ill.: Northwestern University Press, 1971. $9.50.

Select Bibliography of Music in Africa. L. J. Gaskin, ed. New
York: International Publications Service, 1965. $11.25.

Studies in African Music. A. M. Jones. New York: Oxford University Press, 1959. 2 vols. $30.75.

MUSIC, AMERICAN
Age of Rock: Sounds of the American Cultural Revolution. Jonathan Eisen, ed. New York: Random House, 1970. $2.95 (paper-
bound).

Age of Rock Two: Sounds of the American Cultural Revolution.
Jonathan Eisen, ed. New York: Random House, 1970. $8.95.

American Composers on American Music. Henry Cowell, ed.
New York: Frederick Ungar Publishing Company, 1962. $4.50
($1.45 paperbound).

American Music Since 1910. Virgil Thomson. New York: Holt,
Rinehart and Winston, 1971. illus. $8.95.

America's Music: From the Pilgrims to the Present. Gilbert Chase.
New York: McGraw-Hill, 1955. $11.25. 2nd ed., 1966. $11.95.

Annals of Music in America (Select Bibliographies Reprint Series).
Henry C. Lahee. Freeport, N.Y.: Books for Libraries, 1922.
$12.50.

Annals of Music in America. Henry C. Lahee. New York: AMS
Press, 1969. reprint of 1922 ed. $10.00.

Ballads, Blues, and the Big Beat. Donald Murus. New York: Macmillan Company, 1966. $5.95.

Country Music Story. Robert Shelton and Burt Goldblatt. New Rochelle, N.Y.: Arlington House, 1971. reprint of 1966 ed. illus. $7.95.

Country Music U.S.A. A Fifty-Year History (Memoir Series, Vol. 54). Bill C. Malone. University of Texas Press, 1968. illus. $7.50.

Dilemma of American Music, and Other Essays. Daniel G. Mason. Westport, Conn.: Greenwood Press, 1928. $12.75.

Handbook of American Music and Musicians (Music Series). F. O. Jones, ed. New York: Plenum Publishing Corporation, 1971. reprint of 1886 ed. $12.50.

History of American Music. Louis C. Elson. New York: Burt Franklin, 1971. reprint. $15.00.

History of American Music. William L. Hubbard, ed. New York: AMS Press. reprint of 1908 ed. $15.00.

History of Popular Music. Sigmund Spaeth. New York: Random House, 1948. $8.95.

Hundred Years of Music in America. William S. Mathews, ed. New York: AMS Press, 1969. reprint of 1889 ed. $30.00.

Inside Music City, USA. Teddy Bart. Nashville, Tenn.: Aurora Publications, 1970. $1.95 (paperbound).

Jazz Masters of New Orleans. Martin T. Williams. New York: Macmillan Company, 1967. $5.95.

Jazz: New Orleans, Eighteen Eighty-Five to Nineteen Sixty-Three (rev. ed.). Samuel B. Charters. New York: Oak Publications. illus. $2.95 (paperbound).

Landmarks of Early American Music, 1760–1800. Richard F. Goldman, ed. New York: AMS Press. reprint of 1943 ed. $7.50.

Listen Here. Vernon Duke. Stamford, Conn.: Astor-Honor, 1963. $5.95 ($2.45 paperbound).

Melodies Linger On. Larry G. Freeman. Watkins Glen, N.Y.: Century House Americana, 1951. illus. $15.00.

Music and Musicians in Early America. Irving Lowens. New York: W. W. Norton and Company, 1964. illus. $8.50.

Music from the Days of George Washington. Carl Engel and W. Oliver Strunk, eds. New York: AMS Press, 1970. reprint of 1931 ed. $5.00.

Music in America. W. T. Marrocco and Harold Gleason, eds. New York: W. W. Norton and Company, 1964. $10.95.

Music in America. Frederic L. Ritter. New York: Johnson Reprint Corporation, 1971. Reprint of 1890 ed. $15.00.

Music in a New Found Land. Wilfrid Mellers. New York: Alfred A. Knopf, 1965. $7.95.

Music in American Life. Jacques Barzun. Bloomington, Ind.: Indiana: University Press, 1962. $1.75 (paperbound).

Music in the Cultured Generation. Musical Life in America, 1870–1900 (Pi Kappa Lambda Studies in American Music). Joseph A. Mussulman. Evanston, Ill.: Northwestern University Press, 1971. $9.75.

Music in the United States (Music Horizon Series). Arthur C. Edwards and W. T. Marrocco. Dubuque, Iowa: William C. Brown and Company, 1968. $3.25 (paperbound). $2.50 (paperbound).

Music of the Americas. An Illustrated Music Ethnology of the Eskimos and American Indian Peoples. Paul Collaer. New York: Frederick A. Praeger, 1971. illus. $25.00.

Music of the Old South. Colony to Confederacy. Albert Stoutamire. Rutherford, N.J.: Fairleigh Dickinson University Press. $10.00.

Nashville Sound: Bright Lights and Country Music. Paul Hemphill. New York: Pocket Books, 1971. reprint of 1970 ed. $1.25 (paperbound).

New Sound: Yes. Ira Peck, ed. New York: Scholastic Book Services, 1967. illus. $3.50.

Our American Music: A Comprehensive History from 1620 to the Present (4th ed.). New York: Thomas Y. Crowell Company, 1965. illus. $12.95.

Outlaw Blues: A Book of Rock Music. Paul Williams. New York: E. P. Dutton and Company, 1969. illus. $4.95 ($1.75 paperbound).

Panorama of American Popular Music. David Ewen. Englewood Cliffs, N.J.: Prentice-Hall, 1957. $9.95.

Short History of Music in America. John T. Howard and George K. Bellows. New York: Apollo Editions. $2.75 (paperbound).

Tin Pan Alley (Suppl. *From Sweet and Swing to Rock and Roll* by Edward Jablonski). Isaac Goldberg. New York: Frederick Ungar Publishing Company. $1.45.

Tin Pan Alley in Gaslight. Maxwell F. Marcuse. Watkins Glen, N.Y.: Century House Americana. illus. $15.00.

Twentieth Century Music (rev. ed.). Marion Bauer and Ethel Peyser. New York: G. P. Putnam's Sons, 1947. illus. $6.00.

MUSIC, AMERICAN—BIBLIOGRAPHY
Catalog of Published Concert Music by American Composers. Angelo Eagon. Metuchen, N.J.: Scarecrow Press, 1971. $5.00.

MUSIC, POPULAR (SONGS, ETC.)
Bacharach–David Songbook. Burt Bacharach and Hal David. New York: Simon and Schuster, 1970. $7.50.

Bacharach and David Songbook (Fireside Paperback Series). Burt Bacharach and Hal David. Simon and Schuster, 1971. $3.95 (paperbound).

Best of Popular Music: Book One. New York: Crown Publishers. $5.95.

Encyclopedia of Country and Western Music. Len Brown and Gary Friedrich. New York: Tower Publications, 1971. $1.25 (paperbound).

Encyclopedia of Folk, Country, and Western Music. Irwin Stambler and Grelun Landon. New York: St. Martin's Press, 1969. illus. $12.50.

Encyclopedia of Popular Music. Irwin Stambler. New York: St. Martin's Press, 1965. illus. $12.50.

Encyclopedia of Rock and Roll. Len Brown and Gary Friedrich. New York: Tower Publications, 1970. $1.25 (paperbound).

Great Songs of the Sixties. Milton Okun ed. Chicago: Quadrangle Books, 1970. illus. $17.50.

Inside Credence (Rock Special Series). John Hallowell. New York: Bantam Books, 1971. illus. $1.00 (paperbound).

Inside Pop, No. 2. David Dachs. New York: Scholastic Book Services, 1970. illus. $.75 (paperbound).

Jefferson Airplane and the San Francisco Sound. Ralph Gleason. New York: Ballantine Books, 1969. $.95 (paperbound).

Jerome Kern Song Book. Oscar Hammerstein, 2nd. New York: Simon and Schuster, 1955. $7.50.

Kaleidoscope. Rod McKuen. New York: Crown Publishing. $3.95 (paperbound).

New Beatles Top Forty Songbook. New York: Crown Publishers. $3.50 (paperbound).

No One Waved Goodbye. A Casualty Report on Rock and Roll. Robert Somma, ed. New York: Outerbridge and Dienstfrey, 1971. $4.95 ($1.95 paperbound).

Panorama of American Popular Music. David Ewen. Englewood Cliffs, N.J.: Prentice-Hall, 1957. $9.95.

Rock Revolution. Arnold Shaw. New York: Macmillan Company, 1969. $4.95.

Rodgers and Hart Songbook. Richard Rodgers and Lorenz M. Hart. New York: Simon & Schuster, 1951. illus. $10.00.

Songs of Leonard Cohen. Leonard Cohen. New York: Macmillan Company, 1969. illus. $2.95 (paperbound).

Songs of Love and Hate. Leonard Cohen. New York: Oak Publications, 1971. $2.95 (paperbound).

Tom Lehrer Song Book. Tom Lehrer. New York: Crown Publishers. illus. $2.95.

Stecheson Classified Song Directory. Anne Stecheson and Anthony Stecheson. New York: Criterion Music Corporation, 1961. $25.00.

World of Rod McKuen. Rod McKuen. New York: Random House, 1968. illus. $4.95.

MUSIC, POPULAR (SONGS, ETC.)—BIBLIOGRAPHY
American Popular Songs from the Revolutionary War to the Present. David Ewen, ed. New York: Random House, 1966. $10.00.

Book of World-Famous Music: Classical, Folk and Popular (rev. ed.). James J. Fuld. New York: Crown Publishers, 1971. $12.50.

Popular Music, an Annotated Index of American Popular Songs. Nat Shapiro, ed. New York: Adrian Press. 5 vols. Including Vol. 1, 1950-1959, 1964. Vol. 2, 1940-1949, 1965. Vol. 3 1960-1964, 1967. Vol. 4, 1930-1939, 1968. Vol. 5 1920-1929, 1969. $16.00 ea.

MUSIC, POPULAR (SONGS, ETC.)—DISCOGRAPHY
Country Music U.S.A.: A Fifty-Year History (Memoir Series, Vol. 54). Bill Malone. Austin, Tex.: University of Texas Press, 1968. illus. $7.50.

Down Home: Country-Western. James Sallis. New York: Macmillan Company, 1971. illus. $3.95 (paperbound).

Encyclopedia of Popular Music. Irwin Stambler. New York: St. Martin Press, 1965. illus. $12.50.

Sound of Soul. Phyl Garland. Chicago: Henry Regnery Company, 1969. $5.95 ($2.95 paperbound).

World of Soul: The Black Contribution to Pop Music. Arnold Shaw. New York: Cowles Book Company, 1970. illus. $6.95.

MUSIC, POPULAR (SONGS, ETC.)—HISTORY AND CRITICISM
Country Music: White Man's Blues. John Grissim. New York: Paperback Library, 1970. $1.25 (paperbound).

Country Music U.S.A.: A Fifty-Year History (Memoir Series, Vol. 54). Bill Malone. Austin, Tex.: University of Texas Press, 1968. illus. $7.50.

Festival: The Book of American Music Celebrations. Baron Wolman. New York: Macmillan Company, 1970. $3.95 (paperbound).

Great Men of American Popular Song. David Ewen. Englewood Cliffs, N.J.: Prentice-Hall, 1970. illus. $12.95.

Guitar Years. Irwin Stambler. New York: Doubleday and Company, 1970. illus. $3.95.

Life & Death of Tin Pan Alley: The Golden Age of American Popular Music. David Ewen. New York: Funk and Wagnalls Company, 1964. $5.95.

Melodies Linger On. Larry G. Freeman. New York: Century House, 1951. $15.00.

Popular Music (Culture and Discovery Series). John Rublowsky. New York: Basic Books, 1967. illus. $5.95.

Ragtime Songbook. Ann Charters, ed. New York: Oak Publications. illus. $2.95 (paperbound).

Sound of the City: The Rise of Rock and Roll. Charlie Gillett. New York: Outerbridge and Dienstfrey, 1970. $6.95 ($2.95 paperbound).

Sound of Soul. Phyl Garland. Chicago: Henry Regnery Company, 1969. $5.95 ($2.95 paperbound).

Sociology and History of Popular American Music and Dance, 1920–1968. Ann Arbor, Mich.: Ann Arbor Publishers. $3.00 (paperbound).

Sweet Saturday Night. Colin McInnes. New York: International Publications Service. 1969. $7.50.

Tin Pan Alley (Suppl. From *Sweet and Swing to Rock and Roll* by Edward Jablonski). Isaac Goldberg. New York: Frederick Ungar Publishers. $1.45.

MUSIC, POPULAR (SONGS, ETC.)—WRITING AND PUBLISHING

How to Make Money Selling the Songs You Write. Henry Boye. New York: Frederick Fell, 1970. $4.95.

How to Write Songs That Sell (rev. ed.). Arthur Korb. Deer Park, New York: Brown Book Company, 1957. $3.50.

Play and Create Pop and Rock Music. Win Stormen. New York: Arco Publishing Company, 1969. illus. $4.00 ($2.45 paperbound).

Successful Songwriting (2nd ed.). Lou Herscher, ed. by Paul Mills. Los Angeles: Solo Music, 1966. $4.95 (paperbound).

Teach Yourself Songwriting. Martin Lindsay. New York: Dover Publications. $2.50.

They All Sang: From Tony Pastor to Rudy Vallee. Edward B. Marks. New York: Benjamin Blom, 1934. $12.50.

MUSIC AND LITERATURE

Arthurian Romance and Modern Poetry and Music. William A. Nitze. Port Washington, N.Y.: Kennikat Press, 1970. reprint of 1940 ed. $6.00.

Ideas and Music. Martin Cooper. Philadelphia: Chilton Book Company, 1967. $6.50.

Literary Background to Bach's Cantatas. James Day. New York: Dover Publications, 1967. illus. $1.00 (paperbound).

Melody and the Lyric: From Chaucer to Caliers (Studies in Poetry Series, No. 38). New York: Haskell House Publishers, 1969. reprint. $10.95.

Music to Poetry. T. S. Elliot. Philadelphia: Lansdowne Press, 1971. reprint of 1942 ed. $5.00.

Musical Backgrounds for English Literature, 1580–1650. Gretchen L. Finney. New Brunswick, N.J.: Rutgers University Press, 1962. $10.00.

Musical Evenings. Leigh Hunt, ed. by David R. Cheney. Columbia bia, Mo.: University of Missouri Press, 1964. $4.50.

Music and Literature. Calvin S. Brown. Athens, Ga.: University of Georgia Press, 1948. $6.00.

Tenth Muse. Patrick J. Smith. New York: Alfred A. Knopf, 1970. $12.95.

Music Literature for Analysis and Study. Charles W. Walton. Belmont, Calif.: Wadsworth Publishing Company, 1971. $5.95 (paperbound).

Tones Into Words: Musical Compositions As Subjects of Poetry. Calvin S. Brown. Athens, Ga.: University of Georgia Press, 1953. $4.50.

MUSIC AND SOCIETY
How Music Expresses Ideas (rev. ed.). Sidney Finkelstein. New York: International Publishers Company, 1970. $5.95 ($1.95 paperbound).

MUSICAL CRITICISM
Anatomy of Musical Criticism. Alan Walker. Philadelphia: Chilton Book Company, 1968. illus. $5.00.

Be Your Own Music Critic (facsimile ed.) (Essay Index Reprint Series). Robert E. Simon, ed. Freeport, N.Y.: Books for Libraries, 1941. $12.00.

Composer and Critic: Two Hundred Years of Musical Criticism. Max Graf. Port Washington, N.Y.: Kennikat Press, 1969. reprint of 1946 ed. $10.00.

Critical Composer: The Musical Writings of Berlioz, Wagner, Schumann, Tchaikovsky and Others (Essay and General Literature Index Reprint Series). Irving Kolodin, ed. Port Washington, N.Y.: Kennikat Press, 1969. reprint of 1940 ed. $9.00.

How to Become a Musical Critic. George B. Shaw, ed. by Dan H. Laurence. New York: Hill and Wang, 1967. reprint. $2.45 (paperbound).

Lexicon of Musical Invective: Critical Assaults on Composers Since Beethoven's Time (2nd ed.). Nicolas Slonimsky. Seattle: University of Washington Press, 1969. $2.95 (paperbound).

Music and Criticism (Essay and General Literature Index Reprint Series). Richard F. French, ed. Port Washington, N.Y.: Kennikat Press, 1969. reprint of 1948 ed. $8.00.

Music and the Line of Most Resistance (Music Series). Artur Schnabel. New York: Plenum Publishing Corporation, 1969. reprint of 1942 ed. $8.50.

Music Observed. Bernard H. Haggin. New York: Oxford University Press, 1964. $7.50.

Schumann as Critic. Leon B. Plantinga. New Haven, Conn.: Yale University Press, 1967. $10.00.

MUSICAL INSTRUMENTS

Ancient European Musical Instruments. Nicholas Bessaraboff. New York: New York Graphic Society, 1941. illus. $17.50.

Ancient Musical Instruments. Pauline Granichstadten. Cambridge, Mass.: Acanthus Press. illus. $8.95.

Antique Musical Instruments and Their Players (rev. ed.). Filippo Bonanni. New York: Dover Publications, 1923. illus. $3.00 (paperbound).

Dictionary: Old English Music and Musical Instruments. Jeffrey Pulver. New York: Burt Franklin, 1970. reprint of 1923 ed. $22.50.

Early Keyboard Instruments: From Their Beginnings to 1820. Philip James. New York: Barnes and Noble, 1970. reprint. illus. $18.50.

European and American Musical Instruments. Anthony Baines. New York: Viking Press, 1966. illus. $30.00.

European Musical Instruments. Frank L. Harrison and Joan Rimmer. New York: W. W. Norton and Company, 1965. illus. $12.50.

Harmonie Universelle: The Books on Instruments. M. Mersenne, tr. by R. E. Chapman. New York: W. S. Heinman, 1964. illus. $35.00.

History of Musical Instruments. Curt Sachs. New York: W. W. Norton and Company, 1940. illus. $10.00.

Horns, Strings and Harmony. Arthur H. Benade. New York: Doubleday and Company. illus. $1.45 (paperbound).

Instruments of Music. Robert Donington. New York: Barnes and Noble, 1970. illus. 3rd ed., rev. and enlarged: $5.50 (paperbound).

Interpretation of Early Music (2nd ed.). Robert Donington. New York: St. Martin's Press, 1965. illus. $27.50.

Music in Print: Fifty-two Prints Illustrating Musical Instruments from the 15th Century to the Present. Sydney Beck and Elizabeth Roth. New York: New York Public Library, 1965. illus. $6.75.

Musical Instruments. Anthony Barnes, ed. New York: Walker and Company, 1966. illus. $10.00.

Musical Instruments: A Comprehensive Dictionary. Sibyl Marcuse. New York: Doubleday and Company, 1964. illus. $17.50.

Musical Instruments in Art and History. Roger Bragard and Ferdinand J. De Hen. New York: Viking Press, 1968. illus. $18.50.

Musical Instruments and Audio. G. A. Briggs. Boston: Cahners Publishing Company, 1966. illus. $7.95.

Musical Instruments: Their History in Western Culture from the Stone Age to the Present. Karl Geiringer, tr. by Bernard Miall. New York: Oxford University Press, 1945. illus. $15.00.

Musical Instruments through the Ages. Anthony Baines, ed. Baltimore: Penguin Books, 1961. $1.95 (paperbound).

Observer's Book of Music (Observer's Pocket Series). Freda Dinn. New York: Frederick Warne and Company, 1953. illus. $1.95.

Old English Instruments of Music (4th ed.). Francis W. Galpin, ed. by Thurston Dart. New York: Barnes and Noble, 1965. $12.00.

Old Musical Instruments (Pleasures and Treasures Series). Rene Clemencic. New York: G. P. Putnam's Sons, 1968. $5.95.

Old Musical Instruments. Gyorgy Gabry. New York: International Publications Service, 1971. illus. $2.85.

Orchestral Instruments and What They Do. Daniel G. Mason. Westport, Conn.: Greenwood Press, 1971. reprint of 1909 ed. illus. $8.50.

Pictorial History of Music. Paul H. Lang and Otto L. Bettmann. New York: W. W. Norton and Company, 1960. illus. $15.00.

Showcase of Musical Instruments. Filippo Bonanni. Gloucester, Mass.: Peter Smith. illus. $4.00.

Story of Musical Instruments, from Shepherd's Pipe to Symphony (facsimile ed.). Harry W. Schwartz. Freeport, N.Y.: Books for Libraries, 1938. $13.75.

Talking Drums of Africa. John F. Carrington. Westport, Conn.: Negro Universities Press, 1949. reprint. illus. $7.00.

Thesaurus of Orchestral Devices. Gardner Read. Westport, Conn.: Greenwood Press, 1953. $34.25.

MUSICAL INSTRUMENTS (MECHANICAL)
From Music Boxes to Street Organs. Romke De Waard. Vestal, N.Y.: Vestal Press, 1967. $6.95.

Player Pianos and Music Boxes: Keys to a Musical Past. Harvey N. Roehl. Vestal, N.Y.: Vestal Press. $2.00 (paperbound).

Put Another Nickel In. Q. David Bowers. Vestal, N.Y.: Vestal Press, 1966. $8.95.

MUSICAL REVUES, COMEDIES, ETC.
American Musical (International Film Guide Series). Tom Vallance. Cranbury, N.J.: A. S. Barnes and Company, 1970. illus. $3.50 (paperbound).

American Musical Stage Before 1800. Julian Mates. New Brunswick, N.J.: Rutgers University Press, 1962. $10.00.

Broadway's Greatest Musicals: The New Illustrated Edition. Abe Laufe. New York: Funk and Wagnalls Company, 1970. illus. $10.00.

Great Songs of the Sixties. Milton Okun, ed. Chicago: Quadrangle Books, 1970. illus. $17.50.

Guide to Broadway Musical Theatre (Theatre Student Series). Tom Tumbusch. New York: Richards Rosen Press, 1971. illus. $10.50.

Musical Comedy: A Story in Pictures. Raymond Mander and Joe Mitchenson. New York: Taplinger Publishing Company, 1970. $10.00.

Tambo and Bones: A History of the American Minstrel Stage. Carl Wittke. Westport, Conn.: Greenwood Press, 1968. $12.50.

MUSICIANS

American Writers and Compilers of Sacred Music. Frank J. Metcalf. New York: Russell and Russell Publishers, 1967. reprint of 1925 ed. illus. $10.00.

Anecdotes of Music and Musicians. Helen L. Kaufmann. New York: Grosset and Dunlap, 1960. $2.50.

Biographical Dictionary of Musicians. James D. Brown. New York: Adler's Foreign Books, 1968. reprint of 1886 ed. $34.50.

Blow My Blues Away. George Mitchell. Baton Rouge, La.: Louisiana State University Press, 1971. illus. $10.00.

Bossmen: Bill Monroe and Muddy Waters. James Rooney. New York: Dial Press, 1971. $5.95.

Complete Book of the Great Musicians, 3 Vols. in One. Percy A. Scholes. New York: Oxford University Press, 1949. illus. $7.00.

Concise Encyclopedia of Music and Musicians. Martin Cooper, ed. New York: Hawthorn Books, 1958. illus. $17.95.

Count Basie and His Orchestra. Raymond Horricks. Westport, Conn.: Negro Universities Press. reprint of 1957 ed. $13.50.

Dictionary of Modern Music and Musicians. Arthur E. Hull, ed. New York: AMS Press. reprint of 1924 ed. $22.50.

Dictionary of Musical Information. John W. Moore. New York: Burt Franklin, Publisher, 1967. reprint of 1876 ed. $35.00.

Forgotten Musicians. Paul Nettl. Westport, Conn.: Greenwood Press, 1951. $12.50.

From Bach to Stravinsky: The History of Music by Its Foremost Critics. David Ewen, ed. New York: AMS Press, 1970. $9.00.

Handbook of American Music and Musicians (Music Series). F. O. Jones, ed. New York: Plenum Publishing Corporation, 1971. reprint of 1886 ed. $12.50.

Hollywood Studio Musicians: Their Work and Careers in the Recording Industry. Robert R. Faulkner. Chicago: Aldine Publishing Company, 1971. $7.50.

Hundred Years of Music in America. William S. Mathews, ed. New York: AMS Press, 1969. reprint of 1889 ed. $30.00.

Masters in Music, 3 Vols. Daniel G. Mason, ed. New York: AMS Press, 1930. $24.00 ea. ($72.00 set).

Masters and Their Music. William S. Mathews. New York: AMS Press, 1898. $11.00.

Modern Music: Composers and Music of Our Time (Essay and General Literature Index Reprint Series). Max Graf. Port Washington, N.Y.: Kennikat Press, 1969. reprint of 1946 ed. $12.50.

Musicians' Wit, Humour, and Anecdote. Frederick J. Crowest. Highland Park, N.J.: Gryphon Press, 1971. reprint of 1902 ed. illus. $15.00.

Music's Glamorous Hall of Fame. J. H. Powers. New York: Carlton Press, $3.75.

My Life and Music (rev. ed.). including *Reflections on Music.* Artur Schnabel. New York: St. Martin's Press, 1971. $3.50 (paperbound).

On Music and Musicians. Robert Schumann. New York: W. W. Norton and Company, 1969. $6.95.

Pergamon Dictionary of Musicians and Music: Vol. 1, Musicians, Vol. 2, Music. Robert Illing. Elmsford, N.Y.: Pergamon Press. $3.75 ea. ($2.95 ea. paperbound).

Some Musicians of Former Days (facsimile ed.) (Essay Index Reprint Series. Romain Rolland. Freeport, N.Y.: Books for Libraries, 1915. $11.75.

Toscanini Legacy (2nd ed.). Spike Hughes. Gloucester, Mass.: Peter Smith. illus. $6.00.

Waltz Kings of Old Vienna (facsimile ed.) (Select Bibliographies Reprint Series). Ada B. Teetgen. Freeport, N.Y.: Books for Libraries, 1939. $11.50.

Who's Who in Music: Musicians' International Directory. New York: Hafner Publishing Company, 1969. $15.50.

World of the Virtuoso. Marc Pincherle. New York: W. W. Norton and Company, 1963. illus. $4.50.

MUSICIANS—CORRESPONDENCE, REMINISCENCES, ETC.
American Folksong. Woody Guthrie, ed. by Moses Asch. New York: Oak Publications. $1.95 (paperbound).

Arnold Schoenberg Letters. Arnold Schoenberg, ed. by E. Stein. St. Martin's Press, 1958. illus. $8.75.

Autobiographical Reminiscences with Family Letters and Notes on Music (Music Series). Charles Gounod. New York: Plenum Publishing Corporation, 1970. reprint of 1896 ed. $12.50.

Autobiography, 1829-1889 (Music Series, No. 42). Anton Rubinstein. New York: Haskell House, 1969. reprint of 1890 ed. $8.95.

Autobiography of Karl Von Dittersdorf (Music Series). Karl D. Von Dittersdorf, tr. by A. D. Coleridge. New York: Plenum Publishing Corporation, 1970. reprint of 1896 ed. $15.00.

Beethoven: The Man and the Artist. Ludwig Van Beethoven, ed. by Krehbiel. Gloucester, Mass.: Peter Smith. $3.00.

Best Regards to Aida. Hans W. Heinsheimer. New York: Alfred A. Knopf, 1968. illus. $6.95.

Big Bill Blues (new ed.). Bill Bronzy and Yannick Bruynoghe. New York: Oak Publications, 1964. illus. $2.95 (paperbound).

Black and White Baby. Robert Short and Mary E. Durant. New York: Dodd, Mead and Company, 1971. $7.95.

Bound for Glory (new ed.). Woody Guthrie. New York: E. P. Dutton and Company, 1968. reprint of 1943 ed. illus. $6.95. New York: New American Library, 1970. reprint of 1968 ed. $1.25 (paperbound).

Business of Music. Ernst Roth. New York: Oxford University Press, 1969. $7.50.

Chaliapin. Maxim Gorky. New York: Stein and Day, 1968. illus. $10.00.

Correspondence of Wagner and Liszt (rev. ed.) Richard Wagner and Franz Liszt, tr. by W. Ashton Ellis & Francis Hueffer. New York: Haskell House, 1968. 2 vols. reprint of 1897 ed. $23.95.

Daybreak. Joan Baez. New York: Dial Press, 1968. orig. title: *Sad Carnival.* $3.95.

Encyclopedia of Country and Western Music. Irwin Stambler and Grelun Landon. New York: St. Martin's Press, 1969. illus. $12.50.

Farewell My Youth. Arnold E. Bax. Westport, Conn.: Greenwood Press, 1943. $8.00.

Franz Schubert's Letters and Other Writings. Franz P. Schubert, ed. by Otto E. Deutsch, tr. by Venetia Savile. Westport, Conn.: Greenwood Press. reprint of 1928 ed. illus. $7.75.

Gentlemen, More Dolce Please. Harry E. Dickson. Boston: Beacon Press, 1969. illus. $7.50.

Great People I Have Known. Florizel Von Reuter. Waukesha, Wis.: Cultural Press, 1962. illus. $3.50.

Gustav Mahler: Memories and Letters (rev. and enlarged ed.). Alma Mahler, ed. by Donald Mitchell, tr. from German by Basil Creighton. Seattle, Wash.: University of Washington Press, 1971. reprint of 1969 ed. illus. $3.95 (paperbound).

Harold Bauer: His Book. Harold Bauer. Westport, Conn.: Greenwood Press, 1948. $12.00.

Hear Me Talkin to Ya. Nat Shapiro and Nat Hentoff. Gloucester, Mass.: Peter Smith. $4.50.

Hector Berlioz: A Selection from His Letters. Hector Berlioz, ed., tr. by Humphrey Searle. New York: Harcourt Brace Jovanovich, 1966. $5.75.

Here I Stand. Paul Robeson. Boston: Beacon Press, 1971. reprint of 1958 ed. $5.95 ($2.45 paperbound).

I Remember It Well. Maurice Chevalier. New York: Macmillan Company, 1970. illus. $5.95.

In Spite of Myself: A Personal Memoir. Winthrop Sargeant. New York: Doubleday and Company, 1970. $6.95.

Interrupted Melody: The Story of My Life. Marjorie Lawrence. Carbondale, Ill.: Southern Illinois University Press, 1969. $7.00 ($2.85 paperbound).

It's a Long Way from Chester County. Eddy Arnold. Old Tappan, N.J.: Hewitt House, 1969. illus. $4.95.

Joys and Sorrows. Pablo Casals and Albert E. Kahn. New York: Simon and Schuster, 1970. $7.50.

Lena. Lena Horne and Richard Schickel. New York: New American Library. $.75 (paperbound).

Letters of Beethoven. Ludwig Van Beethoven. New York: St. Martin's Press, 1961. 3 vols. $40.00 (set).

Letters of Composers. Gertrude Norman and Miriam L. Shrifte, eds. New York: Grosset and Dunlap. $2.25 (paperbound).

Letters of Composers Through Six Centuries. P. Weiss, ed. Philadelphia: Chilton Book Company, 1967. illus. $13.95.

Letters of Franz Liszt, 2 Vols. (Music Series, No. 42). Franz Liszt. New York: Haskell House, 1969. reprint of 1894 ed. $28.95.

Letters of Giacomo Puccini. Giacomo Puccini, ed. by Edna Makin. New York: AMS Press, 1931. $12.00.

Life and Liszt. Arthur Friedheim, ed. by Theodore L. Bullock. New York: Taplinger Publishing Company, 1961. illus. $6.00.

Lost Letters of Jenny Lind. Thaddeus Lockard. New York: International Publications Service, 1966. $7.00.

Man and the Artist Revealed in His Own Words. Wolfgang A. Mozart, tr. by Krehbiel. Gloucester, Mass.: Peter Smith. $3.25.

Man and Mask. Fedor I. Chaliapin, tr. by Phyllis Megroz. Westport, Conn.: Greenwood Press. reprint of 1932 ed. illus. $15.00.

Masters of the Keyboard. Donald Brook. Westport, Conn.: Greenwood Press, 1971. reprint of 1946 ed. $9.50.

Melodies and Memories (Select Bibliographies Reprint Series). Nellie Melba. Freeport, N.Y.: Books for Libraries, 1926. $13.50.

Memoirs. Mikhail I. Glinka, tr. by Richard B. Mudge. Norman, Okla.: University of Oklahoma Press, 1963. illus. $7.50.

Men, Women and Tenors (facsimile ed.) (Select Bibliographies Reprint Series). Frances Alda. Freeport, N.Y.: Books for Libraries, 1937. $13.50.

Midway in My Song, the Autobiography of Lotte Lehman (Select Bibliographies Reprint Series). Lotte Lehman. Freeport, N.Y.: Books for Libraries, 1938. $12.50.

Mine Eyes Have Seen the Glory. Anita Bryant. Old Tappan, N.J.: Fleming H. Revell Company, 1970. $3.95.

Movin' on Up: The Mahalia Jackson Story. Mahalia Jackson and Evan M. Wylie. New York: Hawthorn Books, 1966. $5.95.

Music in My Time and Other Reminiscences (Select Bibliographies Reprint Series). Daniel G. Mason. Freeport, N.Y.: Books for Libraries, 1938. $17.50.

Musical Memories (Music Reprint Series). Camille Saint-Saens. New York: Plenum Publishing Corporation, 1969. reprint of 1919 ed. $15.00.

Musicians Talk (facsimile ed.) (Essay Index Reprint Series). Leonora W. Armsby. Freeport, N.Y.: Books for Libraries, 1935. $9.75.

My Life in Jazz. Max Kaminsky and V. E. Hughes. New York: Harper and Row, 1963. illus. $4.95.

My Lord, What a Morning. Marian Anderson. New York: Viking Press, 1956. illus. $5.75.

My Musical Life. Walter J. Damrosch. Westport, Conn.: Greenwood Press, 1923. $14.75.

My Recollections (Select Bibliographies Reprint Series). Jules E. Massenet, tr. by H. Villiers Barnett. Freeport, N.Y.: Books for Libraries, 1919. $12.50.

My Time Is Your Time. Rudy Vallee and Gil McKean. Stanford, Conn.: Astor-Honor, 1962. illus. $5.95.

Notes of a Pianist. Louis M. Gottschalk, ed. by Jeanne Behrend. New York: Alfred A. Knopf, 1964. illus. $7.95.

Notes without Music (Music Series). Darius Milhaud. New York: Plenum Publishing Corporation, 1970. reprint of 1953 ed. $12.50.

Of Music and Music-Making. Bruno Walter. New York: W. W. Norton and Company, 1961. $1.65 (paperbound).

Overture and Beginners. Eugene Goossens. Westport, Conn.: Greenwood Press, 1963. reprint of 1951 ed. $14.00.

Pages from a Musician's Life. Fritz Busch, tr. by Marjorie Strachey. Westport, Conn.: Greenwood Press. reprint of 1953 ed. illus. $10.25.

Rachmaninoff's Recollection Told to Oskar Von Riesmann (Select Bibliographies Reprint Series). Sergei Rachmaninoff. Freeport, N.Y.: Books for Libraries, 1934. $12.50.

Raw Pearl. Pearl Bailey. New York: Harcourt Brace Jovanovich, 1968. $5.75. New York: Pocket Books, 1969. reprint. $.95 (paperbound).

Selected Letters of Beethoven. Ludwig Van Beethoven. New York: St. Martin's Press, 1967. $2.95 (paperbound).

Singing Family of the Cumberlands. Jean Ritchie. New York: Oak Publications. illus. $2.95 (paperbound).

Song of Motley. Leo Slezak. Westport, Conn.: Greenwood Press. reprint of 1938 ed. illus. $13.75.

Sound of Music: Story of the Trapp Family Singers. Maria A. Trapp. New York: Dell Publishing Company, 1966. $.60 (paperback).

Space Between the Bars. Donald Swann. New York: Simon and Schuster, 1969. $4.95.

Stardust Road. Hoagy Carmichael. Westport, Conn.: Greenwood Press, 1946. $8.50.

Such Sweet Compulsion: The Autobiography of Geraldine Farrar (Select Bibliographies Reprint Series). Geraldine Farrar. New York: Plenum Publishing Corporation, 1970. reprint of 1938 ed. $12.50.

Theme and Variations: An Autobiography. Bruno Walter. New York: Alfred A. Knopf, 1946. illus. $6.95.

Then Sings My Soul. George B. Shea and Fred Bauer. Old Tappan, N.J.: Fleming H. Revell, 1971. $3.95.

They All Had Glamour: From the Swedish Nightingale to the Naked Lady. Edward B. Marks. New York: Benjamin Blom, 1944. $12.50.

This Is My Story, This Is My Song. Jerome Hines. Old Tappan, N.J.: Fleming H. Revell, 1970. $3.95 ($.95 paperbound).

Too Strong for Fantasy. Marcia Davenport. New York: Charles Scribner's Sons, 1967. illus. $8.95.

Troubadour: A Different Battlefield. William Crofut. New York: E. P. Dutton and Company. illus. $6.95.

Vibrations. David Amram. New York: Macmillan Company, 1968. $6.95.

Virgil Thomson. Virgil Thomson. New York: Alfred A. Knopf, 1966. illus. $8.95.

We Called It Music: A Generation of Jazz. Eddie Condon. Westport, Conn.: Greenwood Press, 1947. $13.50.

Wheel of Fortune: Autobiography of Edith Piaf. Edith Piaf. Philadelphia: Chilton Book Company, 1966. illus. $4.50.

With Strings Attached (2nd ed.). Joseph Szigeti. New York: Alfred A. Knopf, 1967. illus. $7.95.

PHONORECORD COLLECTING
How to Build a Record Library. Hyman H. Taubman. Westport, Conn.: Greenwood Press. reprint of 1953 ed. $6.00.

PHONORECORDS
Blues Records: Nineteen Forty-Three to Nineteen Sixty-Six. Mike Leadbitter and Neil Slaven. New York: Oak Publications, 1969. $15.00 ($4.95 paperbound).

Fabulous Phonograph. Roland Gelatt. New York: Hawthorn Books, 1966. $6.95.

Record Industry Book (Entertainment Industry Series, Vol. 1). Walter E. Hurst and William S. Hale. Hollywood, Calif.: Seven Arts Press, 1961. illus. $25.00.

World of Sound Recording. Don M. Murray. Philadelphia: J. B. Lippincott Company, 1965. illus. $3.95.

PHONOTAPES—BIBLIOGRAPHY
History in Sound: Descriptive Listing of the Kiro-CBS Collection of Broadcasts of the World War Two Years and After, in the Phonoarchive of the University of Washington. Milo Ryan. Seattle, Wash.: University of Washington Press, 1963. $15.00.

RADIO ADVERTISING
Blacklisting: Two Key Documents (History of Broadcasting Series). New York: Arno Press. reprint of 1956 ed. $31.00.

Commercial Television Yearbook 1971–72 (5th ed.). New York: International Publications Service, 1970. $15.00.

How to Sell Radio Advertising. S. Willing. Blue Ridge Summit, Pa.: TAB Books, 1970. illus. $12.95.

Successful Television and Radio Advertising. Eugene F. Seehafer and J. W. Laemmar. New York: McGraw-Hill, 1959. illus. $13.50.

RADIO ANNOUNCING
Announcer's Handbook. Ben G. Henneke and Edward S. Dumit. New York: Holt, Rinehart and Winston, 1959. $6.50 (paperbound).

How to Become a Radio Disc Jockey. Hal Fisher. Blue Ridge Summit, Pa.: TAB Books, 1971. $7.95.

Man Behind the Mike: A Guide to Professional Broadcast Announcing. Hal Fisher. Blue Ridge Summit, Pa.: TAB Books, 1967. illus. $7.95 (paperbound).

Television and Radio Announcing (2nd ed.). Stuart W. Hyde. Boston: Houghton Mifflin Company, 1970. $9.95. $6.36 record.

RADIO AS A PROFESSION

Careers in Broadcasting. John H. Lerch, ed. New York: Appleton-Century Crofts, 1962. illus. $3.95.

Modern Broadcaster: The Station Book. Sherman P. Lawton. New York: Harper and Row, 1961. $8.50.

Your Career in Motion Pictures, Radio and Television. Charles R. Jones. Yonkers, N.Y.: Sheridan House. $5.00.

Your Career in TV and Radio. George N. Gordon and Irving A. Falk. New York: Julian Messner, 1966. illus. $3.95.

RADIO AUDIENCES

Great Audience. Gilbert V. Seldes. Westport, Conn.: Greenwood Press, 1950. $11.00.

Radio Programming in Action. Sherril W. Taylor, ed. New York: Hastings House Publishers, 1967. $6.50.

RADIO AUTHORSHIP

Writing for Television and Radio (2nd ed.) (Communications Arts Books Series). Robert L. Hilliard. New York: Hastings House Publishers, 1967. $7.95.

Writing Television and Radio Programs (Rinehart Editions). Edgar E. Willis. New York: Holt, Rinehart and Winston, 1967. $7.50.

RADIO BROADCASTING

AM-FM Broadcast Station Planning Guide. Harry A. Etkin. Blue Ridge Summit, Pa.: TAB Books, 1970. illus. $12.95.

Alfred I. DuPont—Columbia University Survey of Broadcast Journalism 1969–1970. Marvin Barrett, ed. New York: Grosset and Dunlap, 1970–1971. $5.95 ($1.95 paperbound).

Audio Control Handbook (3rd ed.) (Communication Arts Book Series). Robert S. Oringel. New York: Hastings House Publishers, 1968. illus. $7.95.

Broadcasting and Public Policy. E. G. Wedell. New York: Fernhill House, Ltd., 1968. $7.50.

Big Business and Radio (History of Broadcasting Series). Gleason L. Archer. New York: Arno Press. reprint of 1939 ed. $24.00.

Broadcasting and the Bill of Rights. National Association of Broadcasters. New York: Burt Franklin, 1947. $10.00.

Broadcasting and the Community. John Scupham. New York: International Publications Service, 1967. $3.75.

Broadcasting and the Public. Robert E. Summers and Harrison B. Summers. Belmont, Calif.: Wadsworth Publishing Company, 1966. $11.35.

Broadcasting and the Public Interest. John H. Pennybacker and Waldo W. Braden. New York: Random House, 1969. $2.50 (paperbound).

Broadcasting in America. Sydney Head. Boston: Houghton Mifflin Company, 1956. $9.50.

Case Studies in Broadcast Management. Howard Coleman. New York: Hastings House Publishers, 1970. $4.95 ($3.60 paperbound).

Guide to Radio-TV Broadcast Engineering Practices. Edward L. Safford, Jr. Blue Ridge Summit, Pa.: TAB Books, 1970. $12.95.

Handbook of Broadcasting (4th ed.). Waldo M. Abbott and R. L. Rider. New York: McGraw-Hill, 1957. illus. $9.50.

History of Broadcasting in the United States, Vol. 3. Erik Barnouw. New York: Oxford University Press, 1970. $9.75.

I Looked and I Listened (rev. ed.). Ben Gross. New Rochelle, N.Y.: Arlington House, 1970. illus. $8.95.

Invasion from Mars: A Study in the Psychology of Panic. Hadley Cantril. New York: Harper and Row. $2.75 (paperbound).

Licensing of Radio Services in the United States, 1927 to 1947. Murray Edelman. Urbana, Ill.: University of Illinois Press, 1950. $2.00 (paperbound).

Listening: A Collection of Critical Articles on Radio (facsimile ed.) (Essay Index Reprint Series). Albert N. Williams. Freeport, N.Y.: Books for Libraries, 1948. $9.00.

Mass Communitations and American Empire. Herbert I. Schiller. Clifton, N.J.: Augustus M. Kelley, Publishers, 1969. $9.00.

Modern Broadcaster: The Station Book. Sherman P. Lawton. New York: Harper and Row, 1961. $8.50.

National and International Systems of Broadcasting: Their History, Operation and Control. Walter B. Emery. East Lansing, Mich.: Michigan State University Press, 1969. illus. $12.50.

Public Arts. Gilbert Seldes. New York: Simon and Schuster, 1957. $1.95 (paperbound).

Radio and Television Acting. Edwin Duerr. Westport, Conn.: Greenwood Press. reprint of 1950 ed. $29.50.

Radio and Television: Readings in the Mass Media. Allen Kirschner and Linda Kirschner. Indianapolis, Ind.: Odyssey Press. $4.35 (paperbound).

Radio Broadcasting: An Introduction to the Sound Medium (Communication Arts Books Series). Robert L. Hilliard, ed. New York: Hastings House Publishers, 1967. illus. $6.95 ($4.40 paperbound).

Radio Director's Manual. Edgar E. Willis. Ann Arbor, Mich.: Campus Publishers, 1961. $4.00 (paperbound).

Radio Program Ideabook. Hal Fisher. Blue Ridge Summit, Pa.: TAB Books, 1968. $12.95.

Radio Today: The Present State of Broadcasting (History of Broadcasting Series). Arno Huth. New York: Arno Press. reprint of 1942 ed. $9.00.

RADIO BROADCASTING—HISTORY
Broadcasting: Its New Day (History of Broadcasting Series). Samuel L. Rothafel and Raymond F. Yates. New York: Arno Press. reprint of 1925 ed. $19.00.

Cavalcade of Broadcasting. Curtis Mitchell. Chicago: Follett Publishing Company, 1971. illus. $9.95.

The History of Broadcasting in the United Kingdom. 2 vols., including Vol. 1: *The Birth of Broadcasting*, Vol . 2: *The Golden Age of Wireless.* Asa Briggs, ed. New York: Oxford University Press, 1961 (Vol. 1), 1965 (Vol. 2). $8.00 (Vol. 1), $12.00 (Vol. 2).

A History of Broadcasting in the United States. 2 vols., including *A Tower in Babel: To 1933, The Golden Web: 1933 to 1953.* Erik Barnouw. New York: Oxford University Press, 1966 (Vol. 1), 1968 (Vol. 2). $9.00 ea.

A History of Broadcasting: Radio and Television. New York: Arno Press. 32 bks. $652.00.

Pictorial History of Radio (rev. ed.). Irving Settel. New York: Grosset and Dunlap, 1967. illus. $6.95.

History of Radio to 1926 (History of Broadcasting Series). Gleason L. Archer. New York: Arno Press. reprint of 1938 ed. $21.00.

RADIO JOURNALISM
History in Sound: Descriptive Listing of KIro-CBS Collection of Broadcasts of the World War Two Years and After, in the Phono-

archive of the University of Washington. Milo Ryan. Seattle, Wash.: University of Washington Press, 1963. $15.00.

On-the-Spot Reporting: Radio Records History. George N. Gordon and Irving A. Falk. New York: Julian Messner, 1967. illus. $3.95.

News in America (Library of Congress Series in American Civilization). Frank L. Mott. Cambridge, Mass.: Harvard University Press, 1952. $7.00.

News & How to Understand It in Spite of the Newspapers, in Spite of the Magazines, in Spite of the Radio. Quincy Howe. Westport, Conn.: Greenwood Press, 1968. reprint of 1940 ed. illus. $11.50.

Radio New Handbook (2nd ed.). David Dary. Blue Ridge Summit, Pa.: TAB Books, 1970. $7.95.

Radio and the Printed Page (History of Broadcasting Series). Paul F. Lazarsfeld. New York: Arno Press. reprint of 1940 ed. $19.00.

Workbook for Radio and News Editing and Writing (3rd ed.). Arthur Wimer and Dale Brix. Dubuque, Iowa: William C. Brown Company, 1970. illus. $6.95 (paperbound).

RADIO PLAYS—PRODUCTION AND DIRECTION
Radio Drama. Loren E. Taylor. Minneapolis, Minn.: Burgess Publishing Company, 1965. $1.75 (paperbound).

RADIO PROGRAMS
Great Radio Comedians. Jim Harmon. New York: Doubleday and Company, 1970. $6.95.

Great Radio Heroes. Jim Harmon. New York: Ace Books, 1969. $.75 (paperbound).

Radio Programming in Action. Sherril W. Taylor, ed. New York: Hastings House Publishers, 1967. $6.50.

Remember Radio. Ron Lackman. New York: G. P. Putnam's Sons, 1970. illus. $6.95.

Thirty Year History of Programs Carried on National Radio Networks in the United States, 1926–1956 (History of Broadcasting Series). Harrison B. Summers, ed. New York: Arno Press. reprint of 1958 ed. $10.00.

RADIO RESEARCH
Advances in Radio Research. John A. Saxton, ed. New York:
Academic Press, 1964. 2 vols. $8.50 ea.

Forty Years of Radio Research. George C. Southworth. New
York: Gordon and Breach Science Publishers, 1962. illus. $12.50.

Radio Experiments (Pegasus Books Series, No. 20). F. G. Rayer,
ed. by P. Pringle. New York: International Publications Service,
1968. $4.00.

RADIO STATIONS
AM-FM Broadcast Station Planning Guide. Harry A. Etkin. Blue
Ridge Summit, Pa.: TAB Books, 1970. illus. $12.95.

North American Radio-TV Station Guide (7th ed.). Vane A. Jones.
Indianapolis, Ind.: Howard W. Sams and Company, 1971. $2.95
(paperbound).

Not Just a Sound: The Story of WLW. Dick Perry. Englewood
Cliffs, N.J.: Prentice-Hall, 1971. illus. $6.95.

Organization and Operation of Broadcast Stations. Jay Hoffer.
Blue Ridge Summit, Pa.: TAB Books, 1971. illus. $12.95.

Radio Promotion Handbook. William A. Peck. Blue Ridge Summit, Pa.: TAB Books, 1968. $9.95 (paperbound).

Radio Station Management (2nd ed.). J. Leonard Reinsch and E.
I. Ellis. New York: Harper and Row, 1960. $6.95

Radio Stations: Installment, Design and Practice. G. A. Chappel.
Elmsford, N.Y.: Pergamon Press, 1959. $7.50.

Radio, Television and Electronic Data Book. Bernard B. Babani.
Hackensack, N.J.: Wehman Brothers. illus. $1.00 (paperbound).

TELEVISION
Enjoying Radio and Television (Excursions Series for Young
People). Robert Dunnett. New York: International Publications
Service, 1970. illus. $3.75.

First Principles of Television (History of Broadcasting Series).
Alfred Dinsdale. New York: Arno Press. reprint of 1932 ed.
$17.00.

Focal Encyclopedia of Film and Television Techniques (Communication Arts Books Series). Raymond Spottiswoode, ed. New
York: Hastings House Publishers, 1969. illus. $37.50.

Fundamentals of Television. Walter A. Buchsbaum. New York: Hayden Book Company. illus. $7.45 ($5.95 paperbound).

Handbook of Radio Publicity and Promotion. Jack Macdonald. Blue Ridge Summit, Pa.: TAB Books, 1970. $29.95.

Marconi: Father of Radio. David Gunston. New York: Macmillan Company, 1967. $3.50.

One Hundred and One Questions and Answers About CATV-MATV. Theodore B. Baum and Robert E. Baum. Indianapolis, Ind.: Howard W. Sams and Company, 1968. illus. $2.50 (paperbound).

The Outlook for Television (History of Broadcasting Series). Orrin E. Dunlap, Jr. New York: Arno Press. reprint of 1932 ed. $16.00.

Paying for TV (Hobart Paperback Series, No. 43). Sydney Caine. Levittown, N.Y.: Transatlantic Arts, 1969. illus. $1.95 (paperbound).

Radio and TV (It's Made Like This Series). Kenneth Ullyett. New York: Roy Publishers, 1971. $3.50.

Radio-Television—the Hard Way. Ray C. Smucker. New York: Vantage Press. $4.50.

Radio and Television: Readings in the Mass Media. Allen Kirschner and Linda Kirschner, eds. Indianapolis Ind.: Bobbs-Merrill Company, 1971. $4.35 (paperbound).

Radio and Television in the USSR. S. V. Kaftanov et al. New York: CCM Information Corporation, 1960. $20.00 (paperbound).

Sound and Vision (Design Centre Publications Series). Peter E. Sharp. New York: International Publications Service, 1968. illus. $3.00.

Technique of Special Effects in Television. Bernard Wilkie. New York: Hastings House Publishers, 1970. $16.50.

Technological History of Motion Pictures and Television. Raymond Fielding, ed. Berkeley, Calif.: University of California Press, 1967. $14.00.

Television. Les Brown. New York: Harcourt Brace Jovanovich, 1971. $8.95.

Television. B. Cole. New York: Free Press, 1970. $12.50 ($5.95 paperbound).

Television: A Struggle for Power (History of Broadcasting Series). Frank Waldrop and Joseph Borkin. New York: Arno Press. reprint of 1938 ed. $16.00.

Television and Radio (3rd ed.). Giraud Chester et al. New York: Appleton-Century Crofts. illus. $8.25.

Ten Years of Television. Mungo MacCallum, ed. San Francisco: Tri-Ocean Books. $2.50 (paperbound).

Understanding Television (Communication Arts Books Series). Robert L. Hilliard, ed. New York: Hastings House Publishers, 1964. illus. $6.95 ($3.95 paperbound).

TELEVISION—PRODUCTION AND DIRECTION
Hollywood TV Producer. Muriel G. Cantor. New York: Basic Books, 1971. $7.95.

Technique of the Television Cameraman (Library of Communication Techniques Series). Peter Jones. New York: Hastings House Publishers, 1965. illus. $10.00.

Technique of Television Production (rev. ed.) (Library of Communication Techniques Series). Gerald Millerson. New York: Hastings House Publishers, 1968. illus. $13.50 ($7.20 paperbound).

Techniques of Television Production (2nd ed.). Rudy Bretz. New York: McGraw-Hill, 1962. illus. $12.50.

Television Acting and Directing: A Handbook (Rinehart Editions). Walter K. Kingson and Rome Cowgill. New York: Holt, Rinehart and Winston, 1965. $8.95 (paperbound).

Television Director Interpreter (Communication Arts Books Series). Colby Lewis. New York: Hastings House Publishers, 1968. illus. $8.95 ($5.95 paperbound).

Television Production Handbook (2nd ed.). Herbert Zettl. Belmont, Calif.: Wadsworth Publishing Company, 1968. $13.25.

Television Program: Its Direction and Production (rev. ed.). Edward Stasheff and Rudy Bretz. New York: Hill and Wang, 1968. illus. $2.95 (paperbound).

Window on the World: The Story of Television Production. Charles I. Coombs. Cleveland: World Publishing Company, 1965. $4.50.

TELEVISION ANNOUNCING

Announcer's Handbook. Ben G. Henneke and Edward S. Dumit. New York: Holt, Rinehart and Winston, 1959. $6.50 (paperbound).

Man Behind the Mike: A Guide to Professional Broadcast Announcing. Hal Fisher. Blue Ridge Summit, Pa.: TAB Books, 1967. illus. $7.95 (paperbound).

Technique of Television Announcing (Library of Communication Techniques Series). Bruce Lewis. New York: Hastings House Publishers, 1966. $10.00.

Television and the News: A Critical Appraisal. Harry J. Skornia. Palo Alto, Calif.: Pacific Books, 1968. $5.75.

Television and Radio Announcing (2nd ed.). Stuart W. Hyde. Boston: Houghton Mifflin Company, 1970. $9.95.

TELEVISION AUDIENCES

Great Audience. Gilbert V. Seldes. Westport, Conn.: Greenwood Press, 1950. $11.00.

Living with Television. Ira O. Glick et al. Chicago: Aldine Publishing Company, 1962. $6.75.

People Look at Television: A Study of Audience Attitudes. Gary A. Steiner. New York: Alfred A. Knopf, 1963. illus. $7.95.

Television and Delinquency. J. D. Halloran et al. New York: Humanities Press, 1970. $4.50 (paperbound).

Uses of the Mass Media by the Urban Poor: Findings of Three Research Projects and an Annotated Bibliography. Bradley S. Greenberg and Brenda Dervin. New York: Frederick A. Praeger, 1970. $13.50.

TELEVISION AUTHORSHIP

Audiovisual Script Writing. Norton S. Parker. New Brunswick, N.J.: Rutgers University Press, 1968. $12.50.

Practical Manual of Screen Playwriting for Theater and Television Films. Lewis Herman. Cleveland: World Publishing Company. $3.95 (paperbound).

Teleplay: An Introduction to Television Writing. Coles Trapnell. San Francisco: Chandler Publishing Company, 1966. $4.75 (paperbound).

Television Writer. Erik Barnouw. New York: Hill and Wang, 1962. $3.95.

Television Writing and Selling (3rd ed.). Edward B. Roberts. Boston: Writer, 1968. $8.95.

Writing for Television. Gilbert V. Seldes. Westport, Conn.: Greenwood Press, 1968. reprint of 1952 ed. illus. $11.75.

Writing for Television. Max Wylie. New York: Cowles Book Company, 1970. $9.95.

Writing for Television and Radio (2nd ed.) (Communication Arts Books Series). Robert L. Hilliard. New York: Hastings House Publishers, 1967. $7.95.

Writing Television and Radio Programs (Rinehart Editions). Edgar E. Willis. New York: Holt, Rinehart and Winston, 1967. $7.50.

TELEVISION BROADCASTING

Age of Television (3rd ed.). Leo Bogart. New York: Frederick Ungar Publishing Company. $12.00.

Behind the Scenes in Television (rev. ed.). David C. Cooke. New York: Dodd, Mead and Company, 1967. illus. $3.95.

Broadcasting and the Public. Robert E. Summers and Harrison B. Summers. Belmont, Calif.: Wadsworth Publishing Company, 1966. $11.35.

Broadcasting and the Public Interest. John H. Pennybacker and Waldo W. Braden. New York: Random House, 1969. $2.50 (paperbound).

Broadcasting in America. Sydney Head. Boston: Houghton Mifflin Company, 1956. $9.50.

Broadcast Management (Studies in Media Management). Ward L. Quaal and Leo Martin. New York: Architectural Book Publishing Company, 1968. illus. $8.95 ($5.60 paperbound).

Documentary in American Television (Communication Arts Books Series). William A. Bluem. New York: Hastings House Publishers, 1964. illus. $8.95.

Due to Circumstances Beyond Our Control. Fred W. Friendly. New York: Random House, 1967. $8.95 ($1.95 paperbound).

ETV in Controversy. John C. Schwarzwalder, ed. Minneapolis: Dillon Press, 1970. $3.95.

Eighth Art. CBS. New York: Holt, Rinehart and Winston, 1962. $5.00.

Factual Television (Communication Arts Books Series). Norman Swallow. New York: Hastings House Publishers. $7.50.

Handbook of Broadcasting (4th ed.). Waldo M. Abbott and R. L. Rider. New York: McGraw-Hill, 1957. illus. $9.50.

How to Talk Back to Your Television Set. Nicholas Johnson. Boston: Little, Brown and Company, 1970. $5.75.

Kemp's Film and Television Yearbook 1971 (16th ed.). New York: International Publications Service, 1971. $20.00.

Living-Room War. Michael J. Arlen. New York: Viking Press, 1969. $5.95.

Mass Communications and American Empire. Herbert I. Schiller. New York: Augustus M. Kelley, Publishers, 1969. $9.00.

Meaning of Commercial Television. Stanley T. Donner, ed. Austin, Tex.: University of Texas Press, 1967. $2.50 (paperbound).

Modern Broadcaster: The Station Book. Sherman P. Lawton. New York: Harper and Row Publishers, 1961. $8.50.

National and International Systems of Broadcasting: Their History, Operation and Control. Walter B. Emery. East Lansing, Mich.: Michigan State University Press, 1969. illus. $12.50.

North American Radio-TV Station Guide (7th ed.). Vane A. Jones. Indianapolis, Ind.: Howard W. Sams Company, 1971. $2.95 (paperbound).

Open Letter from a Television Viewer (Open Letter Series). Robert Montgomery. New York: James H. Heineman Publishers, 1968. $2.25 (paperbound).

Radio and Television Acting. Edwin Duerr. Westport, Conn.: Greenwood Press. reprint of 1950 ed. $29.50.

Television: The Dream and the Reality. Robert L. Shayon. Milwaukee: Marquette University Press, 1960. $.50 (paperbound).

Television Broadcasting. Howard Chinn. New York: McGraw-Hill, 1953. illus. $17.00.

Television Dilemma (Communication Arts Books Series). Yale Roe. New York: Hastings House Publishers, 1962. $4.50.

To Kill a Messenger: Television News and the Real World. William Small. New York: Hastings House Publishers, 1970. $8.95.

Who Owns the Air. Marya Mannes. Milwaukee: Marquette University Press, 1960. $.50 (paperbound).

TELEVISION BROADCASTING—BIOGRAPHY
Funny Men. Steve Allen. New York: Simon and Schuster, 1956. $3.95.

TELEVISION BROADCASTING—HISTORY
Cavalcade of Broadcasting. Curtis Mitchell. Chicago: Follett Publishing Company, 1971. illus. $9.95.

Glorious Decade. Tedd Thomey. New York: Ace Books, 1971. illus. $.95 (paperbound).

So You Think You Know Television. Donald Kennedy. New York: Ace Books, 1971. illus. $.75 (paperbound).

TELEVISION BROADCASTING OF NEWS
Left-Leaning Antenna: Political Bias in Television. Joseph Keely. New Rochelle, N.Y.: Arlington House Publishers, 1971. $8.95.

Network News is Biased. Edith Efron. Los Angeles: Nash Publishing Corporation, 1971. $7.95.

Television News: Anatomy and Process. Maury Green. Belmont, Calif.: Wadsworth Publishing Company, 1969. $10.60.

Television News: Writing, Filming, Editing, Broadcasting (Communication Arts Books Series). Irving E. Fang. New York: Hastings House Publishers, 1968. illus. $8.95 ($5.60 paperbound).

TV Covers the Action. George N. Gordon and Irving A. Falk. New York: Julian Messner, 1968. illus. $3.95.

Writing News for Broadcast. John Patterson and Edward Bliss, Jr. New York: Columbia University Press, 1971. $13.50.

TELEVISION BROADCASTING OF SPORTS
Playback: The Set-Side Sports Guide to the Fifteen Major Television Sports. Tony Verna. Chicago: Follett Publishing Company, 1971. $4.95 (paperbound).

Super Spectator and the Electric Lilliputians. William O. Johnson. Boston: Little, Brown and Company, 1971. illus. $6.95.

TELEVISION GRAPHICS
Film and TV Graphics (Visual Communication Books Series). John Halas, ed. by Walter Herdeg. New York: Hastings House Publishers, 1967. illus. $17.95.

TV Graphics. Roy T. Laughton. New York: Van Nostrand-Reinhold Books, 1966. illus. $5.50 ($2.75 paperbound).

TELEVISION IN ADVERTISING

Anatomy of Local Radio-TV Copy (3rd ed.). William A. Peck. Blue Ridge Summit, Pa.: TAB Books, 1968. $5.95 (paperbound).

Anatomy of a Television Commercial. Lincoln Diamont. New York: Hastings House Publishers, 1970. $12.50.

Commercial Television Yearbook 1971–72 (5th ed.). New York: International Publications Service, 1970. $15.00.

Down the Tube, or Making Television Commercials Is Such a Dog-Eat-Dog Business It's No Wonder They're Called Spots. Terry Galanoy. Chicago: Henry Regnery Company, 1970. $5.95.

Power Technique for Selling Broadcast Advertising (Broadcast Books). Neil Terrell. Blue Ridge Summit, Pa.: TAB Books, 1971. $12.95.

Successful Television and Radio Advertising. Eugene F. Seehafer and J. W. Laemmar. New York: McGraw-Hill, 1959. illus. $13.50.

Television Advertising. Dan Ingman. New York: International Publications Service, 1965. illus. $15.75.

Television's Classic Commercials: The Golden Years, 1948–1958. Lincoln Diamont. New York: Hastings House Publishers, 1970. $14.50.

TELEVISION PLAYS

Best Television Plays. Incl. *Mother*, Paddy Chayefsky; *Thunder on Sycamore Street*, Reginald Rose; *My Lost Saints*, Tad Mosel; *Man on the Mountaintop*, Robert A. Arthur; *Young Lady of Property*, Horton Foote; *Strike*, Rod Serling; *Rabbit Trap*, J. P. Miller; *Visit to a Small Planet*, Gore Vidal. Gore Vidal, ed. New York: Ballantine Books. $.95 (paperbound).

Great Television Plays. William I. Kaufman, ed. New York: Dell Publishing Company, 1969. $.75 (paperbound).

In the Presence of Death. Chalmers Dale, ed. St. Louis: Bethany Press, 1964. $1.50 (paperbound).

Primer for Playgoers (2nd ed.) (Speech and Drama Series). Edward A. Wright and Lenthiel H. Downs. Englewood Cliffs, N.J.: Prentice-Hall, 1969. $8.95.

Seeking Years. John M. Gunn, ed. St. Louis: Bethany Press, 1959. $1.50 (paperbound).

Television Plays for Writers. A. S. Burack. Boston: Writer. illus. $6.95 ($8.95 text ed.).